# DK EYEWITNESS TRAVEL

# TOP 10
# BERLIN

IN

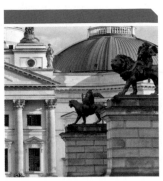

# Top 10 Berlin Highlights

# The Top 10 of Everything

# CONTENTS

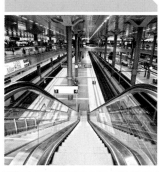

## Berlin Area by Area

## Streetsmart

Within each Top 10 list in this book, no hierarchy
of quality or popularity is implied. All 10 are, in
the editor's opinion, of roughly equal merit.

***Front cover and spine*** *The Berliner Dom
on Museumsinsel*
***Back cover*** *Nikolaiviertel with the Fernsehturm
in the background*
***Title page*** *Unique roof of the Sony Center at
Potsdamer Platz*

# Welcome to
# Berlin

Few European cities have witnessed as much upheaval and renewal as Berlin. From Prussian powerhouse and Nazi bastion to Cold War zombie and revitalized capital of a reunited Germany – Berlin has seen it all, and then some. This fascinating city is perpetually in a state of becoming, and with Eyewitness Top 10 Berlin, it's yours to explore.

Even today, the layers of history are evident. A stroll along **Unter den Linden** leads you from the classical columns of **Brandenburger Tor** past former Third Reich ministries to the world-class treasures of **Museumsinsel**. Just beyond lies the Socialist architecture of **Alexanderplatz**, compelling in an entirely different way. This kaleidoscope of eras lends richness to Berlin's ecclectic charm.

For many visitors, the city's star attractions are its exciting arts scene and variety of bars, cafés and nightclubs. The spirit of the Golden Twenties lives on here, and Berlin keeps going around the clock. How late you stay out depends on your stamina – as any bleary-eyed reveller will tell you, this isn't a city of morning people (the after-parties don't count). For a buzzing metropolis, Berlin is surprisingly green, with vast parks such as the **Tiergarten** or **Volkspark Friedrichshain** teeming with lazing couples, families having a barbecue, joggers and cyclists – in a country known for its *autobahns*, people are increasingly trading in their cars for bicycles.

Whether you're visiting for a weekend or a week, our Top 10 guide brings together the best of everything that Berlin has to offer, from the hip cafés of **Prenzlauer Berg** to the gritty nightclubs of **Kreuzberg** and the royal stamping grounds of **Charlottenburg**. There are tips throughout, from seeking out what's free to avoiding the crowds, plus 14 easy-to-follow itineraries, designed to tie together a clutch of sights in a short space of time. Add inspiring photography and detailed maps, and you've got the essential pocket-sized travel companion. **Enjoy the book, and enjoy Berlin.**

Clockwise from top: Berliner Dom, Sony Center at Potsdamer Platz, Hackescher Markt near Hackesche Höfe, Schloss Charlottenburg, Marx-Engels-Forum, the Philharmonie concert hall

# Exploring Berlin

For a sprawling, historic metropolis whose charms are widely scattered, Berlin is a surprisingly easy place to navigate. There's something for every interest and budget, and excellent public transport whisks you from sight to sight with clockwork efficiency. Here are a few ideas to maximize your fun and minimize your planning.

**The Kaiser-Wilhelm-Gedächtnis-Kirche** stands as a reminder of the horrors of war.

**Key**
— Two-day itinerary
— Four-day itinerary

## Two Days in Berlin

### Day ❶

**MORNING**
Begin at **Alexanderplatz** (see pp102–9) and ascend the **Fernsehturm** (see p104) for an unequalled Berlin panorama. View Babylonian treasures at the **Pergamonmuseum** (see pp24–6).

**AFTERNOON**
Stroll along historic **Unter den Linden** (see pp16–19). Admire the iconic **Brandenburger Tor** (see pp12–13) and take a guided tour of the **Reichstag** (see pp14–15) before enjoying a classical concert at the **Philharmonie** (see pp38–9).

### Day ❷

**MORNING**
Begin with the ruins of the **Kaiser-Wilhelm-Gedächtnis-Kirche** (see pp32–3) before exploring stores along **Kurfürstendamm** (see pp30–31) and in **Kaufhaus des Westens** (see p76).

**AFTERNOON**
After lunch, wander through **Schloss Charlottenburg** (see pp34–7) and linger in its Baroque-style gardens. Seek out **Savignyplatz** for cocktails and an evening bite (see pp120–21).

## Four Days in Berlin

### Day ❶

**MORNING**
Spend time exploring the **Reichstag** and government district (see pp14–15), then take a boat tour through Berlin's waterways (see p170). There are piers in the **Tiergarten** (see p113) next to the Haus der Kulturen der Welt.

**AFTERNOON**
Have lunch at **Aigner** (see p93), and visit pretty **Gendarmenmarkt** (see p86). Promenade on **Unter den Linden** (see pp16–17) before admiring the **Brandenburger Tor** (see pp12–13). Catch an evening show at the **Friedrichstadt-Palast** (see p67).

**The Reichstag,** one of Berlin's most symbolic buildings, is a popular sight.

**The Neues Museum** contains spectacular treasures, including the bust of Nefertiti.

Friedrichstadt-Palast
Pergamon-museum
Neues Museum
Alexander-platz
Fernsehturm
Klosterstrasse station
Unter den Linden
Aigner
Gendarmenmarkt
MITTE
U-BAHN
Potsdamer Platz
Mendelssohn-Bartholdy-Park station
U-BAHN
KREUZBERG
Gneisenaustr. station
Marheineke-Markthalle
SCHÖNEBERG

0 kilometres 1
0 miles 1

**Potsdamer Platz,** untouched for nearly 50 years in rubble, has now been regenerated into a vibrant city hub.

## Day ❷
### MORNING
Take the lift up to the **Fernsehturm** observation deck (see p104). Peruse the collections of **Museumsinsel** (see pp24–7), particularly the **Neues Museum**, home to the Nefertiti bust, and the **Pergamonmuseum** (see p26).
### AFTERNOON
Head to **Potsdamer Platz** (see pp20–23) for daring modern architecture and the Marlene Dietrich exhibit at the **Deutsche Kinamathek** (see p22). Stroll in the **Tiergarten** (see p113).

## Day ❸
### MORNING
Start at the **Kaiser-Wilhelm-Gedächtnis-Kirche** (see pp32–3), then choose between the **Zoologischer Garten** (see pp42–3) or shopping on **Kurfürstendamm** (see pp30–31).
### AFTERNOON
Marvel at Prussian riches at **Schloss Charlottenburg** and wander its beautifully landscaped park (see pp34–7). Stop by the **Gipsformerei** for gift sculptures (see p77). After that, head to **Ana e Bruno** for an excellent Italian meal (see p127).

## Day ❹
### MORNING
Start the day at the **Kulturforum** (see pp38–41). There are several cultural institutions to be explored in this complex, but a wise use of time is to view the Renaissance masters at the **Gemäldegalerie** (see p40). To enjoy some local specialities for lunch, stop by the last market hall in Berlin, the **Marheineke-Markthalle**, which is full of vibrant stores (see p133).
### AFTERNOON
The splendid town of **Potsdam** and the stunning gardens in the palace complex of **Sanssouci** (see pp156–61) are a short trip away from the city by commuter train.

# Top 10 Berlin Highlights

The grand auditorium of the Berlin
Staatsoper Unter den Linden

# ⏺10 Berlin Highlights

Berlin is Germany's liveliest city and one of the most fascinating capitals in the world. You'll find no other place where art and culture, museums and theatres, entertainment and nightlife are more diverse and exciting than around the banks of the Spree River. Once reunited, Berlin quickly developed into a cosmopolitan city, and today there is an air of great energy and vibrancy about it.

### Brandenburger Tor and Pariser Platz ①

The Brandenburger Tor stands in Pariser Platz, where the embassies and the Hotel Adlon Kempinski exude stylish elegance *(see pp12–13)*.

### ② Reichstag

No other building is a more potent symbol of Germany's history than the Reichstag. Its vast egg-shaped dome affords fantastic views across the city *(see pp14–15)*.

### ③ Unter den Linden

This magnificent, leafy boulevard has always been a central axis along Berlin's most important historic buildings *(see pp16–19)*.

### Potsdamer Platz ④

The new heart of the old city is Potsdamer Platz, where exciting modern structures have been erected *(see pp20–23)*.

### 5 Museumsinsel
Among the museums in this complex are the Pergamonmuseum, which houses the Pergamon Altar *(see pp24–7)*, the Altes and the Neues museums.

### 7 Kaiser-Wilhelm-Gedächtnis-Kirche
The tower ruins of the memorial church, built to commemorate Kaiser Wilhelm I, still stand today as a silent reminder of the horrors of war *(see pp32–3)*.

### 6 Kurfürstendamm

Berlin's much visited strolling and shopping avenue is the main thoroughfare in the western part of the city *(see pp30–31)*.

### 8 Schloss Charlottenburg
The former Hohenzollern summer residence and its beautiful Baroque gardens offer visitors a slice of Prussian history *(see pp34–7)*.

### 9 Kulturforum
This complex of museums, which includes the Gemäldegalerie, the Kunstgewerbemuseum and the Neue Nationalgalerie, yields a unique cultural experience *(see pp38–41)*.

### 10 Zoologischer Garten
Germany's oldest and most famous zoo and aquarium, in the centre of the city, boasts over 19,000 animals and nearly 1,500 different species *(see pp42–3)*.

# 🔟 ⭐ Brandenburger Tor and Pariser Platz

The best known of Berlin's symbols, the Brandenburg Gate stands proudly in the middle of Pariser Platz, asserting itself against the modern embassy buildings that now surround it. Crowned by its triumphant Quadriga sculpture, the famous gate has long been a focal point in Berlin's history: rulers and statesmen, military parades and demonstrations – all have felt compelled to march through the Brandenburger Tor.

### Brandenburger Tor ①
Built by Carl G Langhans in 1789–91 and modelled on the temple porticoes of ancient Athens, the Brandenburg Gate **(right)** is the undisputed symbol of Berlin. Since the 19th century, this iconic landmark has been the backdrop for many events in the city's turbulent history.

### ② Quadriga
The 6-m (20-ft) high sculpture **(below)** was created in 1794 as a symbol of peace by Johann Gottfried Schadow. As the model for the goddess of peace, he used his niece, who subsequently became famous throughout Berlin.

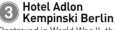

### ③ Hotel Adlon Kempinski Berlin
Destroyed in World War II, the city's most elegant hotel **(below)** is a reconstruction of the original, which hosted celebrities such as Greta Garbo, Thomas Mann and Charlie Chaplin.

### ④ DZ Bank
This modern building, designed by the American architect Frank Owen Gehry, combines the clean lines of Prussian architecture with some daring elements inside (see p57).

### ⑤ Akademie der Künste
Built in 2000–2005 and designed by Günter Behnisch and Manfred Sabatke, the Academy of Arts incorporates, behind a vast expanse of windows, the ruins of the old art academy, which was destroyed in World War II.

### ⑥ French Embassy
Christian de Portzamparc built this elegant building in 2001 on the site of the old embassy, which was ruined in World War II. Its colonnades and windows are a homage to the original.

### 7 Palais am Pariser Platz

This complex by Bernhard Winking is a successful modern interpretation of Neo-Classical architecture. Inside you will find a café, a restaurant and a souvenir shop around a pleasantly shaded courtyard (left).

### NEED TO KNOW

**MAP K3** ■ Pariser Platz

Tourist information centre: Brandenburger Tor southern gatehouse ■ (030) 25 00 25 ■ www.visitberlin.de

**Open** Apr–Oct: 9:30am–7pm daily; Nov–Mar: 9:30am–6pm daily

■ For a quick pit stop between sights, visit the Starbucks on Pariser Platz 4A.

■ You can trace the course of the Wall along the former border patrol road, following the green-and-white Berliner Mauerweg signs. Historic interest and natural beauty alternate along the trail.

### 8 Haus Liebermann

Josef P Kleihues built this in 1996–8, faithfully recreating the original that stood on the same site. The house is named after the artist Max Liebermann, who lived here. In 1933, watching Nazi SA troops march through the gate, he famously said: "I cannot possibly eat as much, as I would like to puke."

### 9 American Embassy

The last gap around Pariser Platz was finally closed in 2008 (above). A dispute had delayed building for years: the US wanted a whole street moved for reasons of security, but had to concede the point in the end.

### 10 Eugen-Gutmann-Haus

With its clean lines, the Dresdner Bank (right), built in 1997 by gmp, recalls the style of the New Sobriety movement of the 1920s. In front of it is Pariser Platz's famous original street sign.

# Reichstag

Of all the buildings in Berlin, the Reichstag, seat of the Bundestag (parliament), is probably one of the most symbolic. The mighty structure, erected in 1884–94 by Paul Wallot as the proud manifestation of the power of the German Reich, was destroyed by arson in 1933 and bombed during World War II. In 1995, the artist Christo wrapped up the Reichstag and, in 1999, the British architect Lord Norman Foster transformed it into one of the most modern parliamentary buildings in the world.

### The Dome

The Reichstag dome by Lord Norman Foster affords breathtaking views of Berlin. It is open at the top to air the building and – a symbolic touch – to allow for the free and open dissemination of debates throughout the country. A ramp winds its way up to the top **(right)**.

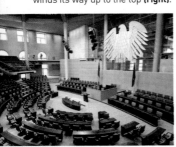

### 2 Plenary Hall

The plenary hall **(above)** is the seat of the Deutscher Bundestag – the German parliament – which has convened here again since 20 April 1999. Technologically, the hall is one of the most advanced parliament buildings in the world. The federal eagle caused a row: considered too "fat", it had to be slimmed down.

### 3 Portico "Dem deutschen Volke"

The dedication "To the German People" was designed in 1916, against the will of Wilhelm II.

### 4 Restored Façade

Despite extensive renovations, small World War II bullet holes are still visible in the building's façade.

**THE REICHSTAG FIRE**

When the Reichstag went up in flames on 27 February 1933, the Dutch Communist van der Lubbe was arrested for arson. It is, however, likely that the Nazis started the fire themselves. Hitler used it as an excuse to get the "Enabling Act" passed, which let him dispose off his opponents and marked the start of a 12-year reign of terror.

### Restaurant Käfer 5

This popular luxury restaurant **(right)** on the Reichstag's roof offers an excellent view of the historical centre of Unter den Linden *(see p117)*.

### 8 The German Flag

The giant German flag **(left)** was first raised on the occasion of the official national celebrations of German reunification on 3 October 1990.

### 9 Weiße Kreuze Memorial

Opposite the southern side of the Reichstag, a memorial recalls the Wall, which stood only a few steps away. The white crosses commemorate the people who died at the Wall while trying to escape to West Berlin.

### 10 Memorial by Dieter Appelt

Unveiled in 1992, the memorial **(below)** in front of the Reichstag commemorates 97 Social Democratic and Communist delegates who were murdered under the Third Reich.

### 6 Platz der Republik

Celebrations often take place on the lawn in front of the Reichstag, as in 2006, when Germany hosted the Football World Cup **(below)**.

### 7 Installation "Der Bevölkerung"

Hans Haacke's work of art "To the People" is a counterpoint to the portico inscription opposite and uses the same style of lettering.

---

**NEED TO KNOW**

**MAP K2** ■ Platz der Republik 1
■ Dome: (030) 22 73 21 52; Käfer: (030) 22 62 99 33 ■ www.bundestag.de

**Open** Dome: 8am–midnight (last entry 10pm); Käfer: 9am–4:30pm, 6:30pm–midnight daily

To visit the Reichstag dome you must register at www.bundestag.de 2–3 days in advance. You can try for same-day admission at the Visitors' Service Centre (Nov–Mar: 8am–6pm daily; Apr–Oct: 8am–8pm daily) next to the Berlin Pavilion on Scheidemannstraße. You will require your passport/identity card.

■ If a meal at Käfer exceeds your budget, many stalls near the Reichstag sell tempting *Bratwurst* (sausages).

# 🔟⭐ Unter den Linden

"As long as the lime trees still blossom in Unter den Linden, Berlin will always be Berlin," sang Marlene Dietrich about this magnificent avenue. The lime trees blossom more beautifully than ever and the street's old buildings have been extensively restored. The Linden, once a royal bridle path linking the king's town residence (the Stadtschloss) and Tiergarten, became Berlin's most fashionable street in the 18th century, and was synonymous with the city that was then the capital of Prussia.

### Deutsches Historisches Museum ①
Germany's largest history museum (right) offers an overview of more than 1,000 years of German history. Housed in the Zeughaus, it is the oldest and architecturally the most interesting building on Unter den Linden (see p18).

### ② Staatsoper Unter den Linden
The richly ornamented State Opera House (above) is one of Germany's most attractive. Neo-Classical in style, it was built by architect Georg Wenzeslaus von Knobelsdorff between 1741–3 as Europe's first free-standing opera house, to plans devised by Frederick the Great himself (see p85).

### ③ St Hedwigskathedrale
Designed by von Knobelsdorff in 1740–2 and modelled on the Pantheon in Rome, this is the seat of Berlin's Catholic archdiocese (below). It was commissioned by Frederick the Great to appease Berlin Catholics after the conquest of Silesia (see p58).

### ④ Humboldt-Universität
Berlin's oldest and most highly regarded university (above) was founded in 1890, on the initiative of Wilhelm von Humboldt. Twenty-nine Nobel Prize winners were educated here, including Albert Einstein.

### 5 Neue Wache

The central German memorial **(above)** for all victims of war was created in 1816–8 by Karl Friedrich Schinkel. A reproduction of Käthe Kollwitz's moving *Pietà* stands here.

### 8 Kronprinzenpalais

Originally created in 1669 as a private residence by Johann Arnold Nering, the building was remodelled in 1732–3 into a Neo-Classical palace by Philip Gerlach and was a residence for several Hohenzollern heirs. After World War I it became an art museum, before the East German government housed state visitors there. The German reunification agreement was signed here in August 1990. It now holds cultural events and exhibitions.

### 9 Bebelplatz

Originally named Opernplatz, this wide open space was designed by Georg W von Knobelsdorff as the focal point of his Forum Fridericianum. The elegant square was meant to introduce some of the splendour and glory of ancient Rome to the Prussian capital. In May 1933, it became the scene of the infamous Nazi book burning.

### NEED TO KNOW

**MAP K5** ▪ Deutsches Historisches Museum: Zeughaus, Unter den Linden 2 ▪ (030) 20 30 40 ▪ www.dhm.de

**Open** 10am–6pm daily

Adm

**MAP K4** ▪ Staatsoper: Unter den Linden 7 ▪ (030) 20 35 45 55 ▪ www.staatsoper-berlin.de

Closed for major renovation; due to reopen in October 2017.

▪ Take a break at the Café im Deutschen Historischen Museum (in the Zeughaus) which can be accessed directly from the street.

### 6 Opernpalais

The charming building next to the Staatsoper, built in 1733–7, was also known as the Kronprinzessinnenpalais and once served as a palace for the daughters of Friedrich Wilhelm III.

### 7 Russische Botschaft

The gigantic Russian Embassy, built in Stalinist "wedding-cake style", was the first building to be erected on Unter den Linden after World War II.

### 10 Frederick the Great's Statue

One of Christian Daniel Rauch's grandest sculptures, this equestrian statue **(above)** shows "Old Fritz" (13.5 m/44 ft high) in his tricorn and coronation mantle *(see p85)*.

# Deutsches Historisches Museum

**1 The Dying Warriors**
The 22 reliefs by Andreas Schlüter, displayed on the walls of the courtyard rather than in one of the museum's exhibitions, portray the horrors of war in an unusually immediate way.

**2 Europe and Asia**
This group of 18th century Meissen porcelain figures reflects the fascinating relationship between the two continents.

**3 Steam Engine**
A full-sized steam engine from the year 1847 marks the entrance to the exhibition on the Industrial Revolution.

**4 Martin Luther**
Luther's portrait, by Lucas Cranach the Elder, is the focal point of exhibition rooms devoted to the Reformation and Martin Luther himself.

*Martin Luther* **by Lucas Cranach**

**5 Clothes from the Camps**
Among the many exhibits here that illustrate the years under Nazi rule is the jacket of a concentration camp inmate – a chilling reminder of the Third Reich.

**6 V2 Rocket**
Exhibited in the section on Nazi Germany is a V2 rocket engine, displayed next to an 88-mm flak gun. The V2 missile was one of the *Wunderwaffen* ("wonder weapons") used by German troops at the end of World War II.

**A Nazi Germany V2 rocket engine**

**7 Soldiers Plundering a House**
This painting by Flemish-Baroque painter Sebastian Vrancx, dating from around 1600, depicts a scene from the wars of religion that tore the Netherlands apart during the 16th century.

**8 Saddle**
A valuable saddle, dating from the middle of the 15th century, is decorated with elaborately carved plaques made of ivory.

**9 The Berlin Wall**
An original section of the Berlin Wall, together with the banners of a peaceful pro-unification demonstration in 1989, commemorates the fall of the Wall.

**10 Gloria Victis**
The moving allegorical figure of Gloria Victis, created by the French sculptor Antonin Mercié, bears witness to the death of his friend during the final days of the Franco-Prussian War of 1870–71.

## ZEUGHAUS UNTER DEN LINDEN

Originally the royal arsenal, the Zeughaus was built in 1706 in the Baroque style according to plans by Johann Arnold Nering. It is an impressive structure, with the building surrounding a historical central courtyard that is protected by a modern glass cupola roof. Especially memorable are Baroque sculptor Andreas Schlüter's figures of 22 dying warriors, lined up along the arcades in the courtyard. They portray vividly the horrors of war. Behind the main building stands a cone-shaped glass annex designed by the Chinese-born architect Ieoh Ming Pei in 2001 for special exhibitions and temporary shows. The permanent exhibition in the main historical building includes a collection entitled "Images and Testimonials of German History". Highlighting the most significant periods and events in the history of the country, the displays include a surprising variety of exhibits dating from the days of the early Medieval German Empire up to 1994. Featured are the period of the Reformation, the Thirty Years' War, the wars of Liberation and the failed Revolution of 1848, and, of course, the two World Wars.

***Entry of Napoleon into Berlin, 27 October 1806*** (1810) by Charles Meynier shows the victorious French at the Brandenburg Gate, Unter den Linden

### TOP 10
### UNTER DEN LINDEN EVENTS

**1  1573** Elector Johann Georg has a bridle path built, linking the royal Stadtschloss and the Tiergarten

**2  1647** During the reign of the Great Elector, the road is planted with *Linden* (lime trees)

**3  From 1740** Frederick the Great has grand buildings erected

**4  1806** Napoleon and his troops march along Unter den Linden

**5  1820** The road turns into a grand boulevard

**6  1928** Unter den Linden and Friedrichstraße epitomize the world city

**7  1933** Troops celebrate Hitler's victory

**8  1945** The avenue is razed to the ground

**9  1948–53** Revival of the boulevard

**10  October 1989** Demonstrations lead to the fall of the East German regime

# TOP 10 ⭐ Potsdamer Platz

The heart of the new metropolis of Berlin beats on Potsdamer Platz. This square, where Berliners and tourists alike now flock to cinemas, restaurants and shops, was a hub of urban life in the 1920s. After World War II, it became a desolate wasteland, but since the fall of the Wall, Potsdamer Platz – for a while Europe's largest building site – has become a city within the city, surrounded by imposing edifices that began to appear in the 1990s, and are still being added to today.

### Sony Center ①
The Sony Center **(right)** is the most ambitious, successful and architecturally interesting building in the new Berlin. The cupola structure, designed by Helmut Jahn, is the German headquarters of the Sony company, and with its cinemas and restaurants it is also a social magnet.

### ② Deutsche Kinemathek
This museum **(below)** takes visitors backstage at Babelsberg and Hollywood with Marlene Dietrich's costumes and other exhibits *(see p22)*.

### Weinhaus Huth ④
The only building on Potsdamer Platz to have survived World War II, the restored Weinhaus **(right)** today accommodates restaurants and the excellent Daimler Contemporary, which showcases modern art.

### ③ Café Josty
Café Josty harkens back to its legendary predecessor, a regular haunt of artists and intellectuals in the 19th century. Today's Josty is partially housed in the historic Kaisersaal (Emperor's Hall) of the former Grand Hotel Esplanade.

### ⑤ Boulevard der Stars
Berlin's walk of fame features stars such as Marlene Dietrich, Werner Herzog, Fritz Lang, Hans Zimmer, Christoph Waltz, Diane Kruger and Romy Schneider **(left)**. The coloured asphalt evokes the red carpet.

**Plan of Potsdamer Platz**

### 6 Potsdamer Platz Arkaden

The arcades **(above)** draw visitors with three floors hosting 130 shops, exclusive boutiques and restaurants. The lower ground floor is a food court serving a range of meals and snacks.

### 7 Spielbank Berlin

Berlin's casino invites visitors to *faites vos jeux*. Apart from roulette, Black Jack is also played, and an entire floor is given over to gambling machines.

**NEED TO KNOW**

**MAP L2** ▪ Deutsche Kinemathek: Potsdamer Str. 2 ▪ (030) 300 90 30 ▪ www.deutsche-kinemathek.de

**Open** 10am–6pm Tue–Sun (to 8pm Thu)

Adm

**MAP F4** ▪ Spielbank Berlin: Marlene-Dietrich-Platz 1 ▪ www.spielbank-berlin.de

**Open** 11–3am daily

Adm

**MAP L2** ▪ LEGOLAND® Discovery Centre: Potsdamer Str. 4 ▪ (030) 301 04 00 ▪ www.legolanddiscoverycentre.de

Adm

**MAP L2** ▪ CinemaxX: Potsdamer Str. 5 ▪ (01805) 24 63 62 99

**MAP L2** ▪ Sony Center Potsdamer Platz ▪ www.sonycenter.de/en/

▪ Apart from visiting Café Josty, try the ice cream at Caffè e Gelato inside the Potsdamer Platz Arkaden.

### 8 CinemaxX

The CinemaxX **(below)**, with its 17 screens, is one of Berlin's largest cinemas. The bigger screens show current Hollywood blockbusters, while the three smallest are for low-budget arthouse and German films.

### 9 Quartier Potsdamer Platz

Leading architects such as Hans Kollhoff and Renzo Piano designed these skyscrapers. One landmark is the terracotta and glass Atrium Tower.

### 10 LEGOLAND® Discovery Centre

This LEGO® wonderland features brick models, a miniature Berlin, a train ride to a land of dragons and a DUPLO® Village with bigger blocks for the little ones (see p65).

# Deutsche Kinemathek Exhibitions

**Costumes of Marlene Dietrich**

film, everyday cinema and the industry's victims: some film stars allowed themselves to be used by the Nazis, others refused to cooperate. The life and work of the actor Kurt Gerron, who was persecuted and murdered, is documented as an exemplary case.

### 1 Marlene Dietrich
This exhibition of the film star's estate includes costumes from her films, her touring luggage, film clips, posters, photographs, letters and notes.

### 2 Metropolis
This iconic film, directed by Fritz Lang in 1927, has an alarming vision of a futuristic urban dystopian world as its subject. Models and props from the film are on display.

### 3 Caligari
The best known German film of the 1920s, *The Cabinet of Dr Caligari* (1920), was an influential masterpiece of Expressionist filmmaking by Robert Wiene.

### 4 Weimar Republic
The exhibits here are dedicated to the works of the legendary directors of German cinema's golden age from 1918 to 1933.

### 5 Olympia
This exhibition reveals the technical tricks used in the Nazi propaganda film *Olympia*, a staged documentary by Leni Riefenstahl made in 1936–8 after the Olympics.

### 6 National Socialism
This exhibition has documents relating to the propaganda uses of

### 7 Post-War Cinema
The story of films and filmmaking in East and West Germany is shown with props and costumes of popular stars of post-war German cinema such as Hanna Schygulla, Romy Schneider, Heinz Rühmann and Mario Adorf.

### 8 Transatlantic
This exhibition of documents, letters, keepsakes and souvenirs retraces the careers of German film stars in Hollywood, both of the silent era and the "talkies" that followed after 1928.

**Exhibits, Transatlantic section**

### 9 Pioneers and Divas
The infant days of cinema are featured here, as well as stars of the silent era such as Henny Porten and the Danish Asta Nielsen.

### 10 Exile
Documents in this exhibition relate the difficulties encountered by German filmmakers when making a new start in the USA in 1933–45.

## THE NEW CENTRE OF BERLIN

In the 1920s, Potsdamer Platz was Europe's busiest square, boasting the first automatic traffic lights in Berlin. During World War II this social hub was razed to the ground. Ignored for almost 50 years, the empty square shifted back into the centre of Berlin when the Wall came down. During the 1990s, it was Europe's largest building site. New skyscrapers were built, old structures were restored – some preserved rooms of the ruined historic Grand Hotel Esplanade were even physically moved into the Sony Center. Millions of people came to follow progress from the famous Red Info Box, which was removed in 2001. Altogether, around €17 billion was invested to create the present square.

**TOP 10**
**POTSDAMER PLATZ ARCHITECTS**

**1 Helmut Jahn**
Sony Center

**2 Renzo Piano and Christian Kohlbecker**
Atrium Tower, Spielbank Berlin, Musical-Theater, Spielbank, Weinhaus Huth

**3 José Rafael Moneo**
Hotel Grand Hyatt, Mercedes-Benz Headquarters

**4 Hans Kollhoff**
Daimler

**5 Giorgio Grassi**
Park Colonnades

**6 Ulrike Lauber and Wolfram Wöhr**
Grimm-Haus, CinemaxX

**7 Sir Richard Rogers**
Office Block Linkstraße

**8 Steffen Lehmann and Arata Isozaki**
Office and Retail House Linkstraße

**9 Heidenreich & Michel**
Weinhaus Huth

**10 Bruno Doedens and Maike van Stiphout**
Tilla-Durieux-Park

**Grand Hotel Esplanade remnants, Sony Center**

**Skyscrapers at dusk on Potsdamer Platz**

# TOP 10 ⭐ Museumsinsel

Formed by the two arms of the Spree River, the Museumsinsel is home to the world's most diverse museum complex. Built between 1830 and 1930, the museums, which hold the Prussian royal collections of art and archaeology, were turned into a public foundation in 1918. Heavily damaged in World War II, the complex was restored and declared a UNESCO World Heritage Site in 1999. Renovation work will go on until 2025 during which a path linking four museums will be created.

### Bode-Museum ①
Located at the northern tip of Museumsinsel, the Bode-Museum is a stately structure dominated by a cupola **(right)**. The building holds the Sculpture Collection, the Museum of Byzantine Art and the Numismatic Collection, made up of a diverse collection of over 500,000 objects.

### ② Pergamonmuseum
Built in 1909–30, this is one of the world's most important museums of ancient art and architecture, with a vast collection of antiquities *(see p26)*. The huge Ishtar gate **(above)** dates from the 6th century BC.

### ③ Neues Museum
Spectacularly revamped by British architect David Chipperfield, the building itself is as fascinating as the exhibits. As well as the Museum of Pre- and Early History, the Ägyptisches Museum is also housed here.

### ④ Ägyptisches Museum
Housed within the Neues Museum, this museum features portraits of Egyptian royals and monumental architecture *(see p50)*.

**MISSING TREASURES**

During World War II, many of the island's exhibits were hidden in underground bunkers. Some pieces of "Priam's Gold", excavated from the site of ancient Troy, were taken by the Red Army as war booty and remain in Moscow. The Neues Museum points out where there are gaps in the collection.

### ⑤ Alte Nationalgalerie
First opened in 1876, the Old National Gallery was beautifully restored in the 1990s **(right)** and now holds 19th-century sculptures and paint-ings, including works by Max Liebermann and Schadow *(see p52)*.

**Plan of the Museumsinsel**

## 6 Altes Museum

The first building to be completed on Museumsinsel in 1830, the Altes Museum resembles a Greek temple (see p55). Originally meant to hold paintings, it now houses the collection of Classical antiquities (right).

## 7 James Simon Gallery

Named in honour of James Simon (1851–1932), a patron of the Berlin State Museums, this will open in 2018 as the central entrance and visitor centre.

## 8 Colonnade Courtyard

This columned court-yard between the Alte Nationalgalerie and Neues Museum frames and connects the museums and provides an atmospheric venue for open-air concerts.

## 9 Lustgarten

This "pleasure park", with a fountain in its centre, is located in front of the Altes Museum. The lawns are popular with tired visitors (see p55).

## 10 Berliner Dom

Easily the island's most overwhelming structure, this Baroque-style cathedral (above) is unusually ornate for a protestant church. Organ concerts and services can be enjoyed in this exquisitely restored church (see p58).

**NEED TO KNOW**

**MAP J5** ■ (030) 266 424 242 ■ www.smb.museum

**Open** 10am–6pm daily, until 8pm Thu (most museums); sections of the Pergamonmuseum may be closed due to a phased remodelling until 2025

Adm €10–12 per museum; Museumsinsel day pass €18; 3-day Berlin Museum Pass €29; extra fee for some exhibitions; free for under-18s

■ Some of the museums have cafés, but the café at the Altes Museum is convenient as it is a little closer than the others to Karl-Liebknecht-Straße, the island's main road.

■ It's best to set aside a whole day for the extraordinary collections of the Museumsinsel. There are several parks nearby in which you can take breaks. Sundays can be very busy with long queues and large groups.

# Pergamonmuseum

**Detail, frieze from Darius's palace**

### 5 Frieze from the Palace of Darius

A frieze dating to around 510 BC from the palace of Darius in Susa (Iran) is made of exquisitely coloured glazed brick and depicts a row of Persian warriors holding lances and carrying bows and quivers.

### 6 Giant Sculpture of a Bird of Prey

The nearly 2-m- (7-ft-) high Riesensonnenvogel (huge sun bird) was discovered during excavations in Tell Halaf, Syria, the centre of the ancient Aramaic city-state of Guzana.

### 1 Pergamon Altar

The colossal Pergamon Altar from the ancient eponymous Greek city (in modern Turkey) dates from 160 BC and is the largest and most significant treasure in the collections of the Berlin museums. This hall is closed for reconstruction until 2019.

### 2 Ishtar Gate

The imposing Ishtar Gate and the Processional Way that led to it are fully preserved. The gate was built under Nebuchadnezar II in the 6th century BC in Babylon. Original faïence tiles depict the sacred lions.

### 3 Market Gate of Miletus

This vast gate (AD 100) is over 16 m (52 ft) high. To the right of the entrance, a hairdresser has carved an advertisement for his shop into the stone.

### 4 Assyrian Palace Room

The reconstructed room of the Assyrian kings' palace (9th century BC) boasts impressive door figures and 13th-century BC wall paintings.

### 7 Aleppo Room

Taken from a Christian merchant's house in Syria and dating from the early 17th century, this small room features magnificent wooden cladding and is a beautiful example of Ottoman architecture.

### 8 Mosaic of Orpheus

This delightful mosaic floor, depicting Orpheus playing his lyre amid animals enchanted by his skill, comes from the dining room of a private home in Asia Minor (AD 200).

### 9 The Mshatta Façade

A gift from Ottoman Sultan Abdul Hamid II to Kaiser Wilhelm II, this stone façade elaborately carved with arabesque and animal forms was the south face of a desert fort built in AD 744 in Mshatta, Jordan.

**Market Gate of Miletus**

### 10 Victory Stele of Esarhaddon

This monumental stele, excavated in 1888 in Zincirli, commemorates Esarhaddon's victory over Pharoah Taharqa (671 BC).

## SAVING THE MUSEUMSINSEL

**Visitors at the spectacular Neues Museum**

The island of museums is a treasury of antique architecture, but until recently it had been slowly decaying. Since 1992, however, €1.8 billion has been spent on the renovation and modernization of Museumsinsel. A master plan created by renowned architects that include David Chipperfield and O M Ungers will transform the complex into a unique museum landscape – just as it was first conceived in the 19th century by Friedrich Wilhelm IV, when he established the "free institution for art and the sciences". Once completed, an "architectural promenade" will serve as a conceptual and structural link between various individual museums, except the old National Gallery. This promenade will consist of a variety of rooms, courtyards and vaults, as well as exhibition halls. The core of the complex will be a new central entrance building. The museums are gradually reopening after extensive individual renovations – the Pergamonmuseum will be completed by 2025.

### TOP 10
### MUSEUMSINSEL EVENTS

**1 1810** Plan for a public art collection created

**2 1830** The Altes Museum, Prussia's first public museum, opens

**3 1859** Completion of the Neues Museum

**4 1876** Opening of the Alte Nationalgalerie

**5 1904** Completion of the Kaiser-Friedrich-Museum (Bode-Museum)

**6 1930** Opening of the Pergamonmuseum

**7 1943** Bombs destroy most of the museums

**8 1958** Most museums reopen after renovation

**9 1999** Museumsinsel declared a UNESCO World Heritage Site

**10 2009** The Neues Museum reopens

**The Altes Museum with the green Lustgarten in front**

# 🔟 ⭐ **Kurfürstendamm**

After years of decline, the Kurfürstendamm, or Ku'damm for short, has once again become a fashionable hot spot. Breathtaking architecture, elegant boutiques and a lively street artist scene around Breitscheidplatz have made this shopping boulevard one of Berlin's most attractive and – at 3.8 km (2.5 miles) – also its longest avenue for strolling.

### Breitscheidplatz ①

Here, in the heart of the western city **(right)**, artists, Berliners and visitors swarm around J Schmettan's globe fountain, known by locals as "Wasserklops" (water meatball).

### ② Kaiser-Wilhelm-Gedächtnis-Kirche

The church tower (the church itself was destroyed during World War II) stands in the centre of the square **(left)**, serving as both memorial and stark reminder of the terrors of war (see pp32–3).

### ③ Europa-Center

The oldest shopping centre in West Berlin, opened in 1962, is still worth a visit. Here you will find fashion boutiques, a comedy theatre and an official Berlin Tourist Info centre.

### ⑤ Bikini Berlin

The Bikini-Haus building **(above)**, built in 1956, was renovated to house the splendid Bikini Berlin, an ultra-hip boutique mall that also offers great views of the nearby zoo.

### ④ Neues Kranzler Eck

This glass and steel skyscraper **(above)** was built in 2000 by architect Helmut Jahn. The legendary Café Kranzler was retained as a bar in front of the office block. There is an official Berlin Tourist Info centre here.

---

**WHEN KU'DAMM WAS NO MORE THAN A LOG ROAD**

In 1542, today's magnificent boulevard was just a humble "Knüppeldamm", or log road. It served the Electors as a bridle path, linking their town residence (Stadtschloss) and their hunting lodge (Jagdschloss). It was not until 1871 that the area around the Ku'damm developed into a fashionable "new west end". Chancellor Otto von Bismarck had the boulevard modelled on the Champs Elysées in Paris, lined with houses, shops, hotels and restaurants.

*Previous pages* The Reichstag and the Paul Löbe legislative building reflected in the Spree

### 8 Lehniner Platz

The square is home to the Schaubühne theatre **(left)**, built as Universum cinema in 1928 by Erich Mendelsohn and converted in 1978.

### 9 Fasanenstraße

A small street off Ku'damm, Fasanenstraße **(below)**, with its galleries, expensive shops and restaurants, is one of Charlottenburg's most elegant areas *(see pp120–21)*.

### 10 Traffic Turret

On the corner of Joachimstaler Straße stands an old-fashioned traffic turret or *Verkehrskanzel*, the last one in the city and now a heritage monument. A policeman sat in the raised glass cabin to control traffic lights manually from 1955 to 1962, when the signals went automatic.

### 6 RT&W Galerie

The Neo-Classical building housing this gallery gives visitors a glimpse of Ku'damm's erstwhile splendour.

### 7 Iduna-Haus

The turreted building at No. 59 at the Leibnitzstraße corner is one of the few surviving bourgeois houses from the late 19th century. The ornamented Jugendstil (Art Nouveau) façade has been lavishly restored **(left)**.

## NEED TO KNOW

**MAP P5** ■ Europa-Center: Tauentzienstr. 9 ■ (030) 348 00 80 ■ www.24EC.de

**Open** 24 hours (shops and Berlin Tourist Info: 10am–8pm Mon–Sat)

**MAP N4** ■ Bikini Berlin: Budapester Str. 38–50 ■ www.bikiniberlin.de

**Open** 10am–8pm Mon–Sat, noon–6pm Sun

■ The Story of Berlin at Kurfürstendamm 207–8 is a multimedia tour of 800 years of Berlin's history from the Great Elector to the fall of the Wall. Visitors can walk through a nuclear bomb shelter, built during the Cold War, beneath the museum. (www.story-of-berlin.de).

■ Few original cafés in the Kurfürstendamm area have survived: the most charming is the Café Wintergarten in the Literaturhaus on Fasanenstraße *(see p126)*.

■ Avoid Ku'damm on Saturday mornings when it is teeming with locals and tourists out on shopping trips.

# TOP10 ⭐ Kaiser-Wilhelm-Gedächtnis-Kirche

This ruined Neo-Romanesque church is one of Berlin's most haunting symbols. It was consecrated in 1895 and named Kaiser Wilhelm Memorial Church in honour of Wilhelm I. Following severe damage by the 1943 bombing raids, the ruins of the tower were left standing as a memorial. Egon Eiermann built a new church next to it in 1957–63.

### Tower Ruins ①
Only the church tower **(right)** survived the Allied bombing raids that razed much of the city to the ground in 1943. Today only 71 m (233 ft) high, the tower once rose to 113 m (370 ft). The rough hole in its roof has given rise to its nickname "the Hollow Tooth".

### New Bell Tower ②
The hexagonal bell tower **(right)** rises 53 m (174 ft) high next to the tower ruins on the site of the old church's main nave.

**A CHURCH WITH TWO LIVES**

The Kaiser-Wilhelm-Gedächtnis-Kirche has the Berliners to thank for its preservation: in 1947, the Senate had planned to demolish the tower ruins for safety reasons. In a referendum only about 10 years later, however, one in two Berliners voted for its preservation. And so the idea came about to build a new church next to the ruin and to preserve the vestibule of the old church as a striking memorial hall to the horrors of war.

### ③ Kaiser's Mosaic
One of the preserved mosaics shows Heinrich I on his throne, with imperial orb and sceptre **(right)**. Originally decorated with scenes from German imperial history, the interior was meant to place the Hohenzollerns within that tradition.

### 8 Coventry Crucifix

This small crucifix was forged from old nails that were found in the ruins of Coventry Cathedral in England. It commemorates the bombing of Coventry by the German Luftwaffe in 1940.

### 9 Tower Clock

The tower bears a clock based on a Classical design, with Roman numerals. At night, it is lit in blue by modern light-emitting diodes to match the lighting inside the new church.

### 4 Main Altar

The golden figure of Christ (above) created by Karl Hemmeter is suspended above the main altar in the modern church. In the evening light, the windows behind the altar glow an overwhelming dark blue.

### 10 Russian Orthodox Cross

This gift from the bishops of Volokolomsk and Yuruyev was given in memory of the victims of Nazism.

### NEED TO KNOW

**MAP N4** ▪ Breitscheidplatz
▪ (030) 218 50 23 ▪ www.
gedaechtniskirche-berlin.de

**Open** Church: 9am–7pm daily; memorial hall: 10am–6pm Mon–Sat, noon–6pm Sun; services 10am and 6pm Sun

Free guided tours at 12:15pm, 1:15pm, 2:15pm & 3:15pm daily and 10:15am & 11:15am Mon, Fri & Sat (donations welcome); group tours in English available for a small fee

▪ Visit the new church on a sunny day around lunchtime, when the blue glass window is at its most impressive.

▪ There are fantastic views of the church from the Mövenpick Café in the Europa-Center opposite.

### 5 Mosaic of the Hohenzollerns

The vividly coloured mosaic (above) of the Hohenzollerns adorns the vestibule of the church ruins. It depicts Emperor Wilhelm I together with Queen Luise of Prussia and her entourage.

### Original Mosaics 6

Glittering Jugendstil-style mosaics showing Prussian dukes and princes are preserved on the walls and ceilings along the stairways (right).

### 7 Figure of Christ

Miraculously, the vast, plain sculpture of Christ, which is suspended from the ceiling, survived the bombing of the church.

# TOP 10 ⭐ Schloss Charlottenburg

The construction of Schloss Charlottenburg, designed as a summer residence for Sophie Charlotte, wife of the Elector Friedrich III, began in 1695. The Orangerie was extended and a cupola was added by Johann Friedrich Eosander between 1701 and 1713. Subsequent extensions were undertaken by Frederick the Great, who added the Neuer Flügel between 1740 and 1746.

### 1 Altes Schloss

The Baroque tower of the oldest part of the palace (dating to 1695) by Johann Arnold Nering is crowned by Richard Scheibe's golden statue of Fortuna **(above)**.

### 2 Porzellankabinett

This small, exquisite mirrored gallery **(below)** has been faithfully restored to its original glory. Among the exhibits on display are valuable porcelain items from China and Japan.

### 3 Schlosskapelle

The luxurious splendour of the palace chapel recalls the once magnificent interior design of the palace, before it was destroyed in World War II. However, apart from the original altar, the entire chapel – including the king's box – is a costly reconstruction.

### 4 Monument to the Great Elector

The equestrian statue of the Great Elector Friedrich Wilhelm **(right)** is thought to be one of his most dignified portraits. Made by Schlüter in 1696–1703, it stood on the Rathausbrücke originally, near the destroyed Stadtschloss.

### 5 Neuer Flügel

Built between 1740 and 1747 by Georg W von Knobelsdorff, the new wing contains Frederick the Great's private quarters, as well as a large collection of 18th-century French paintings.

### 6 Schlosspark

The palace has a lovely Baroque garden, beyond which lies a vast park, redesigned by Peter Joseph Lenné in 1818–1828 in the English style with rivers, artificial lakes and small follies.

### 7 Belvedere

Friedrich Wilhelm II liked to escape to the romantic Belvedere (below), a summer residence built in 1788 by Carl Gotthard Langhans, which served as a tea pavilion. Today it houses a collection of precious Berlin porcelain objects.

**Plan of Schloss Charlottenburg**

### 8 Neuer Pavillon

This Italianate villa, designed by Schinkel for Friedrich Wilhelm III in 1825, was inspired by the Villa Reale del Chiatamone in Naples and clearly shows the Hohenzollerns' love of the Italian style.

### 9 Mausoleum

Slightly hidden, this Neo-Classical building (below) by Schinkel is the final resting place of many of the Hohenzollerns.

### 10 Museum Berggruen

Situated in the Western Stüler Building opposite the Charlottenburg palace, this modern art gallery houses the permanent exhibition "Picasso and his Time", featuring more than 100 works that span the artist's career. Other highlights of the collection include works by Matisse, Klee and Giacometti (see p52).

**NEED TO KNOW**

**MAP A/B3** ■ Spandauer Damm ■ (030) 32 09 10 ■ www.spsg.de
*Altes Schloss:* Apr–Oct: 10am–6pm Tue–Sun (to 5pm Nov–Mar)
*Neuer Flügel:* Apr–Oct: 10am–6pm Wed–Mon (to 5pm Nov–Mar)

*Belvedere:* Apr–Oct: 10am–6pm Tue–Sun
*Neuer Pavillon:* Jan–Mar: 10am–5pm Tue–Sun (to 6pm Apr–Oct; Nov–Dec: noon–4pm Tue–Sun
*Mausoleum:* Apr–Oct: 10am–6pm Tue–Sun
*Museum Berggruen:* Schlossstr. 1

■ www.smb.museum
■ 10am–6pm Tue–Sun Adm (for all)

■ The Orangery Café has an attractive garden.

■ Try a romantic midweek evening stroll to avoid the crowds (park: 6am–dusk).

# Schloss Charlottenburg Rooms

**Goldene Galerie in the Neuer Flügel**

### 5 Winterkammern
Friedrich Wilhelm II's early Neo-Classical rooms contain fine paintings, tapestries and furniture.

### 6 Bibliothek
Frederick the Great's small library has outstanding elegant bookcases and a vibrant, light green colour scheme.

### 7 Konzertkammer
Furniture and gilded panelling in the concert hall have been faithfully recreated as during Frederick the Great's time. Antoine Watteau's *Gersaint's Shop Sign*, considered to be one of his most significant works, hangs here; the king bought the work directly from the artist.

### 1 Goldene Galerie
The festival salon in the Neuer Flügel, 42 m (138 ft) long, was designed in Rococo style by Frederick the Great's favourite architect von Knobelsdorff. The richly ornamented room has a cheerful appearance.

### 2 Eichengalerie
The wooden panelling of the Oak Gallery is carved with expensively gilded portraits of Hohenzollern ancestors.

### 3 Gris-de-Lin-Kammer
This small chamber in Friedrich's second palace apartment is decorated with paintings, including some by his favourite artist, Antoine Watteau. The room was named after its wall coverings in violet-coloured damask (*gris-de-lin* in French).

### 4 Schlafzimmer der Königin Luise
Queen Luise's bedchamber, designed in 1810 by Karl Friedrich Schinkel, features the clear lines typical of the Neo-Classical style. The walls are clad in silk fabrics and wallpaper.

### 8 Grünes Zimmer
The green room in Queen Elisabeth's quarters is an excellent example of royal chambers furnished in 19th-century Biedermeier style.

**Queen Elisabeth's Grünes Zimmer**

### 9 Rote Kammer
The elegant chamber, decorated entirely in red and gold, is adorned by portraits of King Friedrich I and Sophie Charlotte.

### 10 Friedrich I's Audienzkammer
The ceiling paintings and Belgian tapestries depict allegorical figures symbolizing the fine arts and the sciences. There are also magnificent lacquered cabinets, modelled on Asian originals.

# THE HOHENZOLLERNS AND BERLIN

**Friedrich Wilhelm, the Great Elector**

In 1412, Burggraf Friedrich of the Hohenzollern dynasty of Nuremberg was asked by Sigismund of Luxemburg to support him in the princely feuding before the imperial election for the throne. When Sigismund became king, he gave Friedrich, in 1415, the titles of Margrave and Prince-Elector of Brandenburg as a reward for his services – this is where the histories of the Hohenzollerns and Berlin first became entwined, a relationship that was to last for 500 years. From the start, the family tried to limit the powers of the town and of the Brandenburg nobility. Culture, however, flourished under the new rulers, especially the Great Elector 200 years later, who invited 20,000 Huguenot craftsmen to Berlin and founded an art gallery and several schools. His grandson Friedrich Wilhelm I, father of Frederick the Great, transformed the city into a military camp, with garrisons and parade grounds, and scoured the town for tall men to join his bodyguard. In the 19th century, however, relations between Berlin and the Hohenzollerns became decidedly less cordial.

**TOP 10 HOHENZOLLERN RULERS**

1 **Friedrich Wilhelm** the Great Elector (1620–88)

2 **Friedrich I** (1657–1713)

3 **Friedrich Wilhelm I** (1688–1740)

4 **Friedrich II** the Great (1712–86)

5 **Friedrich Wilhelm II** (1744–97)

6 **Friedrich Wilhelm III** (1770–1840)

7 **Friedrich Wilhelm IV** (1795–1861)

8 **Wilhelm I** (1797–1888)

9 **Friedrich III** (1831–88)

10 **Wilhelm II** (1859–1941)

*The Great Elector Receiving Huguenot Refugees*, 18th-century etching by Daniel Chodowiecki

# Kulturforum

The Kulturforum is a unique complex of museums, concert halls and libraries west of Potsdamer Platz. Here, some of the most outstanding European art museums, as well as the famous concert hall of the Berlin Philharmonic Orchestra, attract millions of visitors interested in culture and music. The complex, based in the former West Berlin, has been growing steadily since 1956 as a counterpoint to the Museumsinsel in the former East Berlin. The Kulturforum also contains some of Berlin's best examples of modern architecture.

### Gemäldegalerie

Berlin's largest art museum **(right)** holds masterpieces of European art. They are displayed in the modern Neubau, built in 1998 by Heinz Hilmer and Christoph Sattler. The collection includes Bosch, Holbein, Dürer, Gossaert, Vermeer, Brueghel the Elder, Titian, Caravaggio and Rembrandt.

### 2 Neue Nationalgalerie

Based in a building by Mies van der Rohe **(above)**, this holds mainly 20th-century art, with an emphasis on German Expressionism. Collection highlights are on show elsewhere during the renovation *(see p56)*.

### Philharmonie 3

This tent-like building **(right)** was the first new structure to be built in the Kulturforum in 1960–3. Considered one of the best concert halls in the world, it is the home of the Berlin Philharmonic Orchestra. Sir Simon Rattle will continue to conduct until 2018 *(see p66)*.

### 4 Kunstgewerbe-museum

Craft objects from across Europe from the Middle Ages to the present day are on show at this museum **(left)**, including valuable items like the Guelphs' treasure, Lüneburg's silver and Renaissance faïence *(see p51)*.

### 5 Musikinstrumenten-museum

Concealed behind the Philharmonie is this fascinating little museum of musical instruments. More than 800 exhibits are on show here, particularly early instruments such as harpsichords **(right)** as well as a 1929 Wurlitzer *(see p51)*.

### 6 Kammermusiksaal

The smaller relative of the larger Philharmonie, this concert hall is one of Germany's most highly regarded chamber music venues *(see p57)*.

### 7 Kupferstichkabinett

The Gallery of Prints and Drawings holds more than 550,000 prints and 110,000 drawings from all periods and countries, including a portrait of Dürer's mother.

### 8 St Matthäuskirche

This church **(right)** is the only historical building preserved in the Kulturforum. Built in 1844–6 by Stüler, it is also a venue for art installations and classical music concerts.

**Plan of the Kulturforum**

### 9 Staatsbibliothek

Built in 1978 by Hans Scharoun, the National Library *(see p90)* is one of the world's largest German-language libraries, with five million books, manuscripts and journals.

### 10 Kunstbibliothek

The Art Library has a collection of advertising and art posters, among other items, and also hosts art and architecture exhibitions and design shows.

# Gemäldegalerie

### ① Portrait of Hieronymus Holzschuher

Albrecht Dürer painted this portrait of the mayor of Nuremburg in 1529.

Holbein's *Portrait of Georg Gisze*

### ② Portrait of the Merchant Georg Gisze

This 1532 painting by Hans Holbein, showing the Hanseatic League merchant Georg Gisze counting his money, reflects the rise of the rich citizen during the Renaissance.

### ③ Madonna with Child and Singing Angels

A 1477 painting by Sandro Botticelli depicts the Madonna and Child, surrounded by angels carrying lilies.

### ④ The Birth of Christ

Martin Schongauer's altar painting (c.1480) is one of only a few religious paintings by the Alsatian artist that have been preserved.

### ⑤ Victorious Eros

Caravaggio's 1602 painting, after Virgil's model, shows Eros, the god of love, trampling underfoot the symbols of culture, glory, science and power.

**Floorplan Key**

Exhibition area

Entrance

### ⑥ Portrait of Hendrickje Stoffels

In a 1656–7 portrait of his lover Hendrickje Stoffels, Rembrandt's focus is entirely on the subject.

### ⑦ The French Comedy

This painting by Antoine Watteau belonged to the collection of Frederick the Great.

### ⑧ The Glass of Wine

This skilfully composed scene by Vermeer (1658–61) shows a couple drinking wine.

Detail, Botticelli's *Madonna with Child*

### ⑨ Venus and the Organ Player

This Titian (1550–52) reflects the playful sensuality typical of the Italian Renaissance.

### ⑩ Dutch Proverbs

More than 100 proverbs were incorporated into this 1559 painting by Pieter Brueghel.

Brueghel's *Dutch Proverbs*

## ARCHITECTURE IN THE KULTURFORUM

**The tent-like roof of the Berlin Philharmonie**

The Kulturforum was planned to fill the area between Potsdamer Straße and Leipziger Platz that had been destroyed during the war. The idea for a varied townscape of museums and parks is credited to Berlin architect Hans Scharoun, who had designed plans for this between 1946 and 1957. It was also Scharoun who, with the building of the Philharmonie in 1963, set the character of the Kulturforum: the tent-like, golden roofs of the music hall, the Kammermusiksaal and the national library, designed by him and – after his death – realized by his pupil Edgar Wisniewski, are today among Berlin's top landmarks. All the buildings are characterized by the generous proportions of their rooms and, although controversial when they were built, are today considered classics of modern architecture.

**TOP 10
KULTURFORUM
ARCHITECTS**

**1 Hans Scharoun**
Philharmonie

**2 Mies van der Rohe**
Neue Nationalgalerie

**3 James Stirling**
Wissenschaftszentrum

**4 Heinz Hilmer**
Gemäldegalerie

**5 Christoph Sattler**
Gemäldegalerie

**6 Friedrich August Stüler** St Matthäuskirche

**7 Edgar Wisniewski**
Kammermusiksaal

**8 Rolf Gutbrod**
Kunstgewerbemuseum

**9 August Busse** altes
Wissenschaftszentrum

**10 Bruno Doedens**
Henriette-Herz-Park

**The auditorium of the Berlin Philharmonie**

# 🔟 ⭐ Zoologischer Garten

Berlin's Zoological Garden in the Tiergarten district is the oldest zoo in Germany and, with nearly 1,500 different species, one of the best-stocked in the world. Animals have been kept and bred here since 1844. Today, the zoo hosts about 19,500 animals, ranging from jellyfish to Indian elephants. Many, such as the polar bears and baby gorillas, have become celebrities, and with numerous other fascinating enclosures to explore, a zoo trip is a favourite day out for Berliners and visitors alike.

### 1 Penguin House

Playful Antarctic king and rockhopper penguins inhabit this cool haven, complete with realistic cliffs, illuminated "heavens" and a giant skylight. Happier in warmer climes, Humboldt **(above)** and African penguins swim and waddle outside.

### 2 Monkey House

Monkeys and apes are at home in this house, and here you can watch gorillas, orangutans and chimpanzees playing and swinging from tree to tree. The Eastern Lowland Gorillas are very popular.

### 3 Polar Bear Feeding

The 10:30am public feeding of the polar bears attracts big crowds. Check all the animal feeding times online or at the entrance on arrival.

### 4 Giraffe House

The 1872 North-African-style Giraffe House **(below)** is the oldest enclosure. Visitors enjoy watching as the giraffes nibble the leaves of a tree or slowly bend down to drink.

### 5 Nocturnal Animal House

Located in the Predatory Animal House, this shelters the creatures of the night, including reptiles and birds. Here you can admire striped bandicoots, fruit bats and slender loris **(above)**. Asleep during the day, they have superb hearing and eyes that light up eerily in the dark.

### 6 Elephant House
These huge, good-natured pachyderms have a healthy appetite: Indian elephants **(left)** devour up to 50 kg (110 lb) of hay a day. Since 1998, 16 elephants have been born here.

### 7 Aviaries
Nowhere else in the city can you hear such singing, tweeting and whistling – cockatiels, parrots, hornbills and herons **(right)** sound off in the Bird House.

### 8 Hippo House
Glass domes arch over an aquatic habitat **(left)** at one of the world's most remarkable modern zoo enclosures. An underwater viewing area lets you admire the hippos as they swim with seemingly weightless balletic grace. The animals also have access to an outdoor pool.

### 9 Aquarium
The greatest draw in the aquarium, where fantastic Caribbean and Amazonian habitats have been re-created, are the green morays and blacktip reef sharks, as well as a jellyfish cylinder allowing 360° views of the shimmering aquatic beauties.

### 10 Amphibians' Section
Poisonous snakes, bird spiders and reptiles as well as other amphibians crawl and slither around behind glass **(below)** on the second floor of the aquarium. A particularly spectacular event is the feeding of the spiders.

**NEED TO KNOW**

**MAP N5** ■ Hardenbergplatz 8 and Budapester Str. 34 ■ (030) 25 40 10 ■ www.zoo-berlin.de

**Open** Mid-Mar–Sep: 9am–7pm daily (to 5pm daily in winter)

Adm €15.50; €21 combined entry for zoo and aquarium

■ There is a café and self-service restaurant with a terrace inside the zoo, to the right of the Elephant Gate.

■ A day at the zoo is not complete without a visit to the aquarium. The basins and terraria teem with life, as do the zoo enclosures.

# The Top 10
# of Everything

Gendarmenmarkt's imposing Deutscher Dom,
with the Konzerthaus entrance in the foreground

# 🔟 Moments in History

The Neues Palais in Potsdam, the town where the 1685 edict was signed

### 1 1685: Edict of Potsdam

Berlin's history as a cultural capital began in 1685, when the far-sighted Great Elector announced in the Edict of Potsdam that around 20,000 Huguenots would be taken in by Berlin. Many were excellent craftsmen and scientists, who, having fled Catholic France because of their Protestant beliefs, brought a new age of cultural ascendancy to the provincial town.

### 2 1744: Frederick the Great

Although "Old Fritz", as Frederick the Great was nicknamed, preferred the isolation of Sanssouci to the bustle of Berlin, in 1740 he began to transform the city into a new metropolis. In particular, the "Forum Fridericianum" in Unter den Linden brought new splendours to the town, and masterpieces such as the national opera house helped transform Berlin into one of the most important European cities.

### 3 Golden Twenties

Between 1919 and 1933, Berlin flourished culturally and became an influential metropolis. Film, theatre, cabaret shows and thousands of restaurants and bars transformed the town into a vibrant international centre of entertainment. Berlin also set new standards in the realms of science and industry, and in architecture and fine art, particularly the Bauhaus movement.

### 4 1945: Surrender

Signed in Berlin-Karlshorst on 8 May 1945, Germany's unconditional surrender marked more than the end of World War II. The previous Jewish population of 161,000 had virtually disappeared and Berliners called their city "the empire's fields of rubble".

### 5 1953: Workers' Uprising in East Germany

On 17 June 1953, East Berlin construction workers in Frankfurter Allee demonstrated against an increase in the average rate of production and work quotas. Soviet tanks suppressed the rebellion while, in West Berlin, the uprising was interpreted as a demonstration for German unification.

Soviet tanks during the 1953 uprising

**Worker building the Berlin Wall**

### 6 1961: Building of the Berlin Wall

The building of the Berlin Wall, which commenced during the night of 12 August 1961, was a traumatic event for many Berliners. Many families were torn apart by the concrete wall and more than 100 people were to be killed over the following 30 years at the border dividing East and West.

### 7 1963: "I am a Berliner"

No other politician was as enthusiastically received in Berlin as the US President John F Kennedy. On 17 July 1963, in front of Rathaus Schöneberg, he declared to the cheering crowd: "I am a Berliner". Berliners had forgiven the US for staying silent when the Wall was built. Kennedy confirmed once more that the Western Allies would stand by Berlin and support the town, just as they had done during the blockade of 1948–9, when the US and Britain airlifted food to the "island" of West Berlin.

### 8 1968: The late Sixties

During the late 1960s, West Berlin students transformed Germany. Rudi Dutschke and others proposed political change and a reappraisal of Germany's Nazi past. The movement came to an untimely end when Dutschke was injured in an assassination attempt by Josef Bachmann in April 1968.

### 9 1989: Fall of the Wall

The fall of the Berlin Wall on 9 November 1989 heralded a new dawn for the city and the country. For the first time in 30 years, Berliners from both halves of the divided city were able to visit each other. The town celebrated all along Ku'damm and in front of the Brandenburg Gate. When the Wall was built, Willy Brandt, then governing mayor of West Berlin, had promised: "Berlin will survive!" He was right.

### 10 1991: Berlin becomes the capital of Germany

In June 1991, Berlin was officially declared the capital of the reunified Federal Republic of Germany. Allied Forces left the city during 1994, but it was only when the Bundestag, the German parliament, moved here from Bonn on 19 April 1999 that Berlin became the "real" capital. Today, all the main federal ministries and government authorities, the Bundesrat (upper house), and the Chancellor's and the President's offices are based in Berlin.

**People celebrating the fall of the Wall**

# TOP 10 Famous Berliners

**Actress Marlene Dietrich**

## 1 Marlene Dietrich

The famous filmstar (1901–92), born in Schöneberg, began her career in Berlin in the 1920s. Her breakthrough came with the film *The Blue Angel* (1931). She lies buried in the Friedenau cemetery in Steglitz. Many of her personal possessions are exhibited in the Deutsche Kinemathek *(see p22)*.

## 2 Albert Einstein

In 1914, Albert Einstein (1879–1955) became the director of the Kaiser Wilhelm-Institute for Physics. He was awarded the Nobel Prize for Physics in 1921 for his explanation of the photoelectric effect, though he is now better known for his Theory of Relativity, first developed in 1905. Einstein mostly lived and worked in Potsdam, but stayed closely connected with Berlin through his lectures and teaching activity. In 1933 Einstein, who was Jewish, emigrated to the USA, where he stayed until his death.

## 3 Bertolt Brecht

Born in Augsburg, Bavaria, Bertolt Brecht (1898–1956) wrote some of his greatest works, such as the *Threepenny Opera,* in a small apartment in Charlottenburg. During the Third Reich, the playwright emigrated to the US, but he returned to Germany after World War II and founded the Berliner Ensemble in East Berlin in 1949. Until his death, Brecht lived in Chausseestraße in Berlin-Mitte, with his wife, Helene Weigel. His renovated apartment has been turned into a museum.

## 4 Herbert von Karajan

This famous Austrian conductor (1908–1989) was head of the Berlin Philharmonic Orchestra from 1954 until 1989. During this time he helped create the orchestra's unique sound, which remains legendary until this day. Herbert von Karajan was both revered and feared by his musicians because of his genius and his famously fiery temperament. Berliners still refer to the Philharmonie as "Circus Karajani".

**Conductor Herbert von Karajan**

## 5 Robert Koch

Like few other physicians and microbiologists of his day, Robert Koch (1843–1910) laid the foundations and shaped the face of modern medicine with his pioneering discoveries. The Director of the Institute for Infectious Diseases, Koch also taught and researched at the Charité Hospital. In 1905 he received the Nobel Prize for Medicine for his pioneering discoveries in the field of tuberculosis research.

### 6 Theodor Fontane

A Huguenot, Fontane (1819–98) was one of the most influential 19th-century novelists and poets in Germany. He also worked as a journalist and critic for more than 20 years, penning many of his articles and essays in

**Theodor Fontane**

the Café Josty on Potsdamer Platz. Fontane is particularly well known for his novel *Effi Briest* and five-volume travelogue *Wanderungen durch die Mark Brandenburg (Ramblings through the March of Brandenburg)*, in which he describes the mentality of the people, the historic places, the architecture and the landscapes of the principality of Brandenburg.

### 7 Käthe Kollwitz

The sculptor and painter Käthe Kollwitz (1867–1945) portrayed the social problems of the poor, and her work provides a powerful, haunting commentary on human suffering. Kollwitz spent a large part of her life in a modest abode in the square that is now named after her, in the Prenzlauer Berg district. A monument recalls how she captured the lives of poor Berlin families, burdened with large numbers of children, and of social outcasts. An enlarged reproduction of her *Pietà* now adorns the Neue Wache war memorial *(see p17)*.

### 8 Jacob and Wilhelm Grimm

The brothers Jacob (1785–1863) and Wilhelm (1786–1859) Grimm are known around the world for their collection of classic fairy tales, which include *Little Red Riding Hood, Hansel and Gretel* and *Rumpelstiltskin*. Their linguistic output was equally important – their *German Grammar* and *German Dictionary* are standard reference works even today.

### 9 Georg Wilhelm Hegel

The influential philosopher Hegel (1770–1831) taught at the city's Humboldt University from 1818 until his death.

### 10 Felix Mendelssohn Bartholdy

The composer (1809–47), a grandson of philosopher Moses Mendelssohn, was also the conductor of the Staatskapelle (state orchestra) at the opera house in Unter den Linden. His grave can be found in the Holy Trinity Cemetery I, located in the city's trendy Kreuzberg district.

**Monument to sculptor and painter Käthe Kollwitz by Gustav Seitz**

# 🔟 Museums

**Exhibit at the Pergamonmuseum**

## 1 Pergamonmuseum

This impressive museum on the Museuminsel is a vast treasure trove of antiquities (see p26).

## 2 Ägyptisches Museum

**MAP K5** ■ Museumsinsel, Bodestr. 1 ■ (030) 266 424 242 ■ 10am–6pm daily (until 8pm Thu) ■ Adm ■ www. smb.museum

The star exhibit in the Egyptian Museum, which is a part of the Neues Museum, is the beautiful bust of Nefertiti, wife of Akhenaton. The long-necked limestone bust, discovered in 1912, was copied all over ancient Egypt. Also worth seeing is the "Berlin Green Head", a small bust from the 4th century BC. The museum also holds numerous mummies, sarcophagi, murals and sculptures (see pp24–5).

## 3 Deutsches Historisches Museum

Germany's largest history museum uses unique exhibits, documents and films to take the visitor on a journey through German history, from the Middle Ages to the present day. Special exhibitions are devoted to particular themes (see pp16–19).

## 4 Museum Europäischer Kulturen

This museum specializes in European folk art, lifestyle, tradition and culture, and, with some 280,000 objects, is one of the largest of its kind in the world. It hosts long-running as well as temporary exhibitions, often in conjunction with museums from other European countries. Among the vast collection of exhibits on display are earthenware items, costumes, handicrafts, jewellery, toys and tools (see p151).

## 5 Jüdisches Museum

The Jewish Museum, housed in a spectacular building designed by Daniel Libeskind, documents the German–Jewish relationship through the centuries. There are special exhibitions on the influence of Berlin Jews on the town's cultural life, and on the life of the Enlightenment philosopher Moses Mendelssohn. An empty room commemorates the loss of Jewish culture. There is also an excellent programme of special events (see p129).

A Junkers Ju 52 plane on display at the Deutsches Technikmuseum

### 6 Deutsches Technikmuseum

The fascinating German Museum of Technology, built on the site of a former railway goods yard, has some exciting hands-on displays on the history of technology *(see p129).*

### 7 Kunstgewerbemuseum

MAP L1 ■ Matthäikirchplatz
■ (030) 266 424 242 ■ 10am–6pm Tue–Fri, 11am–6pm Sat & Sun
■ Adm ■ www.smb.museum

European crafts spanning over five centuries are on display here. Its most valuable exhibits are the treasure of the Guelphs from Braunschweig and the silver treasure of the town council in Lüneburg. The museum also holds Italian tin-glazed earthenware, Renaissance faïence and German Baroque glass and ceramics. Popular displays show Neo-Classical porcelain and furniture, Jugendstil art and Tiffany vases *(see pp38–41).*

### 8 Haus am Checkpoint Charlie

The museum at the former Allied checkpoint hosts an exhibition documenting events at the Berlin Wall *(see p129).*

**18th-century hunting horn**

### 9 Museum für Naturkunde

MAP F2 ■ Invalidenstr. 43
■ (030) 20 93 85 91 ■ 9:30am–6pm Tue–Fri, 10am–6pm Sat & Sun
■ Adm ■ www.naturkundemuseum-berlin.de

With over 30 million specimens in its collection, the Natural History Museum is one of the largest of its kind in the world. One of the star features is the world's largest dinosaur skeleton, a brachiosaurus found in Tanzania in 1909. There are six more dinosaur skeletons as well as a variety of fossils. Together, they take the visitor back to prehistoric times. It is also worth making a visit to the glittering exhibition of meteorites and minerals *(see p96).*

### 10 Musikinstrumenten-museum

MAP L2 ■ Ben-Gurion-Str. 1
■ (030) 25 48 10 ■ 9am–5pm Tue–Fri (to 8pm Thu), 10am–5pm Sat & Sun ■ Adm
■ www.sim.spk-berlin.de

Some 800 musical instruments can be heard in this museum, including Frederick the Great's harpsichord *(see p39).* Don't miss the silent-film organ which still works (noon, first Saturday of the month).

# rt Galleries

**Johannes Vermeer's *The Glass of Wine***

## ③ Alte Nationalgalerie

MAP J5 ■ Bodestr. 1–3 ■ 10am–6pm Tue–Sun to 8pm Thu) ■ Adm ■ www.smb.museum

The Old National Gallery, built by Friedrich August Stüler in 1866–76, holds a collection of 19th-century, mainly German paintings, including works by Adolf von Menzel, Wilhelm Leibl, Max Liebermann and Arnold Böcklin. It also has sculptures by Schadow, Rauch and Reinhold Begas *(see pp24–5)*.

## ① Gemäldegalerie

Berlin's best art museum, the Gemäldegalerie holds European art of the 13th–19th centuries, including Vermeer's *The Glass of Wine* and *The Adoration of the Shepherds* by Hugo van der Goes, as well as works by Rembrandt, Dürer, Caravaggio and Rubens *(see pp38–41)*.

## ② Brücke-Museum

Bussardsteig 9 ■ 11am–5pm Wed–Mon ■ Adm ■ www.bruecke-museum.de

Must-see collection of German Expressionist works by the Brücke (bridge) movement, including Kirchner, Schmidt-Rottluff, Nolde, and Pechstein. Many Brücke works were labelled "degenerate" by the Nazis and destroyed.

## ④ Museum Berggruen

The late Heinz Berggruen, born in Berlin in 1914, emigrated to the US in 1936 but returned to Berlin in 1996. His collection, including works from Picasso's Blue Period, is based in a historic Charlottenburg building by Stüler *(see p35)*.

**Museum Berggruen**

**Warhol's *Mao*, Hamburger Bahnhof**

### 5 Hamburger Bahnhof
MAP F2 ■ Invalidenstr. 50–51
■ 10am–6pm Tue–Fri (to 8pm Thu),
11am–6pm Sat & Sun ■ Adm
■ www.smb.museum

The historic Hamburg Station houses modern paintings, installations and multimedia art. One of its highlights is the Erich Marx Collection, with works by Joseph Beuys. Apart from famous artists like Andy Warhol, Jeff Koons and Robert Rauschenberg, it also owns works by Anselm Kiefer, Sandro Chiao and others *(see p114)*.

### 6 Kunsthaus Dahlem
MAP N6 ■ Käuzchensteig 8
■ 11am–5pm Wed–Mon ■ Adm
■ www.kunsthaus-dahlem.de

This exhibition venue for postwar German Modernism from East and West Germany was built during 1939–42 for sculptor Arno Breker. The building was used by US Information Control Division after the war and later became a workspace for artists.

### 7 C/O Berlin
MAP N4 ■ Amerika-Haus, Hardenbergstr. 22–24 ■ 11am–8pm daily ■ www.co-berlin.org

Located in the former Amerika-Haus, this venue hosts regularly changing exhibitions, lectures and historic and contemporary photography events.

### 8 Berlinische Galerie
MAP G5 ■ Alte Jakobstr. 124–128
■ 10am–6pm Wed–Mon ■ Adm
■ www.berlinischegalerie.de

Huge collections of mostly German, east European and Russian painters, photographers, graphic designers and architects from the 20th century, such as Baselitz, Grosz and Kirchner.

### 9 Sammlung Scharf-Gerstenberg
MAP B3 ■ Schlossstr. 70 ■ 10am–6pm Tue–Sun ■ Adm ■ www.smb.museum

This gallery has rare works by surrealists and their forerunners, such as Goya, Klee, Dalí, Max Ernst and Man Ray.

### 10 Bröhan-Museum
MAP B3 ■ Schlossstr. 1a
■ 10am–6pm Tue–Sun ■ Adm
(free 1st Wed of month)
■ www.broehan-museum.de

Jugendstil and Art Deco objects from around Europe, and paintings by Berlin artists, are on display in this design and art museum.

**Impressive exterior of the Bröhan-Museum**

# 🔟 Historic Buildings

### 1 Brandenburger Tor
More than a mere symbol, the Brandenburg Gate is synonymous with Berlin *(see pp12–13)*.

### 2 Schloss Charlottenburg
This palace features Baroque and Rococo splendours and a beautiful park, making it one of the most attractive in Germany *(see pp34–7)*.

**Schloss Charlottenburg**

### 3 Schloss Bellevue
■ MAP E4 ■ Spreeweg 1
■ Not open to the public
■ www.bundespraesident.de/EN/
Built by Philipp Daniel Boumann in 1785–90, this was the residence of the Hohenzollerns until 1861. Since 1994 the stately building with its Neo-Classical façade has been the official residence of the President of the Federal Republic. The modern, egg-shaped Presidential Offices stand next to the old palace.

### 4 Reichstag
The seat of the Deutscher Bundestag, the German parliament, with its spectacular cupola, is a magnet for visitors *(see pp14–15)*.

### 5 Berliner Rathaus
■ MAP K6 ■ Rathausstraße 15 ■ 8am–6pm daily
Berlin's Town Hall, also known as "Red Town Hall" because of the red bricks from Brandenburg province with which it is built, harks back to the proud days when Berlin became the capital of the new Empire. Built in 1861–9 according to designs by Hermann Friedrich Waesemann, the town hall was one of Germany's largest and most magnificent buildings, built to promote the splendour of Berlin. The structure was modelled on Italian Renaissance palaces, and the tower is reminiscent of Laon cathedral in France. The exterior was decorated with *Die Steinerne Chronik* (the stone chronicle) in 1879, depicting scenes from the city's history *(see p103)*.

### 6 Konzerthaus
■ MAP L4 ■ Gendarmenmarkt 2 ■ (030) 203 092 101 ■ Main hall Apr–Oct: 11am–6pm; tours 3:30pm Mon–Fri, 1pm Sun ■ en.konzerthaus.de
The Concert Hall, one of Karl Friedrich Schinkel's masterpieces, was formerly known as the *Schauspielhaus* (theatre). The

**The Neo-Classical exterior of the Konzerthaus**

building has a portico with Ionic columns and statues of allegorical and historical personages, some riding lions and panthers, as well as deities, muses and bacchants.

### 7 Hackesche Höfe
**MAP J5** ■ Rosenthaler Str. 40–41

This complex of 19th-century buildings has eight interlinked courtyards, some of which are decorated in Jugendstil style, originally by August Endell. In the early 1990s the complex was completely renovated. The first courtyard is particularly attractive: coloured glazed tiles with geometric patterns decorate the house from the foundations up to the guttering. In the last courtyard, trees are grouped around an idyllic well. The Hackesche Höfe is one of Berlin's most popular hotspots; restaurants, cafés, a cinema and the Chamäleon musical theatre and variety show *(see p66)* attract visitors from afar.

### 8 Siegessäule
The Victory Column in Tiergarten is topped by the statue of Victoria.

**Siegessäule**

Designed by Heinrich Strack after Prussia's victory in the Danish-Prussian War of 1864, it was refurbished in 2010 *(see p113)*.

### 9 Altes Museum and Lustgarten
The façade of the Old Museum, possibly one of the most attractive Neo-Classical museum buildings in Europe, is remarkable for the 18 Ionic columns supporting a portico. Built in 1830 to Karl Friedrich Schinkel's design, it was at the time one of the first buildings to be created specifically as a museum. Originally it was to house the royal collection of paintings; today it is home to a collection of antiquities. In front of the museum is a garden designed by Peter Joseph Lenné. Conceived as the king's herb garden, it is now decorated with a 70-ton granite bowl by Gottlieb Christian Cantian, and a fountain *(see p25)*.

### 10 Zeughaus
Designed by J A Nering as the first Berlin Baroque building, the former Royal Prussian Arsenal is now the Deutsches Historisches Museum *(see pp16–19)*, with a modern addition by I M Pei.

# TOP 10 Modern Buildings

## 1 Sony Center

The spectacular Sony Center, with its unique roof, is one of Berlin's largest structures *(see p20)*.

**Glass membrane roof, Sony Center**

## 2 Neue Nationalgalerie

MAP E4 ▪ Potsdamer Str. 50
▪ 10am–6pm Tue–Fri (until 8pm Thu), 11am–6pm Sat & Sun ▪ Adm
▪ Closed until 2020 for remodelling
▪ www.smb.museum

This impressive structure was built in 1965–8 by Mies van der Rohe. It was the first building by the pioneering Bauhaus architect after his emigration to the USA. He used his earlier designs for the Havana headquarters of the Bacardi company, which had been abandoned after the Cuban Revolution *(see p38)*.

## 3 Bundeskanzleramt

MAP K2 ▪ Willy-Brandt-Str. 1
▪ Not open to the public

Berliners are not too fond of the Chancellor's modern offices, although this is the only government building to have been designed by a Berlin architect. Axel Schultes developed a vast, elongated office complex, which extends north of the Reichstag, in a bend of the Spree, even stretching across the river. In the centre of the hyper-modern building stands a gleaming white cube with round windows, which Berliners quickly nicknamed the "Washing Machine". Critics describe the design as pompous, while civil servants dislike their small offices. The interior of the building is decorated with valuable modern paintings. The Chancellor's office on the 7th floor has a view of the Reichstag building.

**Exterior of the Bundeskanzleramt**

**Ludwig-Erhard-Haus**

### 4 Ludwig-Erhard-Haus
MAP N4 ■ Fasanenstr. 85
■ 8am–6pm Mon–Fri

The seat of the Berlin Stock Exchange, Ludwig-Erhard-Haus was designed by British architect Nicholas Grimshaw in 1994–8. Locals refer to it as the "armadillo", because the 15 giant metal arches of the domed building recall the animal's armour.

### 5 Philharmonie and Kammermusiksaal

Two modern concert halls in the Kulturforum were designed by Hans Scharoun in 1961 and 1987 respectively – the Kammermusiksaal (chamber music hall) was completed after Scharoun's death in 1972 according to his plans by his pupil Edgar Wisniewski. Both buildings are renowned for their excellent acoustics as well as for their tent-like roof structures *(see pp38–41)*.

### 6 Hauptbahnhof
MAP J2 ■ Hauptbahnhof

Europe's largest train station sits on the site of the historic Lehrter Bahnhof. This impressive glass and steel structure doubles as a retail and hospitality hub.

### 7 Quartiere 205–207 Friedrichstraße

The Galeries Lafayettes and the Friedrichstadtpassagen are based within these three office blocks designed by architects Nouvel, Pei and Ungers *(see p87)*.

### 8 Nordische Botschaften
MAP N6 ■ Rauchstr. ■ Gallery 10am–7pm Mon–Fri, 11am–4pm Sat & Sun ■ www.nordicembassies.org

No other embassy building has caused as much of a stir as the one housing five embassies of the Nordic countries: its green shutters open and close depending on the available light. Regular art exhibitions are held in the building.

### 9 DZ Bank on Pariser Platz
MAP K3 ■ Pariser Platz 3 ■ Lobby 10am–6pm Mon–Fri

This elegant building by Frank Owen Gehry combines Prussian and modern architecture. The giant dome inside is remarkable *(see p12)*.

**Spectacular interior of the DZ Bank**

### 10 Kant-Dreieck
MAP N4 ■ Kantstr. 155
■ 9am–6pm Mon–Fri

The enormous "shark fin" on top of the KapHag-Group's headquarters, built by Josef Paul Kleihues in 1992–5, has become a symbol of the new Berlin. The aluminium weather vane is designed to turn in the wind like a sail. Originally, the structure was to be built one-third higher than it is now, but the plans were vetoed by the Berlin Senate.

# ▒ Churches and Synagogues

**Baroque-style exterior, Berliner Dom**

Hohenzollern residence opposite the cathedral. Members of this powerful ruling dynasty are buried in the crypt. The main nave, topped by an 85-m (279-ft) high dome, is remarkable. The church is dominated by a splendid 20th-century Neo-Baroque pulpit and the giant Sauer organ (see p25).

## ① Berliner Dom
MAP K5 ▪ Am Lustgarten ▪ (030) 20 26 91 19 ▪ Apr–Sep: 9am–8pm daily; Oct–Mar: 9am–7pm daily (Opening hours subject to concert schedule, check website) ▪ Adm ▪ www.berlinerdom.de

Berlin Cathedral, the largest and most lavish church in the city, was reopened in 1993, after almost 40 years of restoration work. Designed by Julius Raschdorf between 1894 and 1905, the building reflects the empire's aspirations to power. In particular, the black marble imperial stairs are a sign of the proximity of the

## ② St Hedwigskathedrale
MAP K4 ▪ Bebelplatz ▪ 10am–5pm Mon–Sat, 1–5pm Sun ▪ www.hedwigs-kathedrale.de

Berlin's largest Catholic church was built by Frederick the Great in 1747–73 after his conquest of Silesia (see p16).

## ③ Marienkirche
Work started in 1270 on the Church of St Mary, which nestles at the foot of the Fernsehturm. Gothic and Baroque in style, it has an impressive Neo-Gothic tower, added in 1790 by Carl Gotthard Langhans. The font (1437) and the fresco *Dance of the Dead* (1485) are among the oldest treasures of the church. The richly ornamented Baroque pulpit was made by Andreas Schlüter in 1703 (see p104).

## ④ Nikolaikirche
MAP K6 ▪ Nikolai-kirchplatz ▪ 10am–6pm daily ▪ Adm ▪ www.en.stadtmuseum.de

Berlin's oldest sacred building, this was built in 1230 in the Nikolaiviertel quarter. The present church dates to around 1300. It is particularly famous for the portal on the west wall of the main nave, created by Andreas Schlüter. It is adorned with a gilded relief depicting a goldsmith and his wife. The church was rebuilt in 1987 and

**Kaiser-Wilhelm-Gedächtnis-Kirche**

completely restored in 2009. It is now a museum exploring the history of the church and the surrounding area. Regular events and concerts are held here.

### 5 Synagoge Rykestraße

Berlin's largest synagogue, this is one of the few Jewish places of worship in Germany to have survived Kristallnacht. It looks the same today as when it was originally built over 100 years ago *(see p139)*.

### 6 Neue Synagoge

Once Berlin's largest synagogue, this was built originally in 1859–66. It was demolished in World War II and partially reconstructed in 1988–95. Its magnificent, ornate dome is visible from afar *(see p95)*.

**Beautiful dome of the Neue Synagoge**

### 7 Kaiser-Wilhelm-Gedächtnis-Kirche

A landmark in West Berlin, the Kaiser Wilhelm Memorial Church successfully combines modern architecture with the ruins of the church tower *(see pp32–3)*.

### 8 Friedrichswerdersche Kirche

**Werderscher Markt ▪ Closed for restoration**

This Neo-Gothic church, built in 1824–30, has an impressive façade. Originally it was meant to serve the German and French communities of the Friedrichswerder district.

### 9 Christi-Auferstehungs-Kathedrale

**MAP B6 ▪ Hohenzollerndamm 166 ▪ Open only during service 10am & 6pm Sat, 10am Sun**

Berlin's largest Russian-Orthodox church, the Church of Christ's Ascension is known for its green onion domes. Services are held in Russian, following Orthodox rituals.

### 10 Französischer Dom

**MAP L4 ▪ Gendarmenmarkt 5 ▪ Summer: 10am–7pm daily; winter: 10:30am–6:30pm daily ▪ www. franzoesischer-dom.de**

At 66 m (216 ft) high, this domed Baroque tower, which dates back to between 1780 and 1789, is a magnificent ornamental addition to the Friedrichstadtkirche serving Berlin's Huguenot community *(see p86)*.

# 🔟 Parks and Gardens

### 1 Großer Tiergarten
**MAP E4** ■ Tiergarten

The Tiergarten – the green lungs of Berlin – is the most famous park in the city. Set in the centre of town, the park covers 203 ha (500 acres). Originally designed in 1833–40 by Peter Joseph Lenné as a hunting estate for the Elector, in the latter half of the 19th century the park became a recreation ground for all Berliners. Today it attracts a happy crowd of cyclists, joggers, sun-bathers and families having picnics, especially at weekends (see p113).

### 2 Schlosspark Charlottenburg
**MAP B3** ■ Schloss Charlottenburg, Spandauer Damm ■ from sunrise to sunset daily ■ www.spsg.de

The Palace Park is one of the most attractive and charming green spaces in Germany. Immediately behind Schloss Charlottenburg is a small but magnificent Baroque garden, and beyond this extends a vast park, dating back to the early 19th century. It was landscaped in the English style and boasts artificial lake and river landscapes, small hidden buildings and idyllic shaded groves on the banks of ponds and streams. The park is ideal for strolling, and it is also a favourite place for sunseekers (see pp34–7).

**The Belvedere, Charlottenburg park**

### 3 Grunewald and Teufelsberg
Grunewald

The Grunewald, or "green forest", is the public woods in the southwest of Berlin (see pp150–55). It is the least built-up area of woodland in the city. Parts of Grunewald are very quiet and isolated indeed, and there are even wild boar in the woods – which can be a nuisance to people who have gardens in the nearby district of Zehlendorf. Grunewald is excellent for hiking and horse-riding.

**The folly at Pfaueninsel**

### 4 Pfaueninsel
Peacock Island, an island in the middle of Großer Wannsee that can be reached only by ferry, is probably the most romantic spot in Berlin. In the 19th century, the island served as a love nest for King Friedrich Wilhelm II. His charming folly of a palace ruin was in keeping with the tastes of the time. Today dozens of proud peacocks live in the area around the building (see p151).

### 5 Botanischer Garten
Königin-Luise-Str. 6–8 (garden and museum) ■ (030) 83 85 01 00 ■ 9am to sunset daily (garden); 10am–6pm daily (museum) ■ Adm ■ www.bgbm.org/en

The 19th-century Botanical Garden is a paradise of flowers and plants in the southwest of the city. The vast area with 15 greenhouses was built in the late 19th century around gentle hills and picturesque ponds. The Great Palm House by Alfred

Koerner has spectacular 26-m (85-ft) high giant bamboo from Southeast Asia. The museum introduces visitors to the world of microbiology.

### 6 Viktoriapark and Kreuzberg

The old municipal park, originally designed in 1888–94 as a recreation area for local workers, is now one of Berlin's most popular green spaces (see p131). The meadows around Kreuzberg, which rise to 30 m (98 ft), are great for sunbathing. On top of the hill, a monument recalls the Prussian Wars of Liberation.

### 7 Volkspark Friedrichshain

Berlin's oldest park (1840) is an artificial landscape of lakes and meadows and two wooded mounds, one of which is nicknamed "Mont Klamott", meaning "mount rubble". There is also a fountain with statues of the most popular fairy-tale characters (see p146).

**Fountain statue**

### 8 Tierpark Berlin

This second, larger zoo is situated in the idyllic palace park of Friedrichsfelde, and houses some 860 animal species (see p147).

### 9 Treptower Park

The 19th-century garden on the banks of the Spree has become famous for the Soviet Memorial, which stands next to the graves of 7,000 Red Army soldiers (see p146).

### 10 Britzer Schloss and Park

Alt-Britz 73 ▪ (030) 60 97 92 30 ▪ 11am–6pm Tue–Sun (palace), 9am to sunset daily (garden) ▪ Adm ▪ www.schlossbritz.de

The palace in Britz, dating from 1706 and situated in a lovely park, has been authentically refurbished with historical furniture from the Gründerzeit period after 1871.

---

**TOP 10 LAKES, RIVERS AND CANALS**

**Boat ride on the Spree River**

**1 Spree River**
MAP J/K 1–6 ▪ Mitte, Tiergarten
Guided boat tours, romantic evening cruises and riverside walks are on offer.

**2 Teufelssee, Grunewald**
One of Berlin's cleanest and most relaxed lakes – nudists and dog lovers enjoy the peaceful banks.

**3 Großer Müggelsee**
Thousands congregate at Berlin's largest lake in summer to swim, row, sail or surf (see p146).

**4 Schlachtensee**
After Wannsee, this small lake is the second most popular. Avoid the crowds by going during the week.

**5 Großer Wannsee**
Europe's largest inland beach is beautifully white (see p152).

**6 Lietzensee**
MAP A4 ▪ Am Kaiserdamm
Not suitable for swimming, but the surrounding meadows are idyllic and the lakeside walks popular.

**7 Krumme Lanke, Fischerhüttenweg**
Although many consider the lake not clean enough for bathing, it seems cleaner (but colder) than Schlachtensee.

**8 Landwehrkanal**
MAP M/N5 ▪ Lützowplatz
Take a boat trip along the canal to see some of Berlin's most attractive bridges.

**9 Tegeler See, Alt-Tegel**
The Greenwich Promenade, from Tegeler Hafen (harbour) to Schwarzer Weg, is an attractive walk.

**10 Neuer See**
MAP M3 ▪ Großer Tiergarten
This tranquil lake is hidden in the vast Großer Tiergarten park. On its banks is the Café am Neuen See (see p117).

# 🔟 Off the Beaten Track

### ① Bearpit Karaoke
MAP G1 ■ Topsstraße 28
■ May–Oct: 3–5pm Sun
■ www.bearpitkaraoke.com

Sunday afternoon karaoke sessions in the Mauerpark's "bearpit" amphitheatre are extremely popular. The show host, Joe Hatchiban, arrives on a fancy bicycle equipped with loudspeaker and laptop. Crowds of up to 2,000 gather to watch hopefuls take turns belting out oldies.

### ② Unterwelten Museum
MAP G1 ■ Brunnenstraße 105 ■ (030) 49 91 05 18 ■ English tours Apr–Oct: 11am, 1pm & 3pm ■ Adm ■ www.berliner-unterwelten. de

Did you know the Nazis made aircraft underground? Or that Cold War nuclear bunkers were largely futile? Find out on guided tours of bomb shelters, tunnels and vaults going back to the 19th century. Exhibits include an Enigma encryption machine, armaments and atmospheric living quarters.

### ③ Boros Art Collection
MAP J3 ■ Reinhardtstraße 20 ■ English tours at 11am and 1pm daily (by reservation only) ■ Adm ■ www.sammlung-boros.de

This World War II air-raid shelter is now a contemporary art gallery owned by the advertising mogul Christian Boros *(see p98)*. Built for the staff of nearby Friedrichstrasse railway station, this concrete behemoth has also served as a prison, a larder for

produce, and a disco. Visits can be made only on 90-minute private tours, which can be booked online.

The Badeschiff in the Spree

### ④ Badeschiff
Eichenstraße 4 ■ (030) 533 20 30 ■ May–Sep: 8am–midnight daily ■ Adm ■ www.arena-berlin.de

A shimmering island of blue, this old cargo container in the Spree is the city's coolest place for a dip. The pool is reached via a pier from a sandy beach. After sunset DJs spin vinyl and guests migrate to a nightclub boat, *Hoppetosse*, moored alongside.

### ⑤ Schwerbelastungskörper
MAP E6 ■ General-Pape-Straße ■ (030) 533 20 30 ■ Apr–Oct: 2–4pm Tue–Wed, 10am–6pm Thu, 1–3pm Sun ■ www.schwerbelastungskoerper.de

Hitler and Albert Speer, the Führer's chief architect, planned to transform Berlin into a "world capital" called Welthauptstadt Germania. To test the feasibility of building a huge triumphal arch on the area's soft ground, they commissioned the Schwerbelastungskörper, a concrete cylinder weighing 12,650 metric tons.

Boros Art Collection

The Welthauptstadt was never built but the cylinder houses a historical exhibition.

### 6 Monsterkabinett

MAP J5 ■ Rosenthaler Straße 39 ■ (0152) 12 59 86 87 ■ 6–10pm Thu, 4–10pm Fri & Sat ■ Adm ■ www.monsterkabinett.de

Run by the Dead Chickens art collective, this installation features robots that interact with visitors. The 20-minute tour with heavy metal soundtrack and lightshow ends with a blast of anti-monster spray that blows the head off one creature.

### 7 Mount Mitte

MAP F2 ■ Caroline-Michaelis-Straße 8 ■ 2pm–sunset Mon–Fri, 10am–sunset Sat & Sun ■ Adm ■ www.beachmitte.de

Don a helmet, strap on a security line and wiggle your way through Berlin's oddest high-rope climbing course, tackling wooden barrels, surfboards and old East German Trabant cars suspended in midair.

### 8 Admiralbrücke

MAP H5 ■ Fraenkelufer 25

This lacy, wrought iron bridge was built in 1882 in Jugendstil style, spanning one of the prettiest stretches on the Landwehrkanal. On balmy summer nights it fills up with beer-drinking revellers listening to street musicians playing their hearts out.

### 9 Currywurst Museum

MAP G4 ■ Schützenstraße 70 ■ (030) 88 71 86 47 ■ 10am–6pm daily ■ Adm ■ www.currywurstmuseum.de

Curried pork sausage is as much a part of Berlin as the Reichstag. This interactive museum's displays delve into the 1940s origins of currywurst and the history of fast food. Look out for a wienerwurst-shaped couch, a spice chamber with sniffing stations, a sausage game and a documentary called *Rest of the Wurst*.

**Currywurst mascot**

### 10 Tieranatomisches Theater

MAP J3 ■ Philippstraße 12 ■ (030) 209 346 625 ■ 2–6pm Tue–Sat ■ www.kulturtechnik.hu-berlin.de

Nestled in a remote university courtyard, the Veterinary Anatomical Theatre is Berlin's oldest surviving academic building, erected in 1789-90. Wander through the historical exhibition to the circular lecture hall with dissection table and spectator galleries.

**Tieranatomisches Theater**

# 🔟 Children's Attractions

**Deutsches Technikmuseum**

## 1 Deutsches Technikmuseum

The technology museum is a giant playground for children, excellent for learning through play. There are locomotives to clamber over, windmills to play with and the Science Center Spectrum, where older children can conduct their own physics and technology experiments *(see p129)*.

## 2 Labyrinth Kindermuseum

Osloer Str. 12 ▪ 9am–6pm Mon–Fri, 1–6pm Sat, 11am–6pm Sun ▪ Adm ▪ www.labyrinth-kindermuseum.de

Berlin's Museum for Children is particularly suitable for children at the preschool stage and in the early school years. Three or four themed exhibitions each year deal with subjects in a child-friendly and entertaining way – for example the "Pots and Pans Orchestra". Every exhibition is interactive, allowing children to join in and experiment. See website for details of special exhibitions and events.

**Labyrinth Kindermuseum**

## 3 Grips-Theater

MAP D3 ▪ Altonaer Str. 22 ▪ Phone for performance times: (030) 39 74 74 47 ▪ Adm ▪ www.grips-theater.de

This famous Berlin theatre for children has been showing the hit musical *Linie 1* since 1986. The play, which is best suited to older children and adolescents, uses a U-Bahn line running from Kreuzberg to the Ku'damm as a metaphor for life in the big city. All shows are in German.

## 4 Museum für Naturkunde

Berlin's museum of natural history has the biggest dinosaur skeleton on show anywhere in the world. The collections here are well presented *(see p51)*.

**Museum für Naturkunde**

## 5 Zoologischer Garten

If you are visiting Berlin with children you should not miss out on the zoo. Particular favourites are the Monkey House (with baby gorillas and chimpanzees) and the Baby Zoo, where kids are allowed to touch and feed the young animas *(see pp42–3)*.

## 6 Zeiss-Großplanetarium

Artificial stars, planets and nebulae take you to faraway galaxies under the silvery dome of the planetarium *(see p140)*.

**LEGOLAND® Discovery Centre**

### 7 Filmpark Babelsberg
Großbeerenstr. 200, Potsdam ■ Late Mar–early Nov: 10am–6pm daily; check website for park closing days ■ Adm ■ www.filmpark-babelsberg.de

Exciting shoot-outs, a walk-on film set with a U-boat and a Wild West town are the film park's most popular attractions – and not just with the children. A tour of the former UFA-Film studios takes you behind the scenes: younger visitors can try out costumes or admire the Little Sandman (Sandmännchen), a TV figure popular with children in East Germany since 1959. Everywhere in the park are figures and props from well-known German films. A stunt show features fight scenes, car chases and pyrotechnics like those seen in *Inglourious Basterds*, *Valkyrie* and *Anonymous*, all shot here *(see p160)*.

**The Little Sandman**

### 8 LEGOLAND® Discovery Centre
MAP L2 ■ Potsdamer Str. 4 ■ 10am–7pm daily (last entry 5pm) ■ Adm ■ www.legolanddiscovery centre.de

Apart from the 4D cinema and rides at the world's first indoor LEGOLAND®, thousands of LEGO® bricks are turned into replicas of Berlin sights *(see p21)*.

### 9 Puppentheatermuseum
MAP H6 ■ Karl-Marx-Str. 135 ■ (030) 687 81 32 ■ 9am–3pm Mon–Fri, 11am–4pm Sun ■ Adm

At the small but excellent and inspirational Puppet Museum, children are allowed to perform their own puppet shows and have a go at being puppet theatre directors.

### 10 AquaDom and Sea Life Berlin
MAP K5 ■ Spandauer Str. 3 ■ 10am–7pm daily (last entry 6pm) ■ Adm ■ www.sealife.de/berlin

Visitors journey from the Spree to the depths of the oceans. A mirror maze and fish feeding add to the fun. The biggest attraction is the lift through the AquaDom, the world's largest cylindrical aquarium *(see p106)*.

# 🔟 Performing Arts Venues

### 1 Staatsoper Unter den Linden

MAP C4 ■ www.staatsoper-berlin.de

Both the theatre troupe and the orchestra of the venerable Berlin Opera enjoy top reputations (see p16). This is the place to see stars of the classical music scene. After a seven-year period of major renovation and modernization, the opera house reopened in October 2017.

**Performance at the Deutsche Oper**

### 2 Philharmonie

MAP L2 ■ Herbert-von-Karajan-Str. 1 ■ (030) 25 48 80 ■ Box Office: 3–6pm Mon–Fri, 11am–2pm Sat & Sun ■ www.berliner-philharmoniker.de

Germany's temple of classical music still presents the best performers in the world. Designed by Scharoun, the concert hall has unique acoustics, much appreciated by artists and audience alike. Concerts by the Berlin Philharmonic Orchestra are very popular and are often sold out for weeks ahead (see pp38–9).

### 3 Deutsche Oper

MAP B4 & M2 ■ Bismarckstr. 35 ■ (030) 34 38 43 43 ■ www.deutscheoperberlin.de

Berlin's most modern opera house, with its elegant retro design, was built in 1961 on the site of the former Deutsches Opernhaus, which was destroyed during World War II. The controversial 88 slabs of washed-out concrete, chosen by architect Fritz Bornemann for the main façade, replaced the classic columned portico that once stood here, leading critics to describe the building as lacking artistic formation. Concerts and opera and ballet performances are held here, along with an extensive children's programme (see p124).

### 4 Chamäleon-Varieté

MAP J5 ■ Rosenthaler Str. 40–1, Hackesche Höfe ■ (030) 400 05 90 ■ 8pm Tue–Fri, 7pm & 10:15pm Sat, 7pm Sun ■ chamaeleonberlin.com

The lack of technology is more than made up for with much wit and ingenuity by the small, alternative Chamäleon stage. If you are seated in the front row, you are likely to get pulled onto the stage.

### ⑤ Friedrichstadt-Palast
MAP J4 ▪ Friedrichstr. 107
▪ www.palast.berlin/en

Shiny glass tiles and a white, plumed neon sign adorn the eyecatching façade of the Friedrichstadt-Palast, whose long-legged dancers are as popular today as they were in the 1920s. The legendary original venue was damaged during World War II and replaced in the 1980s with this building. Long celebrated as being among the world's best revues, the performances have become even more spirited and entertaining today.

### ⑥ Deutsches Theater
MAP J3 ▪ Schumannstr. 13
▪ (030) 28 44 12 21 ▪ www. deutschestheater.de/english

Performances at the German Theatre – one of the best – include mainly classic plays in the tradition of Max Reinhardt. Experimental theatre by young playwrights is performed at the DT Baracke (see p98).

### ⑦ Theater des Westens
MAP N4 ▪ Kantstr. 12 ▪ Ticket Office: 8am–9pm daily ▪ (01805) 44 44

In addition to producing its own shows, such as *La Cage aux Folles*, this theatre also shows guest productions such as *Blue Man Group* and *Tanz der Vampire* (see p124).

### ⑧ Bar jeder Vernunft
MAP C5
▪ Schaperstr. 24 (car park Freie Volksbühne) ▪ (030) 883 15 82 ▪ Box office: noon–7pm Mon–Sat, 3–7pm Sun & hols ▪ www.bar-jeder-vernunft.de/en/

This venue, whose name means "devoid of all reason", is Berlin's most popular comedy theatre. The cabaret offers a humorous and, at times, romantic programme of songs, *chansons*, reviews, cabaret, slapstick

**Friedrichstadt-Palast**

and comedy, all under an amazing mirror tent dating from the 1920s. Many stars of the international and German cabaret scene can be seen regularly among the performers here, including Tim Fischer, Georgette Dee, the Pfister Sisters and Gayle Tufts, as well as older stars such as Otto Sander.

### ⑨ Hebbel am Ufer
MAP F5 ▪ Hallesches Ufer 32 ▪ (030) 25 90 04 27 ▪ performances daily ▪ english. hebbel-am-ufer.de

The Hebbel am Ufer has attained cult status in Berlin, thanks to its modern and varied programme of concerts, dance, music and theatre events. Top performers from around the world appear here.

### ⑩ Volksbühne
MAP H2 ▪ Rosa-Luxemburg-Platz ▪ (030) 24 06 57 77 ▪ www. volksbuehne-berlin.de

Opened in 1914 as a "theatre of the people", the iconic, avant-garde Volksbühne offers cosmopolitan theatre, dance and musical performances, and contemporary visual art.

**Theater des Westens**

# 🔟 Gay and Lesbian Berlin

## 1 Christopher Street Day

MAP P3/4 ■ Kurfürstendamm and Straße des 17. Juni ■ 4th weekend in June

Every summer, Germany's largest gay festival, Christopher Street Day, transforms Berlin into a giant street party, with thousands of people walking in a parade from Kurfürstendamm down the Straße des 17. Juni to Siegessäule *(see p80)*. At night, the party continues in the city's many gay clubs and Kneipen.

**Christopher Street Day parade**

## 2 Siegessäule

Free in gay cafés and shops

Berlin's oldest and best-selling gay magazine is named after the Victory Column, Berlin's landmark. This colourful monthly magazine includes all sorts of useful information, a round-up of what's on, small ads and interviews from the city's gay scene.

## 3 Mann-o-Meter

MAP E5 ■ Bülowstr. 106 ■ (030) 216 80 08 ■ 5–10pm Tue–Fri, 4–8pm Sat & Sun

Berlin's best-known advice centre for the gay community offers all kinds of help. Apart from psychological support relating to AIDS, safe sex and coming out, its counsellors offer help in finding accommodation, give support to those in troubled relationships and provide legal advice. Mann-o-Meter is also a good starting point for gay visitors to Berlin who wish to find out about the gay scene, and, last but not least, the café is also a good place to meet people.

## 4 SchwuZ

Rollbergstr. 26 ■ (030) 629 08 80 ■ Open from 11pm Wed, Fri and Sat ■ Adm ■ www.schwuz.de

Located in a handsome ex-brewery in Neukölln, this is one of the best venues for gay parties in Berlin, drawing a young, lively crowd for dancing, drinking, seeing and being seen. The parties are often themed – details can be found in gay magazines such as *Siegessäule* or *Sergej*, or on the club's Facebook page.

## 5 Tom's Bar

MAP D5 ■ Motzstr. 19 ■ (030) 213 45 70 ■ Open from 10pm daily ■ www.tomsbar.de

One of the traditional pubs in Berlin, in the centre of the city's gay heart in Motzstraße, this is not for those who are shy and timid – Tom's is a well-known pick-up joint. Below the (rather dark and dingy) Kneipe is a darkroom.

### 6 Prinz-Eisenherz-Buchhandlung

MAP D5 ■ Motzstr. 23 ■ (030) 313 99 36 ■ 10am–8pm Mon–Sat

Germany's oldest openly gay bookstore stocks the entire range of German and international gay and lesbian publications. Its knowledgeable bookshop assistants will track down rare or out-of-stock titles at your request. The bookshop also hosts frequent literary readings.

### 7 Factory Club

MAP D5 ■ Fuggerstr. 33 ■ (030) 25 74 09 10 ■ Open Fri–Sat from 11pm–6am ■ Adm ■ www.factory-club.de

Well established as one of the most popular gay night clubs in Berlin, this is where clubbers – mainly scenesters – come to dance to house and techno music late into the night. There is a labyrinth of darkrooms in the basement.

### 8 Schwules Museum

MAP E4 ■ Lützowstr. 73 ■ (030) 69 59 90 50 ■ Open 2–6pm Mon, Wed, Fri & Sun, 2–8pm Thu, 2–7pm Sat ■ Adm ■ www.schwulesmuseum.de

Situated in Tiergarten, this small Gay Museum documents, through temporary exhibitions, the high and low points of gay and lesbian life since the 19th century. Next to the museum is an archive, a small library and a venue for cultural events.

### 9 Café Berio

MAP E5 ■ Maaßenstr. 7 ■ (030) 216 19 46 ■ Open 24 hours

Café Berio is an old-fashioned haunt that has become a long-time favourite of the gay community. In the summer its terrace is a great place to have breakfast while people-watching, or to relax over a great meal or afternoon coffee and cake.

**Band flyers and posters, SO36**

### 10 SO36

MAP H5 ■ Oranienstr. 190 ■ (030) 61 40 13 06 ■ check website for current programmes and opening hours ■ www.so36.de

This famous – and infamous – dance venue has been very popular for many years. The Sunday night club "Café Fatal", when old German chart hits and dance tunes are played, is legendary (see p134).

**Galleries at the small Schwules Museum**

# 🔟 Best Places to Eat

**The stylish interiors of Reinstoff**

and international dishes, with an emphasis on Japanese (sushi) dishes and French-Italian fare. In summer, reserve one of the tables on the terrace outside. Open for breakfast, too.

## ① Reinstoff
MAP F2 ▪ Schlegelstr. 26C ▪ (030) 30 88 12 14 ▪ 7pm–midnight Tue–Sat ▪ €€€

A gourmet temple with two Michelin stars. Reinstoff serves fine regional specialities with a molecular twist: try the Brandenburg rabbit with celery and liquorice.

## ② Vox
MAP F4 ▪ Marlene-Dietrich-Platz 2 ▪ (030) 25 53 17 72 ▪ 6:30–10:30am, 6:30–11pm daily ▪ €€

The exquisite food in this elegant restaurant at the Grand Hyatt is a sleek and modern fusion of Asian

## ③ Hugos
MAP N5 ▪ Budapester Str. 2 ▪ (030) 26 02 12 63 ▪ 6:30–9:30pm Tue–Sat ▪ €€€

The Michelin-starred Hugos at Hotel Intercontinental Berlin *(see p172)* is the city's most affable gourmet restaurant, with impeccable service and stunning views. Wood panelling and plush leather set the tone, while the international cuisine reveals the light touch of German chef Thomas Kammeier. The wine list is extensive, and there are private dining rooms.

## ④ Bocca di Bacco
MAP K4 ▪ Friedrichstr. 167–8 ▪ (030) 20 67 28 28 ▪ noon–midnight Mon–Sat, 6pm–midnight Sun ▪ €€€

Berlin's hippest Italian restaurant offers fresh fish and exceptional meat creations such as *bresaola di*

*cavallo* (cured horse meat served with salad and nuts). Excellent *enoteca* with a good wine list.

### 5 Borchardt
MAP K4 ■ Französische Str. 47 ■ (030) 81 88 62 62 ■ 11:30am–midnight daily ■ €€€

Everyone of importance, including German chancellors, dines at Borchardt. The historic room is furnished in Wilhelminian style (featuring tall columns, wall mosaics and tile flooring) – a stunning setting for the modern French cooking and schnitzel served here. Without a reservation, however, even celebrities can't get a table.

**The simple interiors of Borchardt**

### 6 Rutz
MAP F2 ■ Chausseestr. 8 ■ (030) 24 62 87 60 ■ Open from 6:30pm Tue–Sat (wine bar 4–11pm Tue–Sat) ■ €€€

This rising star in Berlin's gourmet scene has slowly worked towards its second, well-deserved Michelin star by offering consistently high-quality fish and hearty meat dishes based on local recipes, but served with a creative twist. Rutz is cosy and informal, with a prodigious wine list of over 1,000 wines *(see p73)*.

### 7 Fischers Fritz
MAP K4 ■ Hotel Regent Berlin, Charlottenstr. 49 ■ (030) 20 33 63 63 ■ noon–2pm, 6:30–10:30pm daily ■ €€€

This high-profile establishment is one of seven restaurants in Berlin with two Michelin stars. Chef Christian Lohse prepares some of the most inspired and spectacular seafood dishes in the country.

**Courtyard dining at Facil**

### 8 Facil
MAP L2 ■ Potsdamer Str. 3 ■ (030) 590 051 234 ■ noon–3pm, 7–11pm Mon–Fri ■ €€€

This Michelin-starred restaurant, in a green oasis in the courtyard of the Mandala Hotel *(see p173)*, is a study in understated elegance. Chef Michael Kempf creates stylish Mediterranean dishes with a French accent.

### 9 Bandol sur Mer
MAP G2 ■ Torstraße 167 ■ (030) 67 30 20 51 ■ 6–10pm Thu–Mon ■ €€€

This Michelin star restaurant offers modern French cuisine, seating 20 in a relaxed, intimate setting. Diners can watch chefs prepare and plate their meals in the bistro-style open kitchen. The ambitious menu changes with the seasons, comprising creatively plated meat and fish dishes and clever wine pairings.

### 10 Horváth
MAP H5 ■ Paul-Lincke-Ufer 44a ■ (030) 61 28 99 92 ■ 6:30–10:30pm Wed–Sun ■ €€€

The culinary inventiveness of Austrian chef Sebastian Frank helped earn this restaurant its second Michelin star in 2015. Diners should allow themselves at least three hours to enjoy the seven-course menu and the accompanying wine.

*For a key to restaurant price ranges see p93*

# 🔟 Kneipen (Pubs) and Bars

## ① Green Door
MAP E5 ▪ Winterfeldstr. 50
▪ (030) 215 25 15 ▪ 6pm–2am Sun–
Thu, 6pm–3am Fri & Sat

This Berlin classic never goes out of style. A young urban crowd enjoys some of the best drinks and cocktails money can buy in Germany, mingling at the minimalist retro-style bar and along the curved, green walls. At weekends, the place is packed to bursting. There's an outdoor bell, but the door policy is pretty liberal as long as you look sober.

## ② E & M Leydicke
MAP E6 ▪ Mansteinstr. 4
▪ (030) 216 29 73 ▪ 6pm–1am daily

This slightly dated winery is still a big hit with tourists as well as groups of pupils and students. Try the sweetish strawberry and raspberry wines.

## ③ Newton Bar
MAP L4 ▪ Charlottenstr.
57 ▪ (030) 20 29 54 21 ▪ 11–3am
Sun–Wed, 11–4am Thu–Sat

To see and be seen is the name of the game at this elegant venue. Service is charming and the fastest in town, and in summer there's even a fold-down bar on the pavement outside. Heavy leather armchairs make for comfortable sitting, and the walls are adorned with enlarged photographs of nudes by Helmut Newton, after whom the bar is named. Don't miss out on the Caribbean and Latin-American cocktails *(see p92)*.

**The atmospheric Beckett's Kopf**

## ④ Beckett's Kopf
MAP H1 ▪ Pappelallee 64
▪ (030) 44 03 58 80 ▪ 8pm–3am
Sun–Thu, 8pm–4am Fri & Sat

One of Berlin's finest cocktail bars, Beckett's Kopf has a portrait of writer Samuel Beckett in its window. Its dark interior is hung with heavy velvet curtains, as if to keep the secret recipes from prying eyes. The superb concoctions include the "Mother-in-Law", with fruity notes, and the "Prince of Wales", said to be a favourite indulgence of King Edward VII.

**The retro ambience of Berlin's Victoria Bar**

### 5 Victoria Bar
MAP E5 ■ Potsdamer Str. 102
■ (030) 25 75 99 77 ■ 6:30pm–3am
Sun–Thu, 6:30pm–4am Fri & Sat

This cosy bar, with its understated 1960s ambience, subdued lighting and sophisticated lounge music is a great place for a relaxing drink and has become a firm favourite among the well-to-do artsy crowd. The cocktails are mixed by the renowned barman Stefan Weber.

### 6 Weinbar Rutz
MAP F2 ■ Chausseestr. 8 ■ (030) 24 62 87 60 ■ 4–11pm Tue–Sat

Berlin's best (but pricey) wine bar and shop is found downstairs from the award-winning restaurant of the same name (see p71). It offers over 1,000 wines, but Sommelier Billy Wagner is on hand to assist you. Excellent selection of food.

**The traditional Zum Nußbaum pub**

### 7 Zwiebelfisch
MAP N3 ■ Savignyplatz 7–8
■ (030) 312 73 63 ■ noon–6am daily

A classic of the somewhat ageing Charlottenburg scene, where the last survivors of the 1968 student revolt generation come to reminisce. The artists in the photographs on the walls are former patrons. In the summer, there are tables outdoors.

### 8 Café M
MAP E5 ■ Goltzstr. 33
■ (030) 216 70 92 ■ 10am–late
daily (from noon Sat & Sun)

Noisy yet laid-back, the Café M Kneipe in Schöneberg is (in)famous. If you find the rock music too loud, try the tables outside.

### 9 Kumpelnest 3000
MAP E5 ■ Lützowstr. 23
■ (030) 261 69 18 ■ 7pm–5am daily

A very popular venue in a former brothel, complete with chintz wallpaper. They serve a delicious Caipirinha, but for most of the clientele its real attraction is as a great place for people-watching.

### 10 Zum Nußbaum
MAP K6 ■ Am Nußbaum 3
■ (030) 242 30 95 ■ noon–midnight

One of only a few traditional Kneipen in the historic Nikolaiviertel quarter worth checking out, the Nußbaum serves draught beer and traditional Berlin food (see p108).

# 🔟 Lounges and Clubs

### ① Tresor Club
**MAP H4** ■ Köpenicker Str. 70
■ (030) 62 90 87 50 ■ from midnight
Wed, Fri & Sat

Berlin's first techno club, this opened in 1991 in the vaults of the former Wertheim department store. Today, Tresor is sited in the basement and industrial halls of a giant former power station and continues to deliver the latest in electronic music with a full programme of visiting musicians and DJ sets.

### ② Horns & Hooves
**MAP H1** ■ Danziger Str. 1
■ (0176) 70 08 42 69 ■ from 10pm
Tue, Thu & Sat

This venue defines itself as a club, a piano and jazz bar, a cabaret and a circus, with eccentric furnishings complementing the playful atmosphere. You could see anything from a burlesque show or a magic act, to a vaudeville performance. It tends to attract a 30-plus crowd.

### ③ House of Weekend
**MAP J6** ■ (0152) 24 29 31 40
■ Alexanderstr. 7 ■ from 11pm
Thu–Sat

This rooftop club in an old Soviet block with great views of the glittering high-rises on Alexanderplatz is a young, trendy and surprisingly down-to-earth house, techno and electro pop club, frequented by a young, fashionable and music-oriented crowd.

### ④ Prince Charles
**MAP G5** ■ Prinzenstrasse 85f
■ from 11pm ■ www.princecharles berlin.com

Housed in the former employee swimming pool of a disused Bechstein Piano factory, this stylish venue boasts an eclectic programme of DJs and live acts playing house, electro and hip-hop music. The sunken bar and old swimming pool tiles add to the interior's quirky charm, and in summer the fun spills out into the exterior courtyard.

### ⑤ Spindler & Klatt
Köpenicker Str. 16 ■ (030) 319
881 860 ■ kitchen from 8pm daily,
club from 11pm Fri & Sat

This event space doubles as a regular lounge with restaurant, but it is famous for special events, mainly dance nights and funky parties.

### ⑥ Sage Club
**MAP H4** ■ Brückenstr. 1
■ (030) 27 89 83 20 ■ from 7pm Thu,
from 11pm Sat & Sun (Kit Kat Club)

As one of the city's oldest and most successful clubs, the Sage Club (which on weekends hosts the

**The fabulous rooftop location of House of Weekend**

notorious, all-nude Kit Kat Club events) is a sure bet for a thrilling night out. It has a stylish interior and an impressive state-of- the-art sound system.

### 7 Berghain
**Am Wriezener Bahnhof**
■ (030) 29 36 02 10 ■ 8pm–6am **Thu, midnight–open end Fri & Sat, 3pm–6am Sun**

Housed in a Communist-era power station, this is Berlin's hottest bastion of electronic music. Some of the world's top DJs spin to spectacular light shows, and the bouncers are notoriously picky. Party animals have been known to spend entire weekends here with no sleep. The top-floor Panorama Bar affords a fantastic view over the Spree River, while anything goes in the men-only cellar sex club Lab.Oratory (see p148).

### 8 Tausend
**MAP J3** ■ Schiffbauerdamm 11 ■ (030) 27 58 20 70 ■ 7:30pm– late Tue–Sat

A great alternative to techno and house-dominated clubs, this chic bar hidden under the S-Bahn tracks has live music, and also soul, jazz and pop music from the 1970s and 80s. Tausend has on offer professionally mixed cocktails and has an affiliated cantina (see p93).

### 9 Clärchen's Ballhaus
**MAP G2** ■ Auguststr. 24 ■ (030) 282 92 95 ■ from noon daily

The Ballhaus is the last survivor of the 1920s "Tanzcafés" where classic society dances are still fashionable. Apart from its many long-time, mostly working-class clientele, the Ballhaus also attracts a younger hip crowd who enjoy the quirky atmosphere and old-fashioned hits.

**Dancing at Clärchen's Ballhaus**

### 10 Watergate
**Falckensteinstr. 49** ■ (030) 61 28 03 94 ■ from midnight Wed, Fri & Sat

Located on the Spree River with beautiful views of the illuminated Warschauer Brücke, the Watergate, with its stunning LED dance floor, is one of Berlin's cutting-edge clubs, featuring the latest in house, techno and drum 'n' bass styles.

# s and Markets

of buying something splendid. With its street artists and buskers, the market is an ideal weekend spot for a bit of browsing, dawdling and people-watching.

### ③ Galeries Lafayette

Located within Quartier 207, this small branch of the luxury French department store specializes in classic womens- and menswear on one level, and young fashion upstairs. French delicacies are sold in the food department *(see p91)*.

### ④ Art and Fashion House Quartier 206

MAP L4 ■ Friedrichstr. 71 ■ (030) 20 94 60 00 ■ 10:30am–7:30pm Mon–Sat

This renowned shopping centre boasts stunning Art Deco interiors, with mosaic flooring and a marble staircase. Luxury labels such as Moschino, Etro and Bally offer stylish designer clothing and accessories, while the elegant basement and first floor cafes provide a welcome taste of Berlin coffee culture.

**Kaufhaus des Westens**

### ① Kaufhaus des Westens (KaDeWe)

MAP P5 ■ Tauentzienstr. 21–24 ■ (030) 212 10 ■ 10am–8pm Mon–Thu, 10am–9pm Fri, 9:30am–8pm Sat

Whatever you are looking for, you will find it here, in Europe's largest temple of consumption. Over its eight floors, the venerable Kaufhaus des Westens ("department store of the West"), affectionately called KaDeWe, offers more than three million products. On its gourmet floor, West Berlin's former "shop window", you can choose from 1,800 cheeses, 1,400 breads and pastries and 2,000 cold meats. The window displays and inner courtyards are also worth a visit in themselves *(see p170)*.

### ② Antik- und Flohmarkt Straße des 17. Juni

MAP M4 ■ Str. des 17. Juni ■ 10am–5pm Sat & Sun

Berlin's largest art and antiques market specializes in antique furnishings and fittings, cutlery and porcelain, books, paintings, clothing and jewellery. The traders are professionals and demand high prices, but in return you are assured

**Art and Fashion House Quartier 206**

### ⑤ Stilwerk
**MAP C4 ■ Kantstr. 17 ■ (030) 31 51 50 ■ 10am–8pm Mon–Fri, 10am–6pm Sat**

Style is writ large in this trendy shopping centre catering to Charlottenburg's well-to-do residents. Stilwerk specializes in designer furniture, lamps and fittings – basically anything good and expensive *(see p125)*.

### ⑥ Gipsformerei Staatliche Museen
**MAP A3 ■ Sophie-Charlotten-Str. 17–18 ■ (030) 326 76 90 ■ 9am–4pm Mon–Fri, to 6pm Wed**

If you fancy a Schinkel statue for your home or an elegant Prussian sculpture from the Charlottenburg Palace gardens, you'll find moulded plaster reproduction here.

### ⑦ Königliche Porzellan-Manufaktur (KPM)
**MAP M4 ■ Wegelystr. 1 ■ (030) 39 00 90 ■ 10am–6pm Mon–Sat**

Prussia's glory and splendour to take away – traditional KPM porcelain for your dining table at home. Apart from elegant porcelain dinner services, figures and accessories made in the Berlin factory are also on sale here.

### ⑧ Winterfeldtmarkt
The trendiest and also the most attractive weekly food and clothing market in Berlin has

**Shoppers at Winterfeldtmarkt**

developed into something of a hotspot with the Schöneberg crowd. This is the place for meeting up on Saturday mornings *(see p133)*.

### ⑨ Türkenmarkt am Maybachufer
**MAP H5 ■ Maybachufer ■ 11am–6:30pm Tue & Fri**

Berlin's largest weekday Turkish market lures visitors with its smells and dishes from *A Thousand and One Nights* and sells everything from unleavened bread to goat's cheese Bartering is expected *(see p133)*.

### ⑩ Berliner Antik- und Flohmarkt
**MAP J4 ■ Am Kupfergraben 1 ■ (030) 208 26 45 ■ 11am–6pm Wed–Mon**

Numerous stalls for antiques and souvenirs are scattered along the Kupfergraben in front of the Bodemuseum. Much of it is over-priced, but occasionally browsers will find a bargain.

# 🔟 Berlin for Free

**View from the Reichstag dome**

## 1 Reichstag

Berlin's biggest freebie happens to be a must-see attraction. There's no topping the fabulous 360° view of the city skyline that you get from Lord Foster's beautiful modern dome. Guided tours take in the plenary hall and graffiti left by Russian soldiers in 1945. You have to register in advance and will need your passport to enter *(see pp14–15)*.

## 2 Tempelhofer Feld

MAP G6 ▪ Tempelhofer Damm 1 ▪ (030) 70 09 06 89 ▪ From sunrise to sunset ▪ www.tempelhoferfreiheit.de

A powerful symbol of the new Berlin, the grounds of this historic airport *(see p132)* have been turned into a green space for the people. You will find lolling couples, urban gardeners, cyclists, in-line skaters, go-karters, and people barbequeing, doing T'ai Chi, flying kites and playing baseball.

## 3 Open Door Days

May–Sep ▪ www.visitberlin.de

Beautiful private gardens, interiors of historic monuments and the hallowed halls of government ministries are opened to the public for a few days every year. Chancellor Angela Merkel shakes hands with visitors to her office.

## 4 Free Concerts

MAP L2 ▪ Herbert-von-Karajan-Str. 1 ▪ (030) 25 48 89 99 ▪ Sep–Jun ▪ www.berliner-philharmoniker.de

Churches, universities and even renowned classical orchestras give free concerts. The Berliner Philharmoniker's gratis lunchtime concerts, usually with small ensembles, are held every Tuesday at 1pm *(see pp38–9)*.

## 5 East Side Gallery

MAP H4 ▪ Mühlenstraße ▪ (030) 251 71 59 ▪ Open 24 hours ▪ www.eastsidegallery-berlin.de

The biggest remaining stretch of Berlin Wall is now an artistic statement on Germany's division from 1961 to 1989. Famous murals include a Trabant busting through the masonry, *Heads with Big Lips* by Thierry Noir, and Brezhnev and Honecker kissing *(see p146)*.

**Mural on the Berlin Wall**

## 6 Gedenkstätte Berliner Mauer

MAP 2F ▪ Bernauer Str. 111 ▪ (030) 46 79 86 66 ▪ Centre 9:30am–8pm Tue–Sun ▪ www.berliner-mauer-gedenkstaette.de

The Berlin Wall Memorial is well worth a visit for its recreated "death strip", excellent documentary centre and dramatic stories of how East Germans escaped over (or under) the hated barrier. Listening stations and displays are spread along the former border.

### 7 Free Walking Tours

**Daily, year-round ▪ See websites for times and departure points ▪ www.alternativeberlin.com, www.brewersberlintours.com, www.newberlintours.com**

Join a guided walking tour of the city run by Alternative Berlin Tours, Brewer's Berlin Tours and New Berlin Tours. They're free of charge, although tips are encouraged.

### 8 Museums

Many museums and galleries, including the Alliiertenmuseum *(see p152)* and Knoblauchhaus *(see p104)* have no admission charge. Some of Berlin's most prestigious museums, such as Gemäldegalerie *(see pp38–40)*, the Pergamonmuseum *(see pp24–6)* and Alte Nationalgalerie *(see p52)* are free to visitors under 18.

### 9 Holocaust-Denkmal

Designed by New York architect Peter Eisenman, the Memorial to the Murdered Jews of Europe consists of 2,711 concrete pillars, many of them off-kilter and placed on undulating ground *(see p87)*. The underground Information Centre offers a moving introduction to the horrors of the Holocaust.

### 10 Schlosspark Sanssouci

Fancy a stroll through a Romantic landscape painting? Just a half-hour from Berlin by commuter train, these gardens in Potsdam are strewn with ponds and whimsical follies, including an Orangerie, Roman Baths modelled on an Italian villa and a Rococo-style Chinese house *(see p158)*.

**The charming Schlosspark Sanssouci**

**TOP 10 MONEY-SAVING TIPS**

**Bode-Museum, Museuminsel**

**1** The city's public museums, including the comprehensive complex on the Museuminsel, are covered by the popular Berlin Museum Pass (€24). This offers free entry at participating institutions on three consecutive days.

**2** The berlinScheckheft (€7.50 at newsagents) contains vouchers that offer steep discounts on restaurants, museums, theatres, music events and other attractions.

**3** Theatres and opera houses sell reduced tickets at the door on the day of the performance.

**4** Go gallery-hopping in the arty Mitte district. Here, Auguststrasse and Linienstrasse teem with collections open to the public.

**5** Visit berlin.eintritt-frei.org for an up-to-date list of free events taking place in the city.

**6** Buy discounted public transport tickets (such as a 4-pack or a day pass) or hire a bicycle to get around and see the city like a local.

**7** Bus lines 100 and 200 take in many of Berlin's best sights for the price of a single fare.

**8** Take advantage of the good-value set meals in cafés and restaurants, particularly at lunchtime.

**9** Comb through the vast Mauerpark flea market for unique vintage and retro finds. The market runs all day on Sundays *(see p140)*.

**10** If you are a visitor from outside the EU and are leaving the EU with purchased goods, remember to get a refund on Germany's 19 per cent sales tax. Ask sales staff at stores for an *Ausfuhrbescheinigung* (export papers).

# 🔟 Festivals and Fairs

**Crowds at the Berliner Filmfestspiele**

musicians, artists, producers, labels and audiences is held at various venues in Kulturbrauerei in the Prenzlauer Berg district.

### ③ Internationale Funkausstellung (IFA)
MAP A5 ■ CityCube Berlin ■ (030) 30 38 30 00 ■ every year in early Sep ■ Adm

The latest in high-tech toys and entertainment technology are on show from over 1,500 global exhibitors at the IFA (International Broadcasting Exhibition).

### ① Berliner Filmfestspiele
MAP L2 ■ Filmhaus Potsdamer Platz ■ 2nd & 3rd week in Feb ■ www.berlinale.de

The Berlinale is the top German film festival, and is attended by Hollywood and German stars alike. Until 1999, the film festival took place around the Zoo-Palast cinema; today the area around Potsdamer Platz takes centre stage for the festivities.

### ② Pop-Kultur
Various venues ■ End Aug ■ www.pop-kultur.berlin

As a successor of the Berlin Music Week, this new festival for bands,

### ④ Christopher Street Day
MAP P3/4 ■ Kurfürstendamm and Straße des 17. Juni ■ (030) 23 62 86 32 ■ 3rd or 4th weekend in Jun

This colourful gay parade on Christopher Street Day celebrates sexual diversity. Up to 500,000 people from all around the world boisterously dance, drink and celebrate in the streets of Central Berlin (see p68).

### ⑤ Festival of Lights
Various venues ■ Oct ■ www.festival-of-lights.de

For 10 days, dozens of Berlin's most popular landmarks are illuminated

**Berliner Dom illuminated by light art during the Festival of Lights**

in spectacular ways and light art and creative installations set up around the city. A mecca for photographers and lovers of optical illusions.

### 6 Lange Nacht der Museen
Berlin museums ▪ (030) 24 74 98 88 ▪ last weekend Aug ▪ www.lange-nacht-der-museen.de ▪ Adm

For one night, one ticket gives access to all the city's museums until well after midnight, offering visitors an unusual experience. Many institutions also put on special events, and street artists and sellers entertain the patiently queueing public.

### 7 Grüne Woche
MAP A5 ▪ CityCube Berlin ▪ (030) 38 30 00 ▪ 2nd half of Jan ▪ www.gruenewoche.de ▪ Adm

The largest gourmet feast in the world, Green Week is a tasty agricultural and gastronomical fair for everyone. Nowhere else can you enjoy a culinary journey around the world in such a condensed space.

### 8 Fashion Week
Various venues ▪ Jan & Jul ▪ www.fashion-week-berlin.com/en ▪ Adm

Top designers and local talent present their new collections.

### 9 Karneval der Kulturen
MAP G/H5/6 ▪ Kreuzberg ▪ Whitsun (varying date in May or early Jun)

Multicultural Berlin celebrates for three days in the colourful Kreuzberg district in a street carnival parade.

### 10 Internationale Tourismus Börse (ITB)
MAP A5 ▪ CityCube Berlin ▪ (030) 38 30 00 ▪ Mar ▪ Adm

The world's largest tourism fair offers up-to-date travel information to the general public, often at elaborately designed stalls. The night-time shows put on by many of the exhibiting countries are especially popular.

**TOP 10 SPORTS HIGHLIGHTS**

Runners at the Berlin Marathon

**1 Berlin Marathon**
Str. des 17. Juni ▪ 3rd/4th Sun in Sep
The most exuberant marathon in the world attracts thousands of runners.

**2 Skate by Night**
Str. des 17. Juni ▪ Jun–Aug: Sun evening
In-line skaters from around the world meet for night-time "blading".

**3 Sechstagerennen**
Velodrom ▪ 2nd half of Jan
The Six-Day Race is one of Berlin's most venerable sports events.

**4 Tempelhofer Feld**
MAP F6
This former airport has become the city's largest sports ground (see p78).

**5 Berliner Neujahrslauf**
MAP K3 ▪ Brandenburger Tor ▪ 1st Jan
This New Year's Day Run is for those who are fit and not afraid of the cold.

**6 Internationales Stadionfest (ISTAF)**
Olympiastadion ▪ Summer
Germany's biggest athletics festival.

**7 DFB-Pokalfinale**
Olympiastadion
Germany's second-most important soccer cup final is played here.

**8 Deutsches Traberderby**
Trabrennbahn Mariendorf ▪ 1st week in Aug
The derby for professional trotter races.

**9 Berlin Triathlon**
Treptower Park ▪ early Jun ▪ triathlon-service.de
Amateurs can register online for this.

**10 Berliner Motorradtage**
Kurfürstendamm ▪ end Mar
The international meeting of bikers is a noisy event.

# Berlin
# Area by Area

Nikolaiviertel and Rotes Rathaus with the Berliner
Dom and Fernsehturm in the background

# ⟦TOP 10⟧ Central Berlin: Unter den Linden

The magnificent boulevard of Unter den Linden is the heart of historic Mitte. Many of Berlin's sights are clustered along this grand avenue and around Bebelplatz, creating an impressive picture of Prussian and German history from the early 18th century onwards. To the south lies the Neo-Classical Gendarmenmarkt, one of Europe's most attractive squares; around it are elegant restaurants and cafés. Not far away, chic Friedrichstraße is lined with luxury stores and modern offices and apartments.

**Statue, Unter den Linden**

## CENTRAL BERLIN: UNTER DEN LINDEN

## Brandenburger Tor
**MAP K3 ■ Pariser Platz**

Berlin's best-known landmark on Pariser Platz leads through to Unter den Linden (see pp12–13).

## Humboldt-Box
**MAP K5 ■ Schlossplatz 5 ■ 10am–6pm daily ■ Adm ■ www.humboldt-box.com/en**

This colourful structure on the Museumsinsel provides information on the reconstruction of the Berliner Schloss and is a multimedia introduction to the Humboldt-Forum (see p89). Upon completion of the Forum (scheduled for 2019), the temporary Humboldt-Box will be dismantled. Until then, it will host science, art,

**The futuristic Humboldt-Box**

culture and architecture exhibitions. It also has a sky-lounge restaurant and viewing platform.

## Forum Fridericianum
**MAP K4 ■ Unter den Linden and Bebelplatz**

The historic structures of this complex are among the city's finest. From 1740, Frederick the Great commissioned the prestigious Neo-Classical buildings for the area around today's Bebelplatz and personally influenced their design: Deutsche Staatsoper, the Catholic St Hedwigskathedrale, Alte Bibliothek and Prinz-Heinrich-Palais, later the Humboldt University. A memorial set into the ground at Bebelplatz recalls its dark past – in 1933, it was the site of the Nazi book burning. Frederick's successors commissioned the Altes Palais and a statue of "Old Fritz", surrounded by "his" buildings. Christian Daniel Rauch created the bronze figure in 1840, portraying Frederick wearing his trademark tricorn hat and coronation mantle. The statue has always faced west but wags claim that the East German government mistakenly placed the figure the wrong way around.

### FREDERICK AS ARCHITECT

Forum Fridericianum was not only Frederick the Great's memorial to himself, it also ensured that Unter den Linden became one of the greatest boulevards in Europe. The king, who favoured a Neo-Classical style, himself drew up plans for the buildings, and Knobelsdorff executed his ideas.

Museumsinsel's Bode-Museum, with the Fernsehturm in the background

### 4 Museumsinsel
MAP J5 ▪ Pergamonmuseum, Bodestr. 1–3 ▪ (030) 266 424 242 ▪ 10am–6pm daily, to 8pm Thu ▪ Adm ▪ Alte Nationalgalerie, Bodestr. 1–3 ▪ (030) 266 424 242 ▪ 10am–6pm Tue–Sun, to 8pm Thu ▪ Adm ▪ www.smb.museum

Museum Island, a UNESCO World Heritage Site, is one of the most significant complexes of museums in the world, holding major arts collections and imposing, full-scale ancient structures. Based here are the Pergamonmuseum, the Alte Nationalgalerie, the Bode-Museum and the Altes and Neues Museums, including the famous Ägyptisches Museum *(see pp24–7)*.

### 5 Gendarmenmarkt
MAP L4 ▪ Mitte

This square, whose strict layout is reminiscent of an Italian Renaissance piazza, is probably the most beautiful in Berlin. Named after a regiment of *gens d'armes* stationed nearby, Gendarmenmarkt was built at the end of the 17th century as a market square. The Schauspielhaus (theatre) on the west side of the square, built by Schinkel in 1818–21, was used as a theatre until 1945. Damaged in World War II, it was reopened as Konzerthaus (concert hall) in 1984 *(see p54)*. A statue of the playwright Friedrich Schiller stands in front of the building. To the left and right of the Konzerthaus stand the twin towers of the Deutscher and Französischer Doms (German and French cathedrals), dating back to the late 18th century. Französischer Dom, to its north, is a prestigious late Baroque building *(see p59)*; concealed behind it is the French Friedrichstadtkirche, a church serving Berlin's Huguenot community. The Deutscher Dom opposite, built in 1708 on the south side of the square for the Reformed Protestant Church, did not receive its first tower until 1785. Today it has an exhibition on democracy in Germany.

---

**THE HUGUENOTS IN BERLIN**

In 1685, the Great Elector issued the famous Edict of Potsdam, granting asylum in Berlin to around 20,000 Huguenots, who were persecuted in their native France because of their Protestant faith. Skilled academics and craftsmen, they moulded Berlin's social and cultural life and enriched it with the French art of living. Today, the city's French community still worships at the Friedrichstadtkirche, part of the Französischer Dom complex **(below)**.

### 6 Friedrichstraße
**MAP J–L4 ▪ Mitte**

Friedrichstraße has regained some of the glamour and vibrancy it possessed before World War II. Today, Berlin's Fifth Avenue once again boasts elegant shops and upmarket restaurants and cafés. Especially worth visiting are the three Quartiers 205, 206 and 207 (the latter designed by architect Jean Nouvel) within the Friedrich-stadtpassagen, containing the Galeries Lafayette store (see p91) and Art and Fashion House Quartier 206 (see p76). At the northern end of the street is the famous Dussmann store (books, music, events), S-Bahn station Friedrichstraße and the former entertainment district, which includes the Friedrichstadt-Palast (see p67) and the impressive Admiralspalast (see p90).

**Concrete steles, Holocaust-Denkmal**

### 7 Holocaust-Denkmal
**MAP L3 ▪ Ebertstr. ▪ (06) 26 39 43 36 ▪ Information Centre: 10am–8pm Tue–Sun (Oct–Mar: to 7pm) ▪ www.stiftung-denkmal.de**

The Memorial to the Murdered Jews of Europe serves as Germany's national Holocaust memorial (see p79). After years of debate, US star architect Peter Eisenman completed the monument in 2005. It consists of a large field with dark grey steles of varying heights up to 2 m (6 ft) high, which symbolize the six million Jews and others murdered by the Nazis in their concentration camps between 1933 and 1945. Below the memorial, an information centre explains the causes and history of the genocide.

## HISTORIC MITTE WALK

### ▶ MORNING

Turn back the clock on **Wilhelmstraße** (see p88), Berlin's political nerve centre until 1945. Starting at Hotel Adlon Kempinski, head south past the bold modern British Embassy. Turn right at Behrensstraße to visit the **Holocaust-Denkmal**, then carry on along Wilhelmstraße, where signs point out the old ministries. The Prussian State Council was in the Neo-Classical building at No. 54; its last president was Konrad Adenauer, who became West Germany's first chancellor. At the corner of Vossstraße were Hitler's main offices in the Neue Reichskanzlei. Continue down to No. 97 on the right, the giant structure of the former Ministry of Aviation. Today the Federal Ministry of Finance is based here. Retrace your steps north, turn right into Mohrenstraße then left into **Friedrichstraße**. Head to **Galeries Lafayette** (see p91), whose gourmet food department is perfect for a snack lunch.

### AFTERNOON

After lunch, indulge in a spot of shopping at Galeries Lafayette and at concept store **The Corner** just down the street (see p91). Then head to the beautiful **Gendarmenmarkt** square nearby. Take some time to admire its Konzerthaus and the imposing Deutscher and Französischer Dome. The latter holds regular classical music concerts – check their website for the schedule. Round off your day with a meal at the gourmet Italian restaurant **Malatesta** (see p93) nearby on Charlottenstraße.

*See map on pp84–*

**British Embassy, Wilhelmstraße**

### 8 Wilhelmstraße
MAP L3 ■ Between Unter den Linden and Leipziger Str.

In imperial Berlin, the centre of the German Empire's governmental power was based in Wilhelmstraße. Around 100 years later, nothing remains of the prestigious historic buildings which represented the equivalent of No. 10 Downing Street in London or Quai d'Orsay in Paris. All political decisions were made at Wilhelmstraße: both Chancellor (at No. 77) and President (No. 73) of the German Reich lived here in old town houses. Their gardens became known as "ministerial gardens". Adolf Hitler had the street systematically developed into the nerve centre of Nazi power. The Neue Reichskanzlei (the Chancellor's office) was built in 1937–9 to plans by Albert Speer, at the corner of Vossstraße and Wilhelmstraße. It was blown up in 1945. Behind the Reichskanzlei was the so-called "Führerbunker" where Adolf Hitler committed suicide on 30 April 1945. It is now a car park. Of the historic buildings, only the former Ministry of Aviation (Reichsluftfahrtministerium) remains. Today, Wilhelmstraße is lined by modern residential and office buildings; the British Embassy, built in 2000 by Michael Wilford, creates a link with the international importance of this street.

### 9 Schlossplatz
MAP K5 ■ Mitte

Today Schlossplatz seems deserted, but once the Stadtschloss (town residence) of the Hohenzollerns stood here. It was blown up by the East German government in 1950–51, and today just a few historic fragments of the original can be seen. Remains include the façade of the doorway where Karl Liebknecht supposedly proclaimed the Socialist Republic in 1918. The portal has been incorporated into the former Staatsratsgebäude (State Council Building) on the south side of the square. On its eastern side, the square used to be bordered by the Palast der Republik (Palace of the Republic), the former seat of the East German parliament demolished in 2008. The

**NAZI ARCHITECTURE**

One of few surviving examples of the monumental architectural style favoured by the Nazis is the former Reichsluftfahrtministerium (Ministry of Aviation), commissioned by Hermann Göring in 1935–6 from Ernst Sagebiel. The sandstone office block was the world's largest and most modern, strengthened by steel girders against attack. After reunification, the Treuhandanstalt (privatisation agency) was based here; today it houses the Federal Ministry of Finance (**right**).

Humboldt-Forum cultural centre will be complete in 2019. It will have a façade reminiscent of the old Hohenzollern Palace, a library and the non-European collections of the former Dahlem Museums (of Asian Art and Ethnology) *(see p151)*. Until then, the Humboldt-Box *(see p85)* will provide information on the Forum's development.

**Staatsratsgebäude, Schlossplatz**

### ⑩ Museum für Kommunikation

MAP L4 ▪ Leipziger Str. 16 ▪ (030) 20 29 40 ▪ 9am–5pm Tue–Fri (to 8pm Tue), 10am–6pm Sat & Sun ▪ Adm ▪ www.mfk-berlin.de

The world's largest Post Office Museum opened in 1872. Its excellent displays document the history of communication from the first postage stamps of the Middle Ages to today's satellite technology. Particularly worth seeing are a blue and a red stamp from Mauritius, one of the first telephone installations (dating back to 1863) and three talking robots who interact with the visitors. Younger visitors always enjoy the Computer-galerie, where they can learn and gain new insights while playing.

**Historic letterbox**

---

**A DAY OF CULTURE**

#### ▶ MORNING

Start your stroll on Unter den Linden, which begins in front of the **Brandenburger Tor** on **Pariser Platz** *(see pp12–13)*. This was Berlin's prestigious royal avenue, and the rich and famous still promenade here today. For breakfast, pop into **Café Einstein** *(see p92)*. Afterwards continue east along the boulevard; you will pass the **KunstHalle**, a gallery of contemporary art run by Deutsche Bank. From here you can already see the 13.5-m (44-ft) high equestrian statue of Frederick the Great at **Forum Fridericianum** *(see p85)*. This area and the nearby Bebelplatz are right in the centre of old Berlin, with the Staatsoper, Altes Palais, St Hedwigskathedrale and Humboldt-Universität around them. Stop for an early lunch at the pleasant museum café of the **Zeughaus** *(see p19)*.

#### AFTERNOON

In the early afternoon continue east along Unter den Linden. At the end of the street lies the **Museumsinsel** *(see pp24–7)*. Cross over on the Schloßbrücke to explore the wealth of treasures in the island's museums. Then, if you still have the time and energy, visit the **Berliner Dom** *(see p58)*. Opposite the cathedral you will see **Schlossplatz**, with its modern **Humboldt-Box** *(see p85)* information centre. Round off your day in Mitte with a delicious evening meal at the French brasserie **Dressler Unter den Linden** *(see p93)*. To get there, retrace your steps to return along Unter den Linden in a westerly direction.

*See map on pp84–5*

# The Best of the Rest

**Trabant at the DDR Museum**

## 1 DDR Museum
MAP K5 ■ Karl-Liebknecht-Str.
1 ■ www.ddr-museum.de/en

This museum of everyday life in East Germany recreates socialist-era interiors and displays examples of East German design, including a Trabant car visitors can sit in.

## 2 Staatsbibliothek Unter den Linden
MAP K4 ■ Unter den Linden 8 ■ (030) 26 60 ■ staatsbibliothek-berlin.de/en/

The lovely reading rooms of this Neo-Baroque library contain many books and manuscripts that are of worldwide importance (see p39).

## 3 WMF-Haus
MAP L3 ■ Leipziger Str., corner Mauerstr.

The former headquarters of the porcelain and cutlery manufacturer WMF has remarkable façades decorated with beautiful mosaics.

## 4 Alte Kommandantur
MAP K5 ■ Unter den Linden 1

Rebuilt with the original Classicist façade, this impressive building houses the Berlin offices of the media giant Bertelsmann.

## 5 Maxim-Gorki-Theater
MAP K4 ■ Am Festungsgraben 2 ■ english.gorki.de

This renowned theatre was once Berlin's Singakademie, or singing school. Paganini and Liszt, among others, performed here.

## 6 S-Bahnhof Friedrichstraße
MAP J4 ■ Friedrichstr.

Remodelled several times, this has always been one of Berlin's most famous stations. Between 1961 and 1989, it was the principal crossing point between East and West.

## 7 Komische Oper
MAP K4 ■ Behrenstr. 55–57 ■ english.komische-oper-berlin.de

One of Germany's most magnificent opera houses, dating from 1892, is concealed behind a modern façade. All performances are in German.

## 8 Palais am Festungsgraben
MAP K4 ■ Am Festungsgraben 1 ■ (030) 208 40 00

The 1753 Baroque palace has retained its original elegant interior and magnificent ceiling frescoes.

## 9 Admiralspalast
MAP J4 ■ Friedrichstr. 101 ■ www.mehr.de

Berlin's most legendary venue, dating from the 1920s, stages musicals and comedy shows.

**Façade of the Admiralspalast**

## 10 Dalí Museum
MAP L3 ■ Leipziger Platz 7 ■ (0700) 32 54 23 75 ■ www. daliberlin.de

A rotating exhibition of some 400 works by the 20th-century Surrealist, including drawings, lithographs, etchings, paintings, sculptures and other three-dimensional works.

# Shops

### ① Galeries Lafayette
MAP L4 ▪ Friedrichstr. 76–78
▪ (030) 20 94 80 ▪ 10am–8pm Mon–Sat

Located within Quartier 207, this is the only German branch of the luxury French store *(see p76)*. Here you will find elegant fashion, and gourmet foods on the lower level.

### ② The Corner
MAP G4 ▪ Französiche Straße 40 ▪ (030) 20 67 09 50

This trendy concept store offers newcomer fashion and luxury labels such as Christian Louboutin and Stella McCartney.

### ③ Mall of Berlin
MAP L3 ▪ Leipziger Platz 12 ▪ (030) 20 62 17 70

The Mall of Berlin occupies an entire block and connects Leipziger Straße and Wilhelmstraße with a passage. There are 270 shops and restaurants in this temple of retail commerce.

### ④ Jack Wolfskin
MAP K4 ▪ Behrenstr. 23/corner of Friedrichstr. ▪ (030) 20 64 80 70

Stock up on apparel, equipment and footwear before setting out on any outdoor activities at this branch of Germany's famous outfitter.

### ⑤ Fassbender & Rausch
MAP L4 ▪ Charlottenstr. 60 ▪ (030) 20 45 84 43

Giant chocolate sculptures of the Reichstag and Brandenburger Tor adorn the windows and tempt visitors into this shop. There is a café on the upper floor where you can try some of the store's creations.

### ⑥ Stiche Düssel
MAP G4 ▪ Charlottenstraße 53/54 ▪ (030) 20 16 56 66

Visitors can rifle through a vast collection of over 10,000 antique prints from the 16th to the 19th century, including cityscapes, maps from all over the world, and decorative engravings.

**Kulturkaufhaus Dussmann**

### ⑦ Kulturkaufhaus Dussmann
MAP K4 ▪ Friedrichstr. 90 ▪ (030) 20 25 11 11

A mecca for culture junkies, this store offers books, movies, computer games, sheet music and a large section of classical music. It is open until midnight on weekdays.

### ⑧ Ritter Sport Bunte Schokowelt
MAP K4 ▪ Französische Str. 24 ▪ (030) 20 09 50 80

The chocolate-maker's flagship store has fun merchandise, a chocolate-themed exhibition and workshops.

### ⑨ Escada
MAP L4 ▪ Friedrichstr. 176–179 ▪ (030) 238 64 04

Stylish fashion and accessories label for women, boasting a fantastic selection of luxurious materials.

**Mannequins in Escada**

### ⑩ Bucherer
MAP L4 ▪ Friedrichstr. 176–179 ▪ (030) 204 10 49

A luxury outlet selling quality watches and jewellery.

*See map on pp84–5*

# Pubs and Bars

**1 Newton Bar**
MAP L4 ■ Charlottenstr. 57
■ (030) 20 29 54 21 ■ 10–3am
daily (to 4am Fri & Sat)
One of the trendiest bars in town.
Sink into the deep leather armchairs
and sip your cocktails, surrounded
by enlarged photographs of nudes
by Helmut Newton (see p72).

**2 La Banca Bar**
MAP K4 ■ Behrenstr. 37
■ (030) 460 60 90 ■ noon–11pm daily
The stylish bar in Hotel de Rome
prides itself on an inventive cocktail
list. Enjoy authentic Italian food in
the relaxed ambience on the terrace.

**3 Zosch**
MAP J4 ■ Tucholskystrasse
30 ■ (030) 280 76 64 ■ 4pm–2am
Mon–Sat
One of the last authentic pubs in
the Mitte district, Zosch has an
unpolished charm. Concerts hosted
in the brick vaulted cellar range from
folk to jazz music.

**4 Sra Bua Bar**
MAP K3 ■ Behrenstr. 72
■ (030) 22 61 19 59 ■ 8pm–1am daily
At the back of Hotel Adlon Kempinski,
this elegant bar specializes in Asian
cocktails and creative cuisine by the
team of star chef Tim Raue.

**5 Café LebensArt**
MAP K4 ■ Unter den Linden
69A ■ (030) 44 72 19 30 ■ 9am–11pm
Sun–Thu, 9am–midnight Fri & Sat
A café rather than a bar, offering
breakfast and afternoon cakes,
this is one of the few places open
at night on Unter den Linden.

**6 Café Einstein**
MAP K4 ■ Unter den Linden 42
■ 7am–10pm daily ■ (030) 204 36 32
This small and cosy branch of the
café serves excellent wines and
Austrian specialities.

**7 Ständige Vertretung**
MAP J3 ■ Schiffbauerdamm
8 ■ (030) 282 39 65 ■ 10:30am–
1am daily
The name harks back to the
permanent West German repre-
sentation in East Berlin. The pub
is famous for its Rhine specialities,
such as Kölsch beer.

**8 Oh, Angie!**
MAP L4 ■ Friedrichstr. 67
■ (030) 20 64 41 64 ■ 9am–10pm
Mon–Sat
An elegant lobby bar in the basement
of Q205 shopping centre, perfect for
a quick healthy lunch or a snack.
Definitely try the delicious focaccias
and carrot cake.

**9 Brauhaus Lemke**
MAP J5 ■ Dircksenstr.
S-Bahn arch No. 143 ■ (030)
24 72 87 27 ■ noon–
midnight daily
An atmospheric pub located
under the S-Bahn arches
with a small courtyard.

**10 Windhorst**
MAP K3 ■
Dorotheenstr. 65 ■ (030) 20
45 00 70 ■ from 6pm Mon–
Fri, from 9pm Sat
Sophisticated jazz bar with
bartenders whipping up
your cocktail of choice.

**Wooden interiors of Sra Bua Bar**

# Restaurants

**Atmospheric interiors of Refugium**

**6 Dressler Unter den Linden**

MAP K3 ■ Unter den Linden 39 ■ (030) 204 44 22 ■ 8am–1am daily ■ €€

In season, this French brasserie, decorated in Art Deco style, is excellent for oysters. Their inexpensive three-course set menu is recommended.

**1 Refugium**

MAP L4 ■ Gendarmenmarkt 5 ■ (030) 229 16 61 ■ noon–11pm daily (winter: from 5pm Mon–Fri) ■ €€

A cosy cellar restaurant next to the French cathedral. International and German dishes.

**2 Chipps**

MAP L5 ■ Jägerstr. 35 ■ (030) 36 44 45 88 ■ 9am–late Mon–Sat (to 5pm Sun) ■ €€

Possibly the best vegetarian/vegan restaurant in Berlin. Organic dishes focus on variations of Asian *chipps* (potato pancakes) and rice rolls.

**3 Vapiano**

MAP K4 ■ Mittelstr. 51 ■ (030) 501 541 00 ■ 10am–midnight daily ■ €€

Quality Italian food made in front of you at this self-service restaurant.

**4 Grill Royal**

MAP J4 ■ Friedrichstr. 105b ■ (030) 28 87 92 88 ■ 6pm–midnight daily ■ €€

Steak-lovers can choose from a range of cuts from around the world.

**5 Tausend Cantina**

MAP J3 ■ Schiffbauerdamm 11 ■ (030) 27 58 20 70 ■ 7:30pm–late Tue–Sat ■ €€

Top-notch Asian and Ibero-American cuisine by celebrated chef Duc Ngo, a Berliner with Vietnamese roots.

**7 Opera Court**

MAP K4 ■ Hotel de Rome, Behrenstr. 37 ■ (030) 46 06 09 12 60 ■ 2–6pm Fri–Sun ■ €

Petit fours, scones, sandwiches and tea are served beneath the gilded skylights at this historic café that boasts marble columns and an original glazed ceiling.

**8 Café Nö**

MAP L3 ■ Glinkastr. 23 ■ (030) 201 08 71 ■ noon–1am Mon–Fri, 7pm–1am Sat ■ €

Mediterranean flavours meet German classics at this wine bar and restaurant.

**9 Malatesta**

MAP L4 ■ Charlottenstr. 59 ■ (030) 20 94 50 71 ■ 10am–midnight daily ■ €€

Gourmet Italian food served in stylish, minimalist surroundings.

**10 Aigner**

MAP K4 ■ Französische Str. 25 ■ (030) 203 751 850 ■ noon–2am daily ■ €€

Original Viennese restaurant serving typically Austrian food.

**PRICE CATEGORIES**

For a three-course meal for one with half a bottle of wine (or equivalent meal), taxes and charges included.

€ under €30   €€ €30–60   €€€ over €60

*See map on pp84–5*

# TOP 10 Central Berlin: Scheunenviertel

From the mid-19th-century onwards, the Scheunenviertel ("barn quarter") was home to thousands of poor Jewish migrants. After World War II the area was entirely neglected and fell into decay. It has experienced a regen-eration in recent decades, and today, many historic merchants' yards and narrow side streets have been restored, reviving the quarter's unique and lively character. With its new restaurants, galleries and shops, the district has become fashionable. The tragic history of its former inhabitants, however, remains unforgotten.

**Richly decorated Postfuhramt building**

**CENTRAL BERLIN: SCHEUNENVIERTEL**

### 1 Neue Synagoge

MAP J4 ■ Oranienburger Str. 28–30 ■ 10am–8pm Sun & Mon, 10am–6pm Tue–Thu, 10am–5pm Fri ■ Adm ■ www.cjudaicum.de

Opened in 1866, the New Synagogue was once the largest in Europe. In 1938, it survived Kristallnacht thanks to a brave guard, but it was damaged by bombs during World War II. Behind the splendid Moorish façades are a prayer room and the Centrum Judaicum (see p59).

### 2 Oranienburger Straße

MAP J4 ■ Mitte, between Friedrichstr. and Rosenthaler Str.

In the centre of old Scheunenviertel, Oranienburger Straße symbolizes the rise and fall of Jewish culture in Berlin like no other street.

Striking dome of the Neue Synagoge

Traces of its Jewish past are visible at the Neue Synagoge and several Jewish cafés and restaurants (see p101). Some 18th- and 19th-century buildings attest to the street's former splendour – the Postfuhramt (see p97), for example, or the house at No. 71–72, built in 1789 by Christian Friedrich Becherer for the Grand Lodge of the German Freemasons.

### 3 Hackesche Höfe

MAP J5 ■ Rosenthaler Str. 40–41

Berlin's largest and most attractive group of restored commercial buildings, Hackesche Höfe extends between Oranienburger and Rosenthaler Straße. The complex, comprising eight interconnecting courtyards, was designed around the turn of the 20th century by August Endell and Kurt Berndt, two leading exponents of the Jugendstil. The first courtyard especially has elements typical of the style: geometric motifs on vibrant glazed tiles cover the building from the foundations to the guttering. The complex has been carefully restored and is now a popular centre of nightlife.

### 4 Museum für Naturkunde

The Museum of Natural History – one of the largest of its kind – has the world's largest dinosaur skeleton: a brachiosaurus found in Tanzania. Also displayed are fossils, meteorites and minerals *(see p51)*.

### 5 Sophienstraße
**MAP J5 ▪ Große Hamburger Str. 29**

Narrow Sophienstraße has been beautifully restored and looks as it did in the late 18th century. The buildings and courtyards now host shops and arts and crafts workshops. The Baroque Sophienkirche nearby, the first Protestant parish church, was founded by Queen Sophie Luise in 1712 *(see p98)*. Next to it is a cemetery with some 18th-century tombs.

**Museum für Naturkunde**

### 6 Dorotheenstädtischer Friedhof
**MAP F2 ▪ Chausseestr. 126 ▪ Summer: 8am–8pm daily; winter: 8am–sunset daily**

Many celebrities have found their final resting place in this striking cemetery, dating back to 1762. To the left of the

entrance are the graves of Heinrich Mann (1871–1950) and Bertolt Brecht (1898–1956); further along are the pillar-like tombstones of Johann Gottlieb Fichte (1762–1814) and Georg Wilhelm Friedrich Hegel (1770–1831). On Birkenallee (left off the main path) are the graves of Karl Friedrich Schinkel (1781–1841), Friedrich August Stüler (1800–65) and Johann Gottfried Schadow (1764–1850).

### 7 Brecht-Weigel-Gedenkstätte
**MAP F2 ▪ Chausseestr. 125 ▪ (030) 200 571 844 ▪ 10am–noon, 2–3:30pm Tue; 10–11:30am Wed & Fri; 10am–noon, 5–6:30pm Thu; 10am–3:30pm Sat; 11am–6pm Sun ▪ Adm ▪ www.adk.de/en/archive**

Bertolt Brecht, one of the greatest playwrights of the 20th century, lived here with his wife, Helene Weigel, between 1953 and 1956. On display are original furnishings, documents and photographs.

### 8 me Collectors Room Berlin
**MAP G2 ▪ Auguststr. 68 ▪ (030) 86 00 85 10 ▪ noon–6pm Tue–Sun ▪ Adm ▪ www.me-berlin.com**

Featuring the private collections of Thomas Olbricht and other international art collectors, this gallery has

---

**JEWISH BERLIN**

In the 19th century, Berlin had a population of 200,000 Jews, the largest such community in Germany. Apart from the wealthier Jews who lived in the west of the city, it included many Jewish migrants from Eastern Europe. They settled in Spandauer Vorstadt, primarily in Scheunenviertel, an impoverished part of the district that had the reputation of being a criminal red-light area. Later, Nazi propaganda used that name to denote the whole area to tarnish all Jews by association. Nazi stigmatization of Jews also included the enforced public wearing of a Star of David **(below)**. The Jewish quarter is still known as Scheunenviertel, but very few Jews live here now. Only some 5,000 Jewish Berliners survived the 1933–45 persecution.

works spanning the 16th century to contemporary times. It also organizes exhibitions, themed workshops and concerts on contemporary art. The upper floor houses Olbricht's "cabinet of curiosities", showcasing exotic, mysterious and dark objects.

### ⑨ Gedenkstätte Große Hamburger Straße

**MAP J5** ∎ Große Hamburger Str. ∎ www.jg-berlin.org/en.html

Before 1939, this was a thoroughly Jewish street, with Jewish schools, the oldest Jewish cemetery in Berlin and an old people's home. The latter achieved tragic fame during the Nazi period – the SS used it as a detention centre for Berlin Jews before transporting them to the concentration camps. A monument commemorates thousands of Jews who were sent to their death from here. To the left of the home is a Jewish school, on the site of an earlier school founded in 1778 by the Enlightenment philosopher Moses Mendelssohn (1729–86). To the right is the Alter Jüdischer Friedhof (old Jewish cemetery), where some 12,000 Berlin Jews were buried between 1672 and 1827. It was almost completely destroyed by the Nazis in 1943, and in 1945 it was converted into a park. Only a few Baroque tombstones or *masebas* survived; these are now fixed into the original cemetery wall. The spot thought to be Mendelssohn's tomb is marked by a *maseba*.

**Moses Mendelssohn**

### ⑩ Postfuhramt

**MAP J4** ∎ **Oranienburger Straße 35**

The richly ornamented Postfuhramt (post office transport department) dates from the 19th century. The building was used as an exhibition space, but it is now the head office of a medical technology firm.

**A DAY IN SCHEUNENVIERTEL**

#### ▶ MORNING

Take the S-Bahn to Berlin's former entertainment district at Friedrichstraße and explore this vibrant, glamorous street. Then walk north up to Reinhardtstraße, opposite the Friedrichstadt-Palast, and turn left here towards Bertolt-Brecht-Platz. Continue south to Albrechtstraße to the **Berliner Ensemble** *(see p98)*. Admire the theatre where Bertolt Brecht used to work, then make a detour to visit his home, the **Brecht-Weigel-Gedenkstätte**. The best way to get there is on foot – return to Friedrichstraße and walk north to Chausseestraße. Then retrace your steps and turn left into **Oranienburger Straße** *(see p95)* to get to the heart of fashionable Scheunenviertel. About a 7-minute walk down the street will bring the dome of the **Neue Synagoge** into view *(see p95)*.

#### AFTERNOON

Before exploring further, stop for some refreshments; not far from the synagogue is the **Keyser Soze** café *(see p101)*. Continue along Tucholskystraße, then turn right into Augustraße. Here you will find some of the most attractive courtyards, such as the old-world **Schulhof** at No. 21. A little ahead is the interesting **me Collectors Room Berlin** art gallery. Continue along Augustraße then turn right for the **Gedenkstätte Große Hamburger Straße** and the **Hackesche Höfe** *(see p95)*. Shop a little, then round off your tour of Scheunenviertel with an evening meal at one of its restaurants.

# The Best of the Rest

**Exhibit at the Charité museum**

### 1 Charité

MAP J3 ■ Schumannstr. 20–21 ■ (030) 450 536 156 ■ Medizinhistorisches Museum; 10am–5pm Tue, Thu, Fri, Sun, 10am–7pm Wed & Sat

Many renowned physicians, such as Rudolf Virchow and Robert Koch, worked and taught at this world-famous hospital, founded in 1710. The Museum of Medical History has some 750 remarkable exhibits on display.

### 2 Alte and Neue Schönhauser Straße

MAP J5 ■ Hackescher Markt

Alte Schönhauser Straße is one of the oldest streets in Spandauer Vorstadt. The lively road is still characterized by a colourful jumble of traditional and new fashion shops.

### 3 Deutsches Theater

MAP J3 ■ Schumannstr. 13A ■ (030) 28 44 12 25

Once the place of work of stage and screen actor and director Max Reinhardt, this theatre – widely considered the best German-language theatre – shows mainly German classics, often in new interpretations *(see p67)*.

### 4 Berliner Ensemble

MAP J3 ■ Bertolt-Brecht-Platz 1 ■ (030) 28 40 81 55

This theatre, established in 1891–2 by Heinrich Seeling, was the main venue for Bertolt Brecht's plays.

### 5 Hochbunker

MAP J3 ■ Reinhardtstr 20

One of the last surviving World War II bunkers in Berlin, this imposing building now houses the Boros Art Collection gallery *(see p62)*.

### 6 Monbijoupark

MAP J5 ■ Oranienburger Str./Spree

A small park, in which once stood the little Monbijou palace. It is now an attractive green space for a break.

### 7 Auguststraße

MAP G2 ■ Between Oranienburger and Rosenthaler Str.

The area round this road harks back to old Scheunenviertel, featuring interior courtyards and now brimming with art galleries.

### 8 Koppenplatz

MAP G2 ■ Near Auguststr.

In this small square, a monument of a table and upturned chair recall the expulsion of the Jews.

**The imposing Baroque Sophienkirche**

### 9 Sophienkirche

MAP G3 ■ Große Hamburger Str. 29

This parish church, built in 1712, has managed to preserve its traditional old Berlin charm. Be sure not to miss the Baroque pulpit.

### 10 Tucholskystraße

MAP J4

This narrow street is typical of the transformation of Scheunenviertel – trendy shops next to both decaying and beautifully renovated façades.

# Old Courtyards

**1 Sophie-Gips-Höfe**
MAP G3 ▪ Sophienstr. 21–22

Famous for the Hoffman art collection, which is based here, this former sewing machine factory is a popular meeting place.

**2 Sophienhöfe**
MAP G3 ▪ Sophienstr. 17–18

The 19th-century red-brick artisans' workshops have been transformed into artists' studios and a theatre.

**Courtyards of Heckmann-Höfe**

**3 Heckmann-Höfe**
MAP G3 ▪ Between Oranienburger Str. 32 and Auguststraße 9

These lavishly restored yards in a candy factory attract visitors with a restaurant and fashionable shops.

**4 Sophienstr. 22 and 22A**
MAP G3

Two small inner courtyards, partially planted, are surrounded by yellow and red-brick walls.

**5 Rosenthaler Straße 37**
MAP J5

This green-tiled courtyard is unique. Once part of the Wertheim department store, it now houses a boutique and tapas bar. The 1775 townhouse through which it is accessed has a beautiful wooden staircase.

**6 Schulhof**
MAP G2 ▪ Auguststr. 21

Time seems to have stood still around 1900 in this courtyard, which houses an elementary school.

**7 Hof Auguststraße 5A**
MAP G3

The extensive courtyard of the former Postfuhramt permits a glimpse of the original façade of the building.

**8 Rosenthaler Straße 39**
MAP J5

Berlin's post-Wall subculture of edgy art collectives is still alive and well in this unrenovated courtyard.

**9 Kunsthof**
MAP J4 ▪ Oranienburger Str. 27

A courtyard full of nooks and crannies, which is today occupied by a number of workshops, offices and cafés. Take a look at the richly ornamented staircases.

**10 Kunst-Werke (KW)**
MAP G2 ▪ Auguststr. 69

Large-scale installations by the resident artists are regularly on display at this well-known centre for contemporary art; artists-in-residence have included Susan Sontag. The courtyard has a café designed by US artist and curator Dan Graham in the conservatory.

**The Kunst-Werke courtyard**

*See map on pp94–5* ←

# Pubs, Bars and Nightclubs

**1 Grüner Salon**
MAP H3 ▪ Weydingerstraße 14–16 ▪ (030) 24 00 93 27 ▪ 9pm–4am Thu, 11pm–4am Fri & Sat

An intimate club with retro decor, including crystal lamps and velvet sofas.

**2 Bellini Lounge**
MAP J4 ▪ Oranienburger Str. 42 ▪ (030) 97 00 56 18 ▪ 6pm–2am daily

Some of the most authentic tropical cocktails north of the equator.

**The trendy interior of Grand Rocka**

**3 Grand Rocka**
MAP J5 ▪ Am Zwirngraben 6–7 ▪ (030) 24 63 86 06 ▪ from 9am daily

This bar and restaurant is a great spot to people-watch and enjoy a cold beer.

**4 Reingold**
MAP F2 ▪ Novalistr. 11 ▪ (030) 28 38 76 76 ▪ from 7pm Tue–Sat

A relaxed, fashionable bar with a 1920s atmosphere. Perfect for a nightcap after dinner in Mitte.

**5 Betty F**
MAP G2 ▪ Mulackstr. 13 ▪ (030) 304 717 440 ▪ from 9pm daily

A trashy gay and straight pub paying ironic homage to former US First Lady Betty Ford. Great cocktails.

**6 B-flat**
MAP G3 ▪ Dircksenstr. 40 ▪ (030) 283 31 23 ▪ from 8pm Sun–Thu, from 9pm Fri & Sat

Live jazz, and occasionally dancing, are on offer at this small venue.

**7 Cordobar**
MAP J5 ▪ Große Hamburger Str. 32 ▪ (030) 27 58 12 15 ▪ 7pm–2am Tue–Sat, 6pm–midnight Sun

This relaxed wine bar has an impressive cellar consisting of mainly German and Austrian wines.

**8 Yosoy**
MAP J5 ▪ Rosenthaler Str. 37 ▪ (030) 28 39 12 13 ▪ from 11am daily

Tasty tapas, good wines and exciting cocktails are served at this attractively furnished Spanish restaurant – which is why it is usually crowded late into the night.

**9 Kaffee Burger**
MAP G2 ▪ Torstr. 58–60 ▪ (030) 28 04 64 95 ▪ from 8pm daily

Thanks to its quirky record release parties, readings and movie screenings, this pub and music venue is a firm favourite with East Berlin hipsters.

**10 Oxymoron**
MAP J5 ▪ Rosenthaler Str. 40–41 ▪ (030) 28 39 18 86 ▪ from 9am daily

This small bar, club and restaurant in popular and lively Hackesche Höfe (see p95), features chintz decoration and serves light German and international meals.

**Oxymoron restaurant and bar**

# Restaurants

**PRICE CATEGORIES**
For a three-course meal for one with half
a bottle of wine (or equivalent meal),
taxes and charges included.

€ under €30 €€ €30–60 €€€ over €60

**Fondue at Nola's am Weinberg**

**(1) Chen Che**
MAP G2 ■ Rosenthaler Str. 13 ■
(030) 28 88 42 82 ■ noon–midnight
daily ■ €€
This Vietnamese teahouse-style restaurant offers fresh, affordable food
and has a tranquil bamboo garden.

**(2) Keyser Soze**
MAP G3 ■ Tucholskystr. 33
■ (030) 28 59 94 89 ■ 7:30am–3am
daily ■ €
Unpretentious restaurant serving
breakfast until 6pm and hearty
German snacks.

**(3) Monsieur Vuong**
MAP G2 ■ Alte Schönhauser
Str. 46 ■ (030) 99 29 69 24
■ noon–midnight daily ■ €
This tiny Vietnamese snack joint
serves delicious Asian dishes.

**(4) Pauly Saal**
MAP G2 ■ Auguststr. 11
■ (030) 33 00 60 70 ■ 3–6pm,
6pm–3am Mon–Sat ■ €€€
Classy Michelin star restaurant in a
former school that also houses art
galleries. Its wine list is extensive.

**(5) Beth-Café**
MAP G2 ■ Tucholskystr. 40
■ (030) 281 31 35 ■ 11am–5pm Fri,
11am–8pm Sun–Thu ■ no credit
cards ■ €
Small Jewish café of the Adass-
Jisroel community, serving Jewish
snacks and kosher wines and beers.

**(6) Hackescher Hof**
MAP J5 ■ Rosenthaler Str.
40–41 ■ (030) 283 52 93 ■ from 8am
Mon–Fri, from 9am Sat & Sun ■ €€
The best restaurant in Hackesche
Höfe serves delicious local produce.

**(7) Nola's am Weinberg**
MAP G2 ■ Veteranenstr. 9
■ (030) 44 04 07 66 ■ 10am–1am
daily ■ €€
The Swiss cuisine served here is
surprisingly inspired. Try one of
their delicious fondues. There is
a lovely outdoor terrace.

**(8) Alpenstück**
MAP G2 ■ Gartenstr. 9
■ (030) 21 75 16 46 ■ 6pm–1am
daily ■ €€
The best of the area's homely
restaurants serving traditional,
hearty fare from southern Germany
and Austria in a cosy setting,
decorated in an Alpine style.

**(9) Kamala**
MAP J4 ■ Oranienburger Str. 69
■ (030) 283 27 97 ■ noon–11:30pm
daily ■ €€
This hidden gem offers diners
traditional Thai cuisine alongside
a surprisingly impressive wine list.
Good value for money.

**(10) Barist**
MAP J5 ■ Am Zwirngraben
13–14 ■ (030) 24 72 26 13 ■ 9am–
1am Sun–Thu, 9am–3am Fri & Sat
■ €€
A mixture of French, Italian and
Austrian dishes are on offer here.
There is always a good atmosphere
under the S-Bahn arches; live jazz
plays at the weekends.

*See map on pp94–5*

# ᵀᴼᴾ10 Central Berlin: Around Alexanderplatz

**Berliner Rathaus**

The area around Alexanderplatz – "Alex" to locals – is one of the city's oldest parts. It was here that the twin towns of Cölln and Berlin merged in the 13th century. The square defined the heartbeat of the city before World War II; after the ravages of war, it seemed vast and a little forlorn. The vibrancy described by Alfred Döblin in his novel *Berlin Alexanderplatz*, is only slowly returning. A short walk away is the city's oldest coherent quarter – the 18th-century Nikolaiviertel – with its medieval Nikolaikirche.

**CENTRAL BERLIN: AROUND ALEXANDERPLATZ**

**Alexanderplatz's Neptunbrunnen with Marienkirche in the background**

### 1 Alexanderplatz
**MAP J6** ■ Mitte

The huge, largely desolate square in the centre of East Berlin, called "Alex" by Berliners, was one of the most vibrant places in Berlin before World War II – and no doubt it will be again some day. Alfred Döblin beautifully captured the rhythm of the city in his world-famous novel *Berlin Alexanderplatz* (1929). Not much remains today of the once frenzied atmosphere, although there is plenty of bustle around the Galeria Kaufhof department store *(see p107)*. Alexanderplatz was originally a cattle and wool market. Not many of the prewar buildings have survived – only Berolinahaus and Alexanderhaus remain, next to the historic S-Bahn station Alexanderplatz, both dating back to 1929. The square was almost completely laid to waste in World War II, and most of the surrounding soulless tower blocks were built in the 1960s.

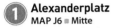

MOLLSTRASSE
BEROLINASTR.
EYDEMEYERSTR.
**U** Schillingstr.
KARL-MARX-ALLEE
JACOBYSTR.
NEUE BLUMENSTR.
SCHILLINGSTRASSE
NEUE BLUMENSTR.
**10**
STRAUSBERGER PLATZ
Strausberger **U** Platz

**Nikolaiviertel**
RATHAUSSTRASSE
SPANDAUER STRASSE
**2**
POST STR.
PROPSTSTR.
NIKOLAI-KIRCH-PLATZ
STRASSE
MÜHLENDAMM
SPREEUFER
Spree
OLZMARKT-TRASSE

### 2 Berliner Rathaus
**MAP K6** ■ Rathausstr. 15
■ (030) 902 60 ■ 9am–6pm Mon–Fri

Berlin's proud town hall, the office of the Governing Mayor, is the political centre of power in Greater Berlin. It was built in 1861–9 to a design by Hermann Friedrich Waesemann on the site of an older town hall. The Rathaus was meant to demonstrate the power and the glory of Berlin, and the architect took his inspiration for the new building from Italian Renaissance *palazzi*. The building is also known as the *Rotes Rathaus* or Red Town Hall – not a reference to its Socialist past, but to the red bricks from Brandenburg province with which it is built *(see also p54)*.

### ③ Berliner Fernsehturm

MAP J6 ■ Panoramastr. 1a
■ (030) 24 75 75 37 ■ Mar–Oct: 9am–midnight; Nov–Feb: 10am–midnight ■ Adm ■ www.tv-turm.de/en/

The 368-m- (1,207-ft-) high TV tower is the tallest building in Berlin, affording views of up to 40 km (25 miles). There is a viewing platform at 203 m (666 ft). The Sphere restaurant above rotates once around its own axis every 30 minutes. The tower, visible from afar, was erected in 1965–9 by the East German government to signify the triumph of their capital East Berlin.

### ④ Nikolaiviertel

MAP K6 ■ Mitte
■ Knoblauchhaus: Poststr. 23
■ (030) 240 020 171
■ 10am–6pm Tue–Sun
■ Adm ■ www.en.
stadtmuseum.de

Centred around the medieval Nikolaikirche (see p58), the small Nikolaiviertel quarter with its nooks and crannies, old Berlin restaurants and souvenir shops is one of the most charming parts of the city. The area extending between the banks of the Spree River and Mühlendamm was razed to the ground in World War II. East Germany restored it after the war, unfortunately not always

successfully: some houses were covered in prefabricated façades. Knoblauchhaus was one of few to escape wartime destruction. Dating from 1835, it was the former home of the Knoblauch family (Neue Synagoge was designed by architect Eduard Knoblauch). Today it houses a museum depicting everyday life in Berlin, and includes a fully furnished apartment in the Biedermeier style.

**Märkisches Museum**

### ⑤ Märkisches Museum

MAP L6 ■ Am Köllnischen Park 5 ■ (030) 24 00 21 62
■ 10am–6pm Tue–Sun
■ Adm ■ www.en.
stadtmuseum.de

Berlin's municipal museum holds artifacts relating to the city's culture and history, including architectural treasures such as doorways and the head of one of the horses from the top of the Brandenburg Gate. There is also a Gothic Chapel room with a collection of medieval sculptures.

### ⑥ Marienkirche

MAP J6 ■ Karl-Liebknecht-Str. 8
■ (030) 242 44 67 ■ 10am–6pm Mon–Sat, noon–6pm Sun

Originally built in 1270, Marienkirche was extensively remodelled in the 15th century. Thanks to its Baroque church tower, it is one of Berlin's loveliest churches. Inside, the alabaster pulpit by Andreas Schlüter (1703) and the main altar (1762) are highlights. The 15th-century Gothic font and a 22-m (72-ft) long fresco from 1485, *Der Totentanz* (The Dance of Death), are its two oldest treasures. The church is now the only reminder of the once densely built-up historic city core here (see p58).

### ⑦ Marx-Engels-Forum

MAP K5

This public park was founded by East German authorities shortly after German reunification in 1989. The words "Next time it will all be

**Buildings in the Nikolaiviertel**

different" were scrawled onto the bronze monument to Friedrich Engels and Karl Marx, the fathers of Socialism, erected in 1986.

### 8 Ephraim-Palais

MAP K6 ■ Poststr. 16 ■ (030) 24 00 21 62 ■ 10am–6pm Tue & Thu– Sun, noon–8pm Wed ■ Adm ■ www. en.stadtmuseum.de

This Rococo palace, built in 1766 for the merchant, court jeweller and mint master Nathan Veitel Heinrich Ephraim, was once regarded as the city's most beautiful spot. Rebuilt using original elements after the old palace was demolished, it houses a museum on Berlin art history.

### 9 Neptunbrunnen

MAP K6 ■ Am Rathaus

The green Neo-Baroque fountain, dating from 1895, depicts the sea god Neptune. He is surrounded by four female figures, symbolizing Prussia's main rivers at the time: the Rhine, Weichsel, Oder and Elbe.

**Neptunbrunnen, Alexanderplatz**

### 10 Karl-Marx-Allee and Frankfurter Allee

MAP H3 ■ Mitte/Friedrichshain

This avenue, lined by Soviet-style buildings, was built as a showpiece for Socialism in 1949–55. Known then as "Stalinallee", it provided ultra-modern apartments that are again in high demand today.

**A DAY AROUND ALEXANDERPLATZ**

**MORNING**

Start your day at Strausberger Platz where you can admire the products of Socialist architecture lining **Frankfurter Allee**. Then take the U-Bahn (or continue on foot) to the vast **Alexanderplatz** *(see p103)* where you can indulge in a bit of people-watching or do a spot of shopping before heading to the beautiful **Marienkirche**. Step back outside to admire the lovely **Neptunbrunnen** fountain a few steps away, then walk to the **Berliner Fernsehturm** and – if the weather is nice – take the lift up to the viewing platform. After that, cross the square to the **Berliner Rathaus** *(see p103)*. Stroll past the statues of Marx and Engels in the **Marx-Engels-Forum,** then turn to the nearby historic **Nikolaiviertel**. For lunch you can enjoy the rustic fare at **Reinhard's** *(see p109)*.

**AFTERNOON**

After lunch, experience the historic ambience of the old Nikolaiviertel quarter by exploring its narrow alleyways and hidden nooks on foot. The **Knoblauchhaus** museum and the Nikolaikirche are especially worth a visit. Then walk down Grunerstraße to reach the opposite bank of the Spree River, where you can immerse yourself in Berlin's culture and history at the **Märkisches Museum**. Round off your day with a meal at the stylish **Zur Gerichtslaube** *(see p109)*.

*See map on pp102–3* ←

# The Best of the Rest

**Lacy balustrades at the Stadtgericht**

### 1 Stadtgericht
MAP K6 ■ Littenstr. 13–15
■ 9am–1pm Mon–Fri

The imposing municipal courts building boasts extravagant stairs in the lobby area, with curved balustrades and elegant columns.

### 2 Franziskanerkirche
MAP K6 ■ Klosterstr. 74

Remnants of a 13th-century Franciscan abbey, these ruins are surrounded by lawns, making this a picturesque spot for a break in the city centre.

### 3 Stadtmauer
MAP K6 ■ Waisenstr.

A fragment of the 13th–14th-century town wall that once surrounded the twin towns of Berlin and Cölln.

### 4 Parochialkirche
MAP K6 ■ Klosterstr. 67

This church, by Johann Arnold Nering and Martin Grünberg, was one of Berlin's most charming Baroque churches, but the magnificent interior and bell tower were destroyed in World War II. In 2016, a replica of the historic tower was mounted, bearing a new carillon with 52 bells.

**Detail, Parochialkirche**

### 5 Palais Podewil
MAP K6 ■ Klosterstr. 68 ■ (030) 24 74 96 ■ 11am–10pm Mon–Sat

The light yellow Baroque palace, built in 1701–4, has been transformed into Podewil, a cultural centre, and a subsidiary of the Grips-Theater (see p64).

### 6 Märkisches Ufer
MAP L6

This picturesque riverside promenade gives a good impression of the city in the late 18th century. Look out for No. 12, a typical Berlin Baroque house that was originally built on Fischerinsel in 1740 and transplanted here in 1969.

### 7 Heiliggeistkapelle
MAP J5 ■ Spandauer Str. 1

A beautiful example of Gothic brick architecture, this hospital church was built around 1300.

### 8 Ribbeckhaus
MAP K5 ■ Breite Str. 36

The only Renaissance house in central Berlin, with a remarkable, lavishly ornamented façade.

### 9 AquaDom and Sea Life Berlin

Discover a host of species living in rivers, lakes and seas, and see amazing corals and tropical fish at this fascinating centre, which boasts the world's largest cylindrical aquarium (see p65).

### 10 Historischer Hafen
MAP L6 ■ Märkisches Ufer ■ Museum May–Sep:1– 6pm Sat & Sun ■ (030) 21 47 32 57

Moored at this port are barges and tugboats that once operated on the Spree River. The *Renate-Angelika* hosts a historical display on inland shipping.

# Shops and Markets

**Vast interiors of the Galeria Kaufhof**

### 1 Galeria Kaufhof
MAP J6 ▪ Alexanderplatz 9
▪ (030) 24 74 30 ▪ 9:30am–8pm
Mon–Sat

The largest department store in eastern Berlin stocks everything your heart could desire. Its food department entices with a range of international gourmet foods.

### 2 Die Puppenstube
MAP K6 ▪ Propststr. 4
▪ (030) 242 39 67 ▪ 9am–6:30
pm Mon–Sat, 11am–6pm Sun

Adorable dolls made from porcelain and other materials await, as do mountains of cute fluffy teddy bears.

### 3 Teddy's
MAP K6 ▪ Propststr. 4
▪ (030) 247 82 44 ▪ 10am–6pm
daily

An old-fashioned toy store with probably the city's best selection of teddy bears, including brands like Steiff. They also have bear clothing and accessories.

### 4 TeeGschwendner
MAP K6 ▪ Propststr. 3 ▪ (030)
242 32 55 ▪ 10am–7pm Mon–Sat

A charming specialist tea shop opposite Nikolaikirche, full of delicious scents. They carry more than 300 varieties of tea.

### 5 Ausberlin
MAP J6 ▪ Karl-Liebknecht Str. 9
▪ (030) 97 00 56 40 ▪ 10am–8pm
Mon–Sat

Whimsical stock, with a fashion focus, all created in Berlin. Exclusive designer items include Breath of Berlin perfume, bags and T-shirts.

### 6 U- and S-Bahnhof Alexanderplatz
MAP J6 ▪ Alexanderplatz

This bustling area has a selection of shops for daily needs, plus late-opening fast food outlets and German *imbisse* (food stands).

### 7 Alexa
MAP K6 ▪ Am Alexanderplatz,
Grunerstr. 20 ▪ (030) 269 34 00
▪ 10am–9pm Mon–Sat

This mall boasts some 180 retail outlets, such as Build-a-Bear Workshop, where kids assemble their own teddy, and LOXX, the world's largest digitally operated model train set.

### 8 Erzgebirgischer Weihnachtsmarkt
MAP K6 ▪ Propststr. 8 ▪ (030)
241 12 29 ▪ 11am–7pm
Mon–Sat

A vast array of stalls laden with a range of German handicrafts, including traditional wooden nutcrackers.

**Wooden nutcracker**

### 9 Münzstraße
MAP J6

This tiny street, just off Alexanderplatz, is full of original fashion boutiques and designer stores. A real mecca for fashion aficionados.

### 10 die mitte
MAP J6 ▪ Alexanderplatz
▪ (030) 263 99 70 ▪ 10am–9pm
Mon–Sat

Visit this large shopping centre for flagship fashion stores Esprit and New Yorker, or multimedia at Saturn.

See map on pp102–3 ⟵

# Pubs, Cafés and Beer Gardens

### 1 Zur letzten Instanz

MAP K6 ▪ Waisenstr. 14–16 ▪ (030) 242 55 28 ▪ noon–1am Mon–Sat, noon–11pm Sun

Berlin's oldest pub dates back to 1621, and former guests include Napoleon, Beethoven, the German artist Heinrich Zille, former Soviet leader Mikhael Gorbachev and Angela Merkel.

**German pub food at Zur letzten Instanz**

### 2 Zum Nußbaum

A charming historic pub in the Nikolaiviertel quarter serving draught beers and *Berliner Weiße* in summer (see p73).

### 3 COME BUY

MAP J5 ▪ Rosenthaler Str. 31 ▪ (030) 93 62 45 15 ▪ 11am–9pm daily

An authentic Taiwanese bubble tea café where customers can choose from more than 30 flavours, such as taro milk tea with tapioca pearls.

### 4 Brauhaus Georgbräu

MAP K6 ▪ Spreeufer 4 ▪ (030) 242 42 44 ▪ summer: 10am–midnight daily; winter: from noon daily

Attracting Bavarians and tourists alike, this beer garden offers a variety of rustic fare and beer from both Berlin and Munich.

**Interior, Brauhaus Georgbräu**

### 5 Deckshaus

MAP H4 ▪ Märkisches Ufer/Historischer Hafen ▪ (030) 21 79 14 04 ▪ noon–10pm Tue–Sat, noon–8pm Sun

This delightful bistro on the deck of an old steamship offers stunning views of the Spree and local specialities such as *apfelstrudel* or fried fish.

### 6 Café Oliv

MAP J6 ▪ Münzstr. 8 ▪ (030) 89 20 65 40 ▪ 8:30am–7pm Mon–Fri, 9:30am–7pm Sat, 10am–6pm Sun

Trendy Berliners get their organic sandwiches, flat whites and home-baked cakes from this sleek venue.

### 7 Café Ephraim's

MAP K6 ▪ Spreeufer 1 ▪ (030) 24 72 59 47 ▪ noon–10pm daily ▪ no credit cards

Hearty German food and excellent coffee and cakes added to the great views of the Spree River attract both locals and tourists.

### 8 tigertörtchen

MAP K6 ▪ Spandauer Str. 25 ▪ (030) 67 96 90 51 ▪ 11am–6pm Thu–Tue

Come here for inventive cupcake creations such as date and walnut or crab and dill.

### 9 Marinehaus

MAP L6 ▪ Märkisches Ufer 48-50 ▪ (030) 279 32 46 ▪ noon–late daily

Traditional pub with maritime decor, serving German food.

### 10 Der Alte Fritz

MAP J6 ▪ Karl-Liebknecht-Str. 29 ▪ (030) 96 20 06 00 ▪ noon–midnight Mon–Sat, noon–10pm Sun

German dishes such as pork knuckles and roasted duck with green cabbage are served here.

# Restaurants

**PRICE CATEGORIES**
For a three-course meal for one with half a bottle of wine (or equivalent meal), taxes and charges included.

€ under €30    €€ €30–60    €€€ over €60

**The simple interior of Zillestube**

**1 Reinhard's**
MAP K6 ▪ Poststr. 28 ▪ (030) 242 52 95 ▪ 9am–midnight daily ▪ €€
One of Mitte's most charming restaurants. Savour the international food, surrounded by photos and paintings of famous contemporaries.

**2 HEat**
MAP K5 ▪ Karl-Liebknecht-Str. 3 ▪ (030) 238 283 472 ▪ 6am–11pm daily ▪ €€
This ultra-chic fusion restaurant at the SAS Radisson Blu *(see p172)* serves an imaginative blend of Oriental and European tastes.

**3 Zur Gerichtslaube**
MAP K6 ▪ Poststr. 28 ▪ (030) 241 56 98 ▪ 11:30am–1am daily ▪ €€
The former court building is a stylish setting for traditional Berlin special- ities such as Prussian sausages.

**4 Le Provençal**
MAP K6 ▪ Spreeufer 3 ▪ (030) 302 75 67 ▪ noon–midnight ▪ €€
Baked oysters, scallop soup and other seafood delicacies are served in this family-run French restaurant. Try the lavender ice cream.

**5 Zum Paddenwirt**
MAP K6 ▪ Nikolaikirchplatz 6 ▪ (030) 242 63 82 ▪ noon–midnight daily ▪ no credit cards ▪ €€
A mecca for fans of traditional Berlin food, including fried herrings and brawn, and a strong beer.

**6 Zillestube**
MAP K6 ▪ Propststr. 9 ▪ (030) 242 52 47 ▪ from 11am daily ▪ €
Named after the 19th-century Berlin illustrator and photographer Heinrich Zille, this tiny pub serves hearty Berlin food and traditional beers in a rustic setting.

**7 Marcellino**
MAP K6 ▪ Poststr. 28 ▪ (030) 242 73 71 ▪ noon–midnight daily ▪ €€
An agreeable Italian restaurant, with a pleasant terrace and a large inviting garden offering shade on a hot summer's day.

**8 Balthasar Spreeufer 2**
MAP K6 ▪ Spreeufer 2 ▪ (030) 30 88 21 56 ▪ noon–10pm daily ▪ €€
Enjoy German and international cuisine with fusion dishes such as tagliatelle with a ginger and tomato sauce, and many more meat- and fish- based mains.

**9 Fernsehturm Sphere**
MAP J6 ▪ Panoramastr. 1a ▪ (030) 242 59 22 ▪ 10am–midnight daily ▪ €€
This revolving restaurant in the TV Tower offers superb views and Berlin-Brandenburg specialities, including cod with beetroot and potato purée.

**10 Mutter Hoppe**
MAP K6 ▪ Rathausstr. 21 ▪ (030) 241 56 25 ▪ 11:30am– midnight daily ▪ €€
Gigantic portions of delicious traditional German food make up for the sometimes brusque service.

*See map on pp102–3*

# 🔟 The Tiergarten and Federal District

In 1999, Berlin's green centre became the government district. Around the Tiergarten, Berlin's largest and most popular park, stand the Reichstag, the Bundeskanzleramt and Schloss Bellevue, official residence of the President of the Federal Republic of Germany. The sprawling Tiergarten itself is a great place for strolling and cycling, and it also boasts the Landwehrkanal, the Neuer See, the Spree River and Berlin's zoo. In summer, its lawns are used for soccer games and barbecue parties.

**Sowjetisches Ehrenmal**

## TIERGARTEN AND FEDERAL DISTRICT

**1** Top 10 Sights
see pp113–15

**1** Restaurants
see p117

**1** Hidden Treasures
see p116

---

*Previous pages* Early summer in the lovely wooded environs of Berlin's Großer Tiergarten

**The majestic Reichstag with its beautiful modern dome**

### 1 Reichstag

More than any of the other landmarks in Berlin, the Reichstag – the seat of the German parliament – has come to symbolize German history *(see pp14–15)*.

### 2 Kulturforum

This unique complex of modern buildings features the best museums and concert halls in western Berlin *(see pp38–41)*.

### 3 Großer Tiergarten
**MAP E4 ▪ Tiergarten**

The Großer Tiergarten is Berlin's largest park, straddling an area of 200 hectares (494 acres) between the eastern and western parts of the town. Formerly the Elector's hunting grounds, it was redesigned in the 1830s as a park by Peter Joseph Lenné. At the end of the 19th century, the Siegesallee was established in the east of the park, more than 500 m (1,640 ft) in length, lined by statues of monarchs and politicians. After World War II, the starving and freezing population chopped down nearly all the trees for firewood and dug up the lawns to grow food. Thanks to reforestation since the 1950s, the Tiergarten is today Berlin's favourite green space and the lungs of the city *(see p60)*.

### 4 Siegessäule
**MAP M6 ▪ Großer Stern ▪ Adm**

In the middle of the Tiergarten stands the 62-m- (203-ft-) high Victory Column, erected to commemorate Prussian victory against Denmark in the war of 1864. After victory over Austria in 1866 and France 1871, the structure was crowned by a 35-ton gilded statue of the goddess Victoria. There are great views from the viewing platform, 285 steps up *(see p55)*.

**PETER JOSEPH LENNÉ**

Lenné (1789–1866), one of Germany's most influential landscape architects, was born into a family of gardeners in Bonn. He studied in Paris and joined the Royal Gardens in Potsdam as an apprentice in 1816. There he met Schinkel and together they set out to design the parks of Berlin and Potsdam in the harmonious style of the time.

### ⑤ Diplomatenviertel
MAP E4 ■ Between Stauffen-bergstr. and Lichtensteinallee as well as along Tiergartenstr.

In the late 19th century, an embassy district sprang up. Most structures were destroyed during World War II, and until German reunification the buildings were left to decay. After the government moved back to Berlin from Bonn in 1999, new life was breathed into the diplomats' quarter and, thanks to its adventurous architecture, it is now one of Berlin's most interesting areas. Especially worth seeing are the Austrian and Indian embassies on Tiergartenstraße, the Nordic embassies (see p57) on Rauchstraße and the Mexican embassy on Klingelhöferstraße.

### ⑥ Hamburger Bahnhof
This former railway station, now the Museum für Gegenwart (Museum of the Present Day), holds contemporary works of art. Former dispatch warehouses were converted and linked to the old railway building, forming the Rieckhallen, and doubling the exhibition space. One of the highlights is the private collection of Erich Marx, with works by Beuys and others (see p53).

**Hamburger Bahnhof**

**Sowjetisches Ehrenmal**

### ⑦ Sowjetisches Ehrenmal
MAP K2 ■ Str. des 17. Juni

The Soviet Memorial was opened on 7 November 1945, the anniversary of the Russian October Revolution. It is flanked by two tanks, supposedly the first to reach Berlin. The memorial commemorates the 300,000 Red Army soldiers who died during World War II in the fight to liberate Berlin. A legend persists that the large column was made from the marble blocks of Hitler's Reich Chancellery. Designed by Nicolai Sergijevski, the column is crowned by a bronze statue by Lev Kerbel. Behind the memorial, 2,500 Russian soldiers are buried.

### ⑧ Hansa-Viertel
MAP D3 ■ Tiergarten, Hanseatenweg

The Hansa estate west of Schloss Bellevue was built for the Interbau architecture exhibition in 1957. World War II bombs had flattened the Tiergarten, and 36 residential complexes were erected in the park, designed by distinguished architects from around the world, including Walter Gropius (Händelallee 3–9), Alvar Aalto (Klopstockstr. 30–32) and Oscar Niemeyer (Altonaer Str. 4–14).

### ⑨ Gedenkstätte Deutscher Widerstand

MAP E4 ▪ Stauffenbergstr. 13–14
▪ (030) 26 99 50 00 ▪ 9am–6pm Mon–
Wed & Fri, 9am–8pm Thu, 10am–6pm
Sat & Sun ▪ www.gdw-berlin.de/en/

Today known as Bendlerblock, this 1930s complex lies behind the former Prussian Ministry of War. During World War II it served as army headquarters. It was here that a group of officers planned the assassination of Adolf Hitler. When the attempt failed on 20 July 1944, Claus Schenk Count von Stauffenberg and the others involved were arrested here, and many of them were shot in the courtyard during the night. A memorial, created by Richard Scheibe in 1953, commemorates these events. On the upper floor is a small exhibition documenting the German resistance against the Nazi regime. Today, the Bendlerblock has been incorporated into the Berlin branch of the Federal Ministry of Defence.

**Gedenkstätte Deutscher Widerstand**

### ⑩ Villa von der Heydt

MAP E4 ▪ Von-der-Heydt-Str.
18 ▪ www.preussischer-kulturbesitz.
de/en

This late Neo-Classical villa, built in 1860–61 by architects Hermann Ende and G A Linke for one of the city's most elegant residential areas at the time, is one of the few extant examples of the architectural villa style typical of the Tiergarten. The Prussian Heritage Foundation now has its headquarters here.

---

### A DAY OUT

#### ▶ MORNING

Start your tour of the Tiergarten near the **Reichstag** *(see pp14–15)*. Explore the government district starting with the Federal Chancellor's Office or the Bundeskanzleramt. Stop at Restaurant Käfer *(see p117)* in the Reichstag building for breakfast. Via John-Foster-Dulles-Allee you will pass the **Carillon** *(see p116)* and the Haus der Kulturen der Welt on the way to **Großer Tiergarten** *(see p113)*. Continue along one of the paths into the park, directly opposite the old Kongresshalle, until you reach Straße des 17. Juni. Turn right to go towards **Siegessäule** *(see p113)*. From there continue along Fasanerieallee in a southwesterly direction until you reach **Café am Neuen See** *(see p117)* for lunch.

#### AFTERNOON

After lunch, take a stroll through the Diplomatenviertel. From Neuer See, it is only a few steps east along Lichtensteinallee and Thomas-Dehler-Straße until you get to Rauchstraße with its Scandinavian embassies. On Tiergartenstraße you will pass, among others, the embassies of Japan, Italy, India and Austria. Head back to Klingelhöferstraße and walk south, making a small detour for refreshments at **Café Einstein** *(see p117)*. Head back to the canal and continue along Lützowufer until you reach the **Kulturforum** *(see pp38–41)* via Potsdamer Brücke. A good place for an evening meal would be **Vox** *(see p70)* at the Grand Hyatt.

*See map on pp112–13* ←

# Hidden Treasures

### 1 Neuer See
**MAP M5 ▪ S-Bahn station Tiergarten**

Shimmering in a mysterious emerald green, the largest lake in the Tiergarten is perfect for rowing. Afterwards you can recover in the Café am Neuen See.

### 2 Löwenbrücke
**MAP M5 ▪ Großer Weg**

The Lion Bridge, which leads across a small stream near Neuer See, was built in 1838 and is "suspended" from the sculptures of four lions. This idyllic spot is a favourite meeting point in Berlin.

### 3 Lortzing-Denkmal
**MAP L1 ▪ Östlicher Großer Weg**

There are 70 statues of philosophers, poets and statesmen in Tiergarten. The statue of the composer Lortzing, at one end of Neuer See, is one of the most beautiful.

### 4 Houseboats
**MAP M4 ▪ Str. des 17. Juni, Tiergartenufer**

Docked on the banks of the Spree River are some of the few remaining houseboats in Berlin – an idyllic haven in the middle of the city's bustle.

### 5 Gaslights in Tiergarten
**MAP M5 ▪ At S-Bahn station Tiergarten**

With 80 beautiful historic gaslights from different cities illuminating the paths, an evening stroll in the Tiergarten can be a romantic affair.

### 6 Englischer Garten
**MAP P3 ▪ An der Klopstockstr.**

The lovely English-style landscaped garden near

Schloss Bellevue is ideal for strolling or relaxing at the Teehaus with coffee and cake.

### 7 Locks
**MAP M5 ▪ At the Zoo, S-Bahn station Tiergarten**

The two Landwehrkanal locks and the quirky Schleusenkrug beer garden (next to the eponymous lock) are very popular with locals and visitors.

**Beer garden on the canal lock**

### 8 Estonian Embassy
**MAP E4 ▪ Hildebrandstr. 5**

In a street next to the ruined Greek Embassy, this building is characteristic of the diplomats' quarter.

### 9 Landwehrkanal
**MAP M/N5/6 ▪ Corneliusstr.**

The grassy banks of the 11-km (7-mile) long Landwehrkanal are ideal for chilling out.

### 10 Carillon
**MAP K1 ▪ John-Foster-Dulles-Allee (Haus der Kulturen der Welt) ▪ Open-air concerts: 3pm Sun May–Sep**

The *carillon*, officially dedicated in 1987, is the largest of its kind in Europe. The 68 bells are rung every day at noon and 6pm in the 42-m (138-ft) high black tower.

**The *carillon* tower**

# Restaurants

### 1 Café am Neuen See

MAP M5 ▪ Tiergarten, Neuer See, Lichtensteinallee 2 ▪ (030) 254 49 30 ▪ Mar–Oct: 9am–11pm daily; Nov–Feb: 10am–8pm Sat & Sun ▪ €

On the shore of the lake, this is a restaurant, café and beer garden. The "Italian breakfast" is delicious.

### 2 Schleusenkrug

MAP M5 ▪ Tiergarten-Schleuse ▪ (030) 313 99 09 ▪ 10–1am daily (to 7pm winter) ▪ no credit cards ▪ €

This small café, right next to a lock, has a rustic beer garden and is very popular with students.

### 3 Café Einstein

MAP E5 ▪ Kurfürstenstr. 58 ▪ (030) 26 39 19 18 ▪ 8–1am daily ▪ €€

Based in the villa belonging to the film star Henny Porten, this is the ultimate in Viennese style.

### 4 Käfer im Reichstag

MAP K2 ▪ Platz der Republik ▪ (030) 22 62 99 35 ▪ 9am–midnight ▪ €€

An ambitious restaurant, better known for its view than its food.

### 5 Joseph-Roth-Diele

MAP E5 ▪ Potsdamer Str. 75 ▪ (030) 26 36 98 84 ▪ 10am–midnight Mon–Fri ▪ €

Popular restaurant/bar serving home-made traditional German food. Accepts cash payments only.

### 6 Panama

MAP E5 ▪ Potsdamer Straße 91 ▪ (030) 983 20 84 35 ▪ from 6pm Tue–Sat ▪ €€

The imaginative dishes at this modern eatery are perfect for tapas-style sharing.

**Lorenz Adlon Esszimmer**

### 7 Lorenz Adlon Esszimmer

MAP K3 ▪ Unter den Linden 77 ▪ (030) 22 61 19 60 ▪ 7–10:30pm Tue–Sat ▪ €€€

Superb European cuisine is on the menu at this restaurant with two Michelin stars in the Hotel Adlon Kempinski.

### 8 Brasserie Desbrosses

MAP L2 ▪ Potsdamer Platz 3 ▪ (030) 337 776 341 ▪ 6:30am–2:30pm, 5:30–11pm daily ▪ €€

An appealing, historic French restaurant in the Ritz-Carlton. Its seafood is particularly good.

### 9 Paris-Moskau

MAP J1 ▪ Alt-Moabit 141 ▪ (030) 394 20 81 ▪ 6pm–midnight daily ▪ €€

A classic restaurant serving seasonal dishes with an emphasis on game and seafood.

### 10 Lutter & Wegner Potsdamer Platz

MAP L2 ▪ Bellevuestr. 1 ▪ (030) 26 39 03 72 ▪ 11am–1am ▪ €€

This tiny outlet of Lutter & Wegner offers great Berlin and Austrian-French dishes in the historic setting of the Kaisersaal of the 1920s Grand Hotel Esplanade, whose remnants were incorporated into the Sony Center.

*See map on pp112–13* ⬅

# TOP 10 Charlottenburg and Spandau

**Palace detail, Charlottenburg**

The sophisticated haute bourgeoisie enclave of Charlottenburg was the only Berlin district that did not touch the Wall. The historical streets off Ku'damm feature galleries, boutiques, cafés and restaurants set in stout early 20th-century residential houses. These streets and the proud town hall remind us that this was once Prussia's richest town, which was only incorporated into the city of Berlin in 1920. Spandau, on the other side of the Spree and Havel, is almost rural in comparison, with a Late Medieval core and citadel that make it seem like a small independent town.

### 1 Kurfürstendamm

This famous Berlin boulevard was frequented by writers, directors and painters in the interwar years. Today it is a lively avenue lined with designer stores and elegant cafés *(see pp30–31)*.

### 2 Schloss Charlottenburg

The Baroque and English-style gardens of this Hohenzollern summer residence are ideal for a stroll. The palace's restored interiors are stunning *(see pp34–7)*.

**SPANDAU AND BERLIN**

Berliners consider the Spandauers to be rather different sorts of people, provincial and rough, and not "real" Berliners at all. But the Spandauers can reassure themselves that Spandau is 60 years older than Berlin, and proudly point to their independent history. The mutual mistrust is not just a result of Spandau's geographical location, isolated from the remainder of the city by the Havel and Spree Rivers. It is also due to the fact that Spandau was only incorporated into Berlin in 1920. Spandauers today still say they are going "to Berlin", even though the city centre is only a few U-bahn stops away.

**CHARLOTTENBURG AND SPANDAU**

0 metres 500
0 yards 500

### 3 Zitadelle Spandau
**Am Juliusturm ■ 10am–5pm daily ■ (030) 354 94 40 ■ Adm**

Berlin's only surviving fortress, this citadel at the confluence of the Havel and Spree is strategically well sited. The structure, built in 1560 by Francesco Chiaramella da Gandino, was based on Italian forts. It has four bastions – Brandenburg, Kronprinz (crown prince), Königin (queen) and König (king). The Juliusturm, a remnant of a fortress that stood here as early as the 12th century, is a keep that was used as a prison in the 19th century. At the time, Berliners used to say "off to the Julio" when they sent criminals to prison. Later, the reparations paid by France after its defeat in the Franco-Prussian War of 1870–71 were kept here.

**The imposing Zitadelle Spandau**

### 4 Zoologischer Garten
Founded in 1844, this is the country's oldest and most prominent zoological garden, combined with an aquarium *(see pp42–3)*.

**1** Top 10 Sights
*see pp119–23*

**1** Restaurants
*see p127*

**1** The Best of the Rest
*see p124*

**1** Cafés and Coffee Shops *see p126*

**1** Shops and Markets
*see p125*

**Exterior of the 15th-century Gotisches Haus in Spandau's Altstadt**

###  Spandau Old Town
**Breite Str., Spandau**

When walking around Spandau's pedestrianized Old Town (Altstadt), it is easy to forget that you are still in Berlin. The narrow alleyways and nooks and crannies around the 13th-century Nikolaikirche are lined by Late Medieval houses, a reminder that Spandau was founded in 1197 and is older than Berlin itself. The Gotisches Haus – the oldest house in Berlin, dating back to the late 15th century – stands at Breite Straße 32. It was built of stone at a time when most houses were made of wood. It is now the Visitor Information Centre, and some of its rooms are used to showcase finds from the house and other artifacts of the period.

### 6 Savignyplatz
**MAP N3 ■ An der Kantstr.**

One of Berlin's most attractive squares is right in the heart of Charlottenburg. Savignyplatz, named after a 19th-century German legal scholar, is the focal point of the neighbourhood's reputation as a district for artists and intellectuals and as a trendy area for dining out and entertainment. The square has two green spaces, either side of Kantstraße. It was built in the 1920s as part of an effort to create parks in the centre of town. Small paths, benches and pergolas make it a pleasant place for a rest. Dotted all around Savignyplatz are street cafés, restaurants and shops, especially in Grolman-, Knesebeck-, and Carmerstraße, all three of which cross the square. Many a reveller has lost his way here after a night out celebrating, which is why the area is jokingly known as the "Savignydreieck" (the Savigny Triangle). North of Savignyplatz it is worth exploring some of the most attractive streets in Charlottenburg, including Knesebeck-, Schlüter- and Goethestraße. This is still a thriving Charlottenburg community; the small shops, numerous bookstores, cafés and specialist retailers are always busy, especially on Saturdays. South of the square, the red-tiled S-Bahn arches also lure visitors with their shops, cafés and bars, particularly the Savignypassage near Bleibtreustraße and the small passageway between Grolman- and Uhlandstraße on the opposite side of the square.

### 7 Fasanenstraße
**MAP N/P4 ■ Charlottenburg**

This elegant street is the most attractive and trendiest street off Kurfürstendamm. Designer shops, galleries and restaurants are tucked away here, a shoppers' paradise for all those who regard Ku'damm as a mere retail strip catering for the masses. The junction of Ku'damm and Fasanenstraße is one of the liveliest spots in Berlin. One of the best known places is the Kempinski Hotel Bristol Berlin at the northern end of Fasanenstraße. The former bank opposite cleverly combines a historic building with a modern structure. Next to it is the Jüdisches Gemeindehaus, the Jewish community house *(see p124)* and a little farther along, at the junction with Kantstraße, is the Kant-Dreieck *(see p57)*. The Berliner Börse (the stock exchange), based in the ultramodern Ludwig-Erhard-Haus *(see p57)*, is just above, at the corner of Hardenbergstraße. The southern end of the street is dominated by residential villas, some of which may seem a little pompous, as well as the Literaturhaus, Villa Grisebach, one of the oldest art auction houses in Berlin, and the Käthe-Kollwitz-Museum *(see p123)*, which holds about 200 of the Berlin artist's works, including several self-portraits. There are also some very expensive fashion stores here, as well as a few cosy restaurants. At its southern end, the street leads to picturesque Fasanenplatz, where many artists lived before 1933.

**Antiques store on Fasanenstraße**

### A DAY IN CHARLOTTENBURG

▶ **MORNING**

Begin your tour of Charlottenburg at Breitscheidplatz and head west along **Kurfürstendamm** *(see pp30–31)*. At **Fasanenstraße** turn left to visit the **Käthe-Kollwitz-Museum** *(see p123)* and the **Literaturhaus**. You could stop for a mid-morning breakfast in the lovely **Café Wintergarten** *(see p126)* in the Literaturhaus, before going back up Fasanenstraße in a northerly direction. You will pass the **Kempinski Hotel Bristol Berlin** on the left, and on the right you can see the Jüdisches Gemeindehaus and the Ludwig-Erhard-Haus. Diagonally opposite across Kantstraße stands the **Theater des Westens** *(see p67)*. Turn left and head west along Kantstraße until you reach the shopping centre **Stilwerk** *(see p77)*, a place no one has ever been known to leave without buying something.

**AFTERNOON**

Carry on west along Kantstraße to **Savignyplatz**. Northwest of the square, at Grolmanstraße 51, the tiny Indian eatery **Ashoka** is a great place for lunch. Explore the small streets around the square, such as Carmer-, Knesebeck- and Mommsenstraße. Browse the small retailers for unique gifts, and visit **Café Savigny** *(see p126)* for coffee and a fruit flan with whipped cream. Head back up Kantstraße and Jebensstraße to end your tour with a visit to the **Museum für Fotografie** *(pp123)* where you can marvel at Helmut Newton's iconic *Big Nudes*.

*See map on pp118–19* ←

**The Funkturm rising above the old ICC building at the Messegelände**

## 8 Funkturm and Messegelände

MAP A4/5 ■ Messedamm 22 ■ (030) 303 80 ■ 10am–8pm Mon, 10am–11pm Tue–Sun (tower) ■ Adm ■ www.messe-berlin.de/en/

The 150-m (492-ft) high Funkturm (TV tower), reminiscent of the Eiffel Tower in Paris, is one of the land-marks of Berlin that can be seen from afar. Built in 1924 to plans by Heinrich Straumer, it served as an aerial and as an air-traffic control tower. The viewing platform at 125 m (410 ft) provides magnificent views, while the restaurant, situated at 55 m (180 ft), overlooks the oldest part of the complex, the exhibition centre and the surrounding pavil-lions. The giant building in the east is the Hall of Honour built to designs by Richard Ermisch in 1936, in the colossal Fascist architectural style. On the opposite side rises the shiny silver ICC, the International Congress Centrum, built in 1975–9 by Ralf Schüler and Ursulina Schüler-Witte. Once considered one of the world's most advanced conference centres, it has fallen into a state of disrepair and may be demolished. Nearby is the two-tier CityCube, Berlin's new trade fair and conference facility. The expansive ExpoCenter grounds (160,000 sq m/40 acres) around it host Grüne Woche (Green Week, an agricultural fair), Internationale Tourismus Börse (ITB, a tourism fair) and Internationale Funkausstellung (IFA, the consumer electronics fair).

### THE HISTORY OF CHARLOTTENBURG

The magnificent Charlottenburger Rathaus or town hall (left) on Otto-Suhr-Allee is a reminder of the time when this district of 200,000 people was an independent town. The town, named after the eponymous palace, arose in 1705 from the medieval settlement of Lietzow. Towards the end of the 19th century, Charlottenburg – then the wealthiest town in Prussia – enjoyed a meteoric rise following the construction of the Westend colony of villas and of Kurfürstendamm. Thanks to its numerous theatres, the opera and the Technical University, the district developed into Berlin's west end during the 1920s.

### 9 Museum für Fotografie

MAP N4 ■ Jebensstr. 2 ■ 10am–6pm Tue–Sun (to 8pm Thu) ■ Adm
■ www.smb.museum

Helmut Newton (1931–2004), the world-famous photographer, has finally returned to his home city. This museum presents changing exhibitions of his early fashion and nude photography, as well as his photos of the famous, rich and beautiful, artfully captured since 1947.

**Museum für Fotografie**

### 10 Käthe-Kollwitz-Museum

MAP P4 ■ Fasanenstr. 24
■ (030) 882 52 10 ■ 11am–6pm daily
■ Adm ■ www.kaethe-kollwitz.de

The museum is dedicated to Berlin artist Käthe Kollwitz (1867–1945), who recorded 1920s workers' lives in prints, graphics and sketches (see p49). After losing a son and a grandson in World War I, she concentrated on the themes of war and motherhood.

## A SPANDAU AND WESTEND WALK

▶ **MORNING**

Start with a journey on the U-Bahn. From the centre of town, take a U2 train in the direction of Ruhleben, and at Bismarckstraße station change to the U7 train in the direction of Rathaus Spandau. Ten minutes later you will have reached the centre of **Spandau Old Town** (see p120), where you can visit Breite Straße and Nikolaikirche. Before returning to Charlottenburg, visit the **Zitadelle Spandau** (see p119). There, in the **Zitadellenschänke**, you can also enjoy a late breakfast. Return by U-Bahn, getting off at the Wilmersdorfer Straße station, one of the few pedestrianized areas in Berlin. This is a particularly good area for shopaholics and bargain hunters.

**AFTERNOON**

From Wilmersdorfer Straße a 30-minute walk west along Kantstraße and Neue Kantstraße will take you to the **Funkturm** and the **Messegelände** with the "Ehrenhalle". Have lunch at the **Funkturm-Restaurant** and enjoy the magnificent views. The Haus des Rundfunks (broadcasting house) nearby and the **Georg-Kolbe-Museum** (see p124), a 25-minute walk (or brief S-Bahn ride) away, are worth visiting. Then, if you still have time and energy, take the S-Bahn to the **Olympiastadion**. In the evening, return to Savignyplatz by S75 from S-Olympiastadion. End your day by enjoying inventive, hearty Franconian cooking at the famed **Florian** (see p127).

*See map on pp118–19*

# The Best of the Rest

**The Fascist-style architecture of the Olympiastadion**

### 1 Georg-Kolbe-Museum
Sensburger Allee 25
■ (030) 304 21 44 ■ 10am–6pm Tue–Sun ■ Adm ■ www.georg-kolbe-museum.de

Sculptures by Kolbe (1877–1947) are exhibited in his home and workshop.

### 2 Le-Corbusier-Haus
Flatowallee 16

This innovative block was built for the 1957 Interbau trade fair. French architect Le Corbusier lived here.

### 3 Jüdisches Gemeindehaus
MAP P4 ■ Fasanenstr. 79–80
■ (030) 88 02 82 06

The Jewish community house stands on the site of the Charlottenburg synagogue. It was damaged during Reichskristallnacht on 9 November 1938 and mostly destroyed during World War II. Only the portal remains.

### 4 Theater des Westens
MAP N4 ■ Kantstr. 12
■ (0180) 544 44

Based in an attractive building from 1895–6, this theatre is regarded as one of Germany's best musical theatres (see p67).

### 5 Technische Universität
MAP M4 ■ Str. des 17. Juni
■ (030) 31 40 ■ 8am–8pm Mon–Fri

Berlin's Technical University was founded in 1879.

### 6 Olympiastadion
Olympischer Platz ■ (030) 25 00 23 22 ■ mid-Mar–Oct: 9am–7pm daily (to 8pm Aug); Nov–mid-Mar: 10am–4pm daily)

Built for the 1936 Olympic Games, the stadium is an example of Fascist architecture favoured by the Nazis.

### 7 Deutsche Oper
MAP B4 ■ Bismarckstr. 34–37
■ (030) 34 38 43 43 ■ Adm

The German Opera, opened in 1961, specializes in Italian and German classics (see p66).

### 8 Denkmal Benno Ohnesorg
MAP B4 ■ Bismarckstr.

Alfred Hrdlicka's 1971 sculpture commemorates the student Benno Ohnesorg, who was shot dead here during a demonstration in April 1967.

### 9 Universität der Künste
MAP N4 ■ Hardenbergstr. 32–33
■ (030) 318 50 ■ 8am–6pm Mon–Fri

The School of Art is one of the best German universities for the fine arts, architecture and design.

### 10 Renaissance Theater
MAP M3 ■ Knesebeckstr. 100 ■ (030) 315 97 30, (030) 312 42 02 (tickets)

A jem of Art Deco architecture, this little venue has been run as an actors' theatre since the 1920s.

# Shops and Markets

### ① Stilwerk
MAP N3 ▪ Kantstr. 17
▪ (030) 31 51 50

A shopping centre specializing in stylish designer home furnishings (see p77).

**Stilwerk in Charlottenburg**

### ② Manufactum Store
MAP M3 ▪ Hardenbergstr. 4-5,
▪ (030) 24 03 38 44 ▪ 10am–8pm Mon–Sat

Unique store with a lovely selection of classic and sustainable textiles, retro design furniture, garden tools, lamps and office supplies.

### ③ Peek & Cloppenburg
MAP P5 ▪ Tauentzienstr. 19
▪ (0800) 555 90 50 ▪ 10am–8pm Mon–Sat

Offering five floors of men's, women's and children's clothing, this is one of Berlin's most popular stores.

### ④ Amorph Black
MAP P3 ▪ Schlüterstrasse 37
▪ (030) 88 72 09 24 ▪ 11am–7pm Mon–Sat

Trendy concept store offering a great choice of top brands and inhouse collection. Shoes are designed by the shop owner, Iris Jorde.

### ⑤ Lindner
MAP N3 ▪ Knesebeckstr. 92
▪ (030) 313 53 75 ▪ 8am–6pm Mon–Fri, 8am–1:30pm Sat

Traditional Berlin store specializing in fresh, homemade delicatessen products. Of its many branches, this is one of the most attractive.

### ⑥ Jil Sander
MAP P2 ▪ Kurfürstendamm 185 ▪ (030) 886 70 20

Simple, elegant designer fashions for men and women are for sale at this cool boutique.

### ⑦ Bücherbogen
MAP N3 ▪ Stadtbahnbogen 593 (Savignyplatz) ▪ (030) 31 86 95 11

Berlin's leading arts and photography bookseller is tucked away within three arches under the S-Bahn viaduct.

### ⑧ Patrick Hellman
MAP P2 ▪ Schlüterstr. 45
▪ (030) 88 48 77 16/19 ▪ 10am–7pm Mon–Fri, 10am–6pm Sat

Gentlemen's fashions made from the best materials, including Hellmann's own collection and clothes from well-known designers.

### ⑨ Tee Gschwendner
MAP P4 ▪ Kurfürstendamm 217 ▪ (030) 881 91 81 ▪ 10am–7pm Mon–Fri, 10am–4pm Sat

This tiny store is a haven for tea lovers, and upstairs you can try out a new flavour in their own tea room.

### ⑩ TITUS Berlin Zooprome
MAP P4 ▪ Meinekestr. 2 ▪ (030) 32 59 32 39 ▪ 10am–8pm Mon–Sat

The latest must-have labels are stocked at this streetwear store.

**Lindner store and deli**

*See map on pp118–19* ←

# Cafés and Coffee Shops

### 1 Café Wintergarten im Literaturhaus

MAP P4 ▪ Fasanenstr. 23 ▪ (030) 882 54 14 ▪ 9am–midnight daily

One of Berlin's most beautiful cafés is based in the conservatory of an old city mansion. In summer guests can sit outside in the garden.

### 2 Café Savigny

MAP N3 ▪ Grolmanstr. 53–54 ▪ (030) 32 89 06 61 ▪ 9am–1am daily

This gay and lesbian café, with traditional 19th-century interior, has a relaxed atmosphere; the tarts are particularly worth trying.

**Berliner Kaffeerösterei**

### 3 Berliner Kaffeerösterei

MAP P4 ▪ Uhlandstraße 173 ▪ (030) 88 67 79 20 ▪ 9am–8pm Mon–Sat, 10am–7pm Sun

A cosy mix of traditional café and coffee bar, this place offers coffee beans from around the world, cakes and breakfast snacks.

### 4 Café Filmbühne am Steinplatz

MAP N4 ▪ Hardenbergstr. 12 ▪ (030) 312 65 89 ▪ 9am–midnight Mon–Fri, 9am–1am Sat & Sun

This coffee shop is popular thanks to its student atmosphere.

### 5 Einstein Coffeeshop

MAP P3 ▪ Kurfürstendamm 50a (off Ku'damm) ▪ (030) 93 93 13 65 ▪ 7:30am–8pm daily (from 8am Sat, 9am Sun)

Probably the most popular outlet of this upmarket chain, this revamped café heaves with the rich and beautiful of Charlottenburg.

### 6 Café Hardenberg

MAP N3 ▪ Hardenbergstr. 10 ▪ (030) 312 26 44 ▪ 9am–1am daily ▪ no credit cards

A favourite of students and artists since the 1850s, this café has a great atmosphere and reasonable prices.

### 7 Balzac Coffee

MAP M3 ▪ Knesebeckstraße 1–2 ▪ 7am–8pm Mon–Fri, 8am–8pm Sat, 8am–7pm Sun ▪ no credit cards

A German gourmet coffee chain offering speciality drinks and snacks.

### 8 Der Kuchenladen

MAP N3 ▪ Kantstr. 138 ▪ (030) 31 01 84 24 ▪ 10am–6:30pm daily ▪ no credit cards

Enjoy lemon tart, crème brûlée cake and other delicious home-made delights at this tiny café.

### 9 Café Kleine Orangerie

MAP A3 ▪ Spandauer Damm 20 ▪ (030) 322 20 21 ▪ 10am–6pm Tue–Sun

A small, pleasant garden café at the Charlottenburg Palace.

### 10 Schwarzes Café

MAP N3 ▪ Kantstr. 148 ▪ (030) 313 80 38 ▪ open around the clock

This alternative rock café offers excellent all-day breakfasts and is often packed until dawn.

**The bohemian Schwarzes Café**

# Restaurants

### 1 Francucci's
MAP B5 ■ Kurfürstendamm 90 ■ (030) 323 33 18 ■ noon–midnight daily ■ €€

This popular Tuscan restaurant serves up excellent pizza, home-made pasta and creative meat and fish dishes.

### 2 Alt-Luxemburg
MAP B4 ■ Windscheidstr. 31 ■ (030) 323 87 30 ■ 5pm–midnight Mon–Sat ■ €€

Since 1982, chef Karl Wannemacher has been dishing up exquisite French and German classics here.

### 3 Eiffel
MAP B5 ■ Kurfürstendamm 105 ■ (030) 891 13 05 ■ 9–1am daily ■ €€

A large but still charming French restaurant with some traditional Berlin and Mediterranean dishes and outside tables.

### 4 Die Quadriga
MAP P4 ■ Eislebener Str. 14 ■ (030) 21 40 50 ■ 6–11pm Tue–Sat ■ €€€

With talented chef André Haufler at the reins, this intimate restaurant, in the Dormero Hotel *(see p173)* pairs creative French cuisine with an excellent wine selection. The elegant Art Deco salons overlook a Japanese garden.

### 5 Kuchi
MAP N3 ■ Kantstr. 30 ■ (030) 31 50 78 16 ■ noon–11pm daily ■ no credit cards ■ €€

Thanks mainly to its exquisite sushi and mixed Asian hot dishes, this minimalist restaurant has a loyal clientele and ranks among the best sushi bars in town.

**Outside tables at Florian**

### 6 Florian
MAP N3 ■ Grolmanstr. 52 ■ (030) 313 91 84 ■ 6pm–3am daily ■ €€

Fine Franconian food – inventive, robust and steadily high-quality – is on offer at this famed restaurant. Trendy and popular with film lovers, particularly during the Berlinale.

### 7 Lubitsch
MAP N3 ■ Bleibtreustr. 47 ■ (030) 882 37 56 ■ 10am–midnight Mon–Sat, 6pm–midnight Sun ■ €€

A small, elegant restaurant, serving fresh, regional cuisine.

### 8 Mine Restaurant
MAP P4 ■ Meinekestrasse 10 ■ (030) 88 92 63 63 ■ 6pm–midnight Tue–Sat ■ €€

This upmarket restaurant serves exciting Italian cuisine. The attached wine bar offers an array of bio-dynamic and natural wines.

### 9 Marjellchen
MAP P3 ■ Mommsenstr. 9 ■ (030) 883 26 76 ■ 5pm–midnight daily ■ €€

This delightful restaurant serves hearty dishes from East Prussia, Pomerania and Silesia.

### 10 Ana e Bruno
MAP A3 ■ Sophie-Charlotten-Str. 101 ■ (030) 325 71 10 ■ 5pm–midnight daily ■ €€€

Friendly and extremely elegant, Ana e Bruno is an excellent Italian restaurant in Berlin.

*See map on pp118–19* ←

# TOP 10 Kreuzberg, Schöneberg and Neukölln

**Checkpoint Charlie**

Before the Wall fell, Kreuzberg was a hotbed of squatters, hippies and anarchists. Despite rapid gentrification it is still the city's most colourful area. Here, a diverse community of doctors, lawyers, artists and students harmoniously coexists in beautifully renovated petit-bourgeois flats. The adjacent Neukölln is Berlin's most trendy area for art galleries, grunge-hip bars and clubs, particularly along Weserstraße. Schöneberg is not as daring as Kreuzberg, but still evokes a free-minded spirit. Here, Winterfeldtplatz is lined with inviting pubs, and Nollendorfplatz is the nexus of Berlin's lively gay scene.

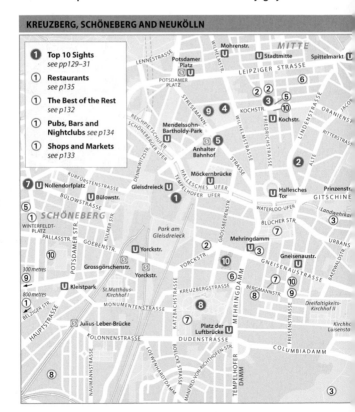

## KREUZBERG, SCHÖNEBERG AND NEUKÖLLN

① **Top 10 Sights**
see pp129–31

① **Restaurants**
see p135

① **The Best of the Rest**
see p132

① **Pubs, Bars and Nightclubs** see p134

① **Shops and Markets**
see p133

## 1 Deutsches Technikmuseum

**MAP F5** ■ Trebbiner Str. 9
■ (030) 90 25 40 ■ 9am–
5:30pm Tue–Fri, 10am–
6pm Sat & Sun ■ Adm
**(kids free after 3pm)**
■ www.sdtb.de

The history of technology
and crafts is the theme of
this museum, located in the
grounds of a former railway
goods yard. Visitors can
learn about developments
in aviation and admire
40 planes, including a
Junkers Ju 52 and a "raisin
bomber", the type of plane used
for the Berlin airlift. Old ships and
steam locomotives hark back to
the Industrial Revolution *(see p64).*

**Exhibits at the Deutsches Technikmuseum**

## 2 Jüdisches Museum

**MAP G5** ■ Lindenstr. 9–14
■ 10am–10pm Mon, 10am–8pm
Tue–Sun ■ Adm ■ www.jmberlin.de

The Jewish Museum's exhibitions and
unique architecture aim to illustrate
the repercussions of the Holocaust.
Narrow, slanting galleries with
zig-zag turns evoke a sense of
dislocation, and are punctured by
voids – empty spaces embodying the
vacuum left behind by the destruction
of Jewish life. Nearly 1,000 years
of German-Jewish cultural
history are documented
here; a special exhibition
evokes everyday Jewish
life in Berlin from
the end of the
19th century *(see
p50).* The two
upper floors of
the Libeskind
building are
closed for
renovation
until late 2019.

**Jüdisches
Museum**

## 3 Haus am Checkpoint Charlie

**MAP G4** ■ Friedrichstr. 43–45 ■ (030)
253 72 50 ■ 9am–10pm daily ■ Adm
■ www.mauermuseum.de

This museum details the history of
the Wall and the means people used
to escape to West Berlin, from a hot-
air balloon to a car with a false floor.
Of the former border only a replica
control hut remains *(see p51).*

### 4 Topographie des Terrors
**MAP F4 ■ Niederkirchnerstr. 8 ■ (030) 254 50 90 ■ 10am–6pm daily (to 8pm May–Sep) ■ www. topographie.de/en**

Between 1933 and 1945, three Nazi institutions of persecution and terror were located in this area: the Secret State Police Office; the SS leadership; and, during World War II, the Reich Security main office. After World War II, all the buildings were bulldozed. A striking documentation centre, designed by Berlin architect Ursula Wilms, was inaugurated in 2010 on this site, providing information about the headquarters of the National Socialist SS and police state during the Third Reich and showing the extent of the Nazi reign of terror throughout Europe.

### 5 Anhalter Bahnhof
**MAP F5 ■ Askanischer Platz 6–7**

Only pitiful fragments remain of the railway station that was once the largest in Europe. The giant structure was erected in 1880 by architect Franz Schwechten as a showcase station: official visitors to the Empire were meant to be impressed by the splendour and glory of the German capital as soon as they reached the

**The ruins of the Anhalter Bahnhof**

**TURKISH BERLIN**

In the 1960s, thousands of Turkish *Gastarbeiter* ("guest workers") came to Berlin in response to a labour shortage. Today the community numbers nearly 240,000 and it is their children and grandchildren who leave their mark on life in the city, with many Turkish Berliners owning shops and businesses. 50 years after their arrival in Berlin, many people of Turkish descent are still plagued by social stagnation. As neighbourhoods like Kreuzberg or Neukölln, once popular amongst Turkish families, gentrify, many are forced into Berlin's outer boroughs.

railway station. In 1943 the station was badly damaged by bombs and in 1960 it was pulled down. The waste ground behind the façade was meant to become a park, but today the Tempodrom is based here, hosting concerts and cabaret shows.

### 6 Oranienstraße
**MAP G4–H5 ■ Between Lindenstr. and Skalitzer Str.**

Oranienstraße is the heart of Kreuzberg. It is the wildest, most colourful and most unusual street of the district, where streetwear shops and pubs jostle for space with doner kebab takeaways and Turkish greengrocers. All aspects of life and politics in Kreuzberg are centred around this road.

### 7 Nollendorfplatz
**MAP E5**

Nollendorfplatz and neighbouring Winterfeldtplatz are right in the centre of Schöneberg. The former square has always been a focal point for Berlin's gay scene, and a plaque at the Nollendorfplatz U-Bahn station commemorates approximately 5,000 homosexuals killed in concentration camps by the Nazis.

Today, gay life is concentrated more in the surrounding streets than the square itself. Before World War II, Nollendorfplatz was also a centre of entertainment. The Metropol-Theater, now a discotheque, then boasted Erwin Piscator as its director. And next door lived the writer Christopher Isherwood, whose novel formed the basis of *Cabaret*, the famous musical and film.

### 8 Viktoriapark
**MAP F6 ■ Kreuzbergstr.**

This rambling park (*see p61*) was set up as a recreational space for workers in Kreuzberg in 1888–94 to plans by Hermann Mächtig. It has an artificial waterfall, and the Neo-Gothic Schinkel memorial, 66 m (216 ft) high, commemorates Prussian victory in the Wars of Liberation against Napoleon.

**Detail, Martin-Gropius-Bau**

### 9 Martin-Gropius-Bau
**MAP F4 ■ Niederkirchnerstr. 7 ■ (030) 25 48 60 ■ 10am–7pm Wed–Mon (check website) ■ Adm ■ www.gropiusbau.de**

The richly ornamented former museum of arts and crafts hosts exhibitions on cultural history.

### 10 Riehmers Hofgarten
**MAP F6 ■ Yorckstr. 83–86**

Over 20 buildings make up this estate, built as officers' quarters in the Gründerzeit (after the founding of the German Empire in 1871). Restored in the 1970s, they include a pleasant hotel with restaurant.

## A DAY IN KREUZBERG

### ▶ MORNING

Start from the ruins of **Anhalter Bahnhof**, which you can reach by S-Bahn. From here continue along Stresemannstraße in a northwesterly direction to the **Martin-Gropius-Bau**. While away a few hours in this impressive building, then take a break in the museum café. Afterwards, a visit to the neighbouring **Topographie des Terrors** exhibition will bring you face to face with the dark Nazi past of this area. Walk along Niederkirchnerstraße, past an original section of the Berlin Wall, to Wilhelmstraße. Continue to Zimmerstrasse and visit some of the many contemporary art galleries lining the street. Walk on to Friedrichstrasse to **Checkpoint Charlie** and the Wall Museum at the former border (*see p129*).

### AFTERNOON

You can have a tasty lunch at **Sale e Tabacchi** (*see p135*) in Rudi-Dutschke-Straße. Continue in an easterly direction to get to the heart of Kreuzberg. Make a detour south on Lindenstraße to the **Jüdisches Museum** (*see p129*) or carry on into **Oranienstraße**. Then take the U6 from U-Bahn station Hallesches Tor to Platz der Luftbrücke. **Viktoriapark** nearby is a good place for a rest, while shopaholics might prefer a stroll up Bergmannstraße. At the end of the street, turn north into Baerwaldstraße and continue to Carl-Herz-Ufer, where you can round off the day with a delicious evening meal at the **Altes Zollhaus** (*see p135*).

*See map on pp128–9* ←

# The Best of the Rest

### 1 Rathaus Schöneberg
**MAP D6** ▪ John-F-Kennedy-Platz

It was from this town hall in 1963 that US President John F Kennedy made his famous "I am a Berliner" speech, expressing his commitment to the freedom of West Berlin.

### 2 Asisi's Wall Panorama
**MAP F4** ▪ Friedrichstr. 205 ▪ 10am–7pm daily ▪ Adm ▪ www.asisi.de

This is a life-size reproduction of the Berlin Wall as it appeared in the early 1980s, with sound and light installations.

**The old Tempelhof terminal**

### 3 Tempelhofer Feld
Tempelhof, built in 1939 by Ernst Sagebiel, at that point Germany's biggest airport, survives as the largest fascist structure in Europe. The airport closed in 2008. The site is now home to a sports ground, park and offices. The old terminal can be visited on a guided tour (see p78).

### 4 Mariannenplatz
**MAP H5**

This park-like square with old trees is dominated by a large Gothic-style building. The former hospital and nursing school Bethanien, is now under landmark protection and is used by cultural and social initiatives.

### 5 Oberbaumbrücke
Warschauer/Skalitzer Str.

Pedestrians and cyclists can cross to the other side of the Spree River from Kreuzberg to Friedrichshain on this red-brick bridge, one of Berlin's loveliest, which was built in 1894–6.

### 6 Mosse-Haus
**MAP G4** ▪ Schützenstrasse 25

One of Berlin's most influential publishing houses was based in this Jugendstil corner house in the former newspaper district.

### 7 Friedhöfe Hallesches Tor
**MAP G6** ▪ Mehringdamm

Many celebrities lie buried in these four cemeteries, including the composer Felix Mendelssohn Bartholdy and the writer E T A Hoffmann, whose work inspired Offenbach to compose his *opéra fantastique The Tales of Hoffmann*.

### 8 Gasometer Schöneberg
**MAP E6** ▪ Torgauer Str. 12–15

Once a massive gas holder, this Schöneberg landmark was decommissioned in the 1990s and turned into a viewing platform.

### 9 Kottbusser Tor
**MAP H5**

Social diversity in Kreuzberg is tucked away in between 1970s prefabricated buildings in the Turkish heart of the district.

### 10 Kammergericht
**MAP E6** ▪ Potsdamer Str. 186

From 1947 to 1990, this magnificent supreme court, built in 1909–13, was used as Allied Control Council.

**The façade of Kammergericht**

# Shops and Markets

**Fruits at Winterfeldtmarkt**

## 1 Winterfeldtmarkt
MAP E5 ■ Winterfeldtplatz
■ 8am–4pm Sat, 8am–1pm Wed

At Berlin's largest market you can buy fresh fruit and vegetables as well as other goods from around the world, such as clothes and New-Age items *(see p77)*.

## 2 Türkenmarkt am Maybachufer
MAP H5 ■ Maybachufer
■ 11am–6:30pm Tue & Fri

The most vibrant market in Berlin. This is where Berliners and Turks alike buy unleavened bread and fresh goat's cheese *(see p77)*.

## 3 Molotow
MAP G6 ■ Gneisenaustr. 112
■ (030) 693 08 18 ■ 1–6pm Mon–Fri

Berlin designer Ute Hentschel's classy outfits are sold off-the-rack, and can be custom-made or altered for a perfect fit.

## 4 Oranienplatz and Oranienstraße
MAP H5 ■ Oranienstr./corner Oranienplatz

Kreuzberg's main square and unofficial high street specialize in all things alternative.

## 5 Hot & Cold
MAP E5 ■ Winterfeldtstr. 48
■ (030) 216 33 54

Irresistible trinkets are sold at this charming Scandinvian design shop.

## 6 Depot 2
MAP H5 ■ Oranienstr. 9
■ (030) 611 46 55

This small boutique sells the latest streetwear and hip-hop fashion of local labels.

## 7 High-Lite
MAP G6 ■ Bergmannstr. 99
■ (030) 691 27 44

Worried about standing out in the alternative crowd in Kreuzberg? This is the place to get your shades, body piercings and other counter-culture essentials.

## 8 Ararat
MAP G6 ■ Bergmannstr. 9
■ (030) 694 95 32

One of Berlin's best-stocked and trendiest stationery, curiosity and gift shops, the colourful Ararat has many designer items for sale.

## 9 Marheineke-Markthalle
MAP G6 ■ Marheinekeplatz
■ 8am–8pm Mon–Fri, 8am–6pm Sat

This is one of the last remaining market-halls in Berlin. It boasts colourful fruit and vegetable stores and a wide range of organic produce, as well as numerous snack bars for hungry shoppers.

## 10 Grober Unfug Comics
MAP G6 ■ Zossener Str. 33
■ (030) 69 40 14 90

Comic books of all periods and in various languages, with an emphasis on Japanese manga. The store, whose name means "complete mischief" has all the latest comics, plus some bargains and rare editions.

**Japanese manga**

*See map on pp128–9*

# Pubs, Bars and Nightclubs

The bar at Ankerklause

### ① Ankerklause
MAP H5 ■ Kottbusser Damm 104 ■ (030) 693 56 49
An unrefined but hugely popular late-night place with a mixed crowd.

### ② Yorckschlösschen
MAP F6 ■ Yorckstr. 15 ■ (030) 215 80 70
A pub-restaurant with a great old Berlin feel. Live jazz at the weekend.

### ③ Kuschlowski
MAP H6 ■ Weserstr. 202 ■ (0173) 36 19 11 85
This Russian vodka bar features bucket-shaped table lamps and bar stools designed by its owner, architect Daniel Neugebauer. Relaxed living-room vibe.

### ④ Van Loon
MAP G5 ■ Carl-Herz-Ufer 5–7 ■ (030) 692 62 93
Enjoy a snack surrounded by nautical artifacts on this old barge moored in Urbanhafen. In summer you can sit on the green banks.

### ⑤ Max & Moritz
MAP H5 ■ Oranienstr. 162 ■ (030) 69 51 59 11
Traditional Berlin tavern with touches of Jugendstil that fronts as a tango salon on Sundays. The bar opens at 5pm; lessons start at 8pm; the club starts at 9pm.

### ⑥ Rauschgold
MAP F6 ■ Mehringdamm 62 ■ (030) 92 27 41 78
Very popular, best late at night and very crowded at weekends. Karaoke, themed nights and a mixed crowd.

### ⑦ Golgatha
MAP F6 ■ Dudenstr. 48–64 (Viktoriapark) ■ (030) 785 24 53
This classic beer garden on the Kreuzberg attracts students and an older clientele, bopping to funk on the small and intimate dance floor.

### ⑧ SO36
A Kreuzberg classic, the SO36 is an über-alternative and very lively dance club. The crowd is a mix of straight and gay (see p69).

### ⑨ Würgeengel
MAP H5 ■ Dresdener Str. 122 ■ (030) 615 55 60
The drinks at the "Angel of Death" are not, in fact, lethal, but the bar staff and most of the clientele are straight out of a Buñuel film.

### ⑩ Klunkerkranich
Karl-Marx-Str. 66 ■ freunde@klunkerkranich.org
You might think a rooftop garden bar above a parking garage is less than glamorous, but it's hard to quibble with the fun-loving DJs, organic bistro stations and gorgeous views.

The rooftop bar at Klunkerkranich

# Restaurants

### 1 Lavanderia Vecchia
MAP H6 ▪ Flughafenstr. 46 ▪ (030) 62 72 21 52 ▪ noon–2:30pm & 7:30–11pm Tue–Fri, 7:30–11pm Sat ▪ €€

Set in an old laundry, this creative Italian eatery excels in Roman tapas. Prepare to linger: a fixed four-course meal requires about 3 hours.

### 2 Entrecôte
MAP G4 ▪ Schützenstr. 5 ▪ (030) 20 16 54 96 ▪ noon–midnight Mon–Fri, 6pm–midnight Sat, 6–11pm Sun ▪ €€

Ever since Madonna enjoyed a meal here the usually low-key Entrecôte has become the talk of the town.

### 3 Altes Zollhaus
MAP G5 ▪ Carl-Herz-Ufer 30 ▪ (030) 692 33 00 ▪ from 6pm Tue–Sat ▪ €€

Former border control point on the banks of the Landwehrkanal serving international and German fare. Try the house speciality *Brandenburger Landente aus dem Rohr* (roast duck).

### 4 Viasko
MAP H5 ▪ Erkelenzdamm 49 ▪ (030) 40 75 19 12 ▪ from 5pm Wed–Fri, from 11am Sat & Sun ▪ €

An imaginative vegan menu using fresh local produce is on offer here.

### 5 Restaurant Tim Raue
MAP G4 ▪ Rudi-Dutschke-Str. 26 ▪ (030) 25 93 79 30 ▪ noon–1:30pm & 7pm–midnight Tue–Sat ▪ €€€

Tasting menus explore combinations such as glazed partridge with Japanese chestnut. The Obamas ate here in 2013. Two Michelin stars.

**Lavanderia Vecchia**

### 6 Defne
MAP H5 ▪ Planufer. 92c ▪ (030) 81 79 71 11 ▪ from 4pm daily ▪ no credit cards ▪ €

An intimate restaurant serving modern Turkish food.

### 7 Long March Canteen
MAP H5 ▪ Wrangelstr. 20 ▪ 0178 884 95 99 ▪ 6pm–midnight daily ▪ €€

A hip dim sum restaurant with communal tables and dim lighting, like a real Chinese street kitchen.

### 8 Henne
MAP H4 ▪ Leuschnerdamm 25 ▪ (030) 614 77 30 ▪ from 6pm Tue–Sat, 5pm Sun ▪ €

Only three dishes are served at this old-Berlin institution but all are cooked to perfection.

### 9 Lochner Weinwirtschaft
MAP D6 ▪ Eisenacher Str. 86 ▪ (030) 23 00 52 20 ▪ 4pm–12:30am Tue–Sun ▪ €€

Wine and dinner bar with an outside terrace. Refined snacks also served.

### 10 Sale e Tabacchi
MAP G4 ▪ Rudi-Dutschke-Str. 23 ▪ (030) 252 11 55 ▪ 10am–11:30pm daily ▪ €€

Elegant Italian restaurant popular with the media crowd. In summer, reserve a table in the courtyard.

*See map on pp128–9*

# 🔟 Prenzlauer Berg

Having undergone dramatic changes in recent decades, this former East Berlin workers' district attracts locals and visitors like no other part of town. Even when Berlin was a divided city, the area was favoured by artists and an alternative crowd, and it exerts a similar pull today. Although it is still possible to find structures that have not yet been restored and give a sense of the old Berlin, Prenzlauer Berg is being steadily and noticeably transformed. Many young professionals, decried as yuppies by locals, are restoring old buildings. Cafés and restaurants have taken over tenement blocks around Kollwitzplatz and Husemannstraße, giving the leafy streets an almost Parisian flair, while Kastanienallee, also known as "Casting Alley", is the catwalk of the hip young scene.

**Gethsemane-kirche, detail**

**Schönhauser Allee, Prenzlauer Berg**

## 1 Schönhauser Allee
MAP H1/2 ■ Prenzlauer Berg

Schönhauser Allee, 3 km (2 miles) long and lined with shops and pubs, is the main artery of the district. Down the centre of the road runs the high-level viaduct of U-Bahn line U2. A couple of buildings are still in their pre-1989 state and give a good impression of the old Prenzlauer Berg, especially between Senefeld-erplatz and Danziger Straße.

## 2 Kollwitzplatz
MAP H2 ■ Prenzlauer Berg

Once a quiet square, Kollwitzplatz is today the noisy heart of the district. All around the green square, locals congregate in the numerous cafés, pubs and restaurants. From the lavishly restored façades it is hard to tell that this was once one of the city's poorest areas. The district's 19th-century tenement blocks and impoverished past are today only recalled by the name of the square. The artist Käthe Kollwitz *(see p49)* once lived and worked at No. 25 (now destroyed), from where she highlighted the poverty of the local workers in her sculptures, drawings and sketches.

## 3 Prater
MAP H1 ■ Kastanienallee 7–9 ■ (030) 448 56 88 ■ 6–11pm Mon–Sat, noon–midnight Sun

The Prater is one of the few remaining entertainment complexes that were once common in big German cities. It was built in 1837 just outside the original city gates, and was first jokingly called "Prater" after its world-famous counterpart in Vienna. A concert hall was added in 1857 and by the turn of the century it had become so popular that the nickname stuck. Today, you can enjoy beer and food at the restaurant of the same name *(see p141)*.

## PRENZLAUER BERG

**1** Top 10 Sights
*see pp136–9*

**1** Restaurants
*see p141*

**1** The Best of the Rest
*see p140*

0 metres 300
0 yards 300

Friedrich-Ludwig-Jahn Sportpark

PRENZLAUER BERG

250 metres

600 metres

Eberswalder Strasse

Jüdischer Friedhof

Kollwitz-Platz

Senefelder-platz

---

**4** Kulturbrauerei

MAP H1 ■ Schönhauser Allee 36–39 (entrance: Knaackstr. 97) ■ (030) 44 35 26 14 ■ kulturbrauerei.de/en

This giant complex of buildings originally housed the Schultheiss brewery, one of the breweries that once made Prenzlauer Berg famous. The complex, parts of which are over 150 years old, was designed by Franz Schwechten. It was completely restored in 1997–9 and has become a lively and popular spot. Cafés, restaurants, a cinema, shops and even a theatre have sprung up in the red and yellow brick buildings and the numerous interior courtyards.

**The Kulturbrauerei complex**

**The peaceful Jewish Cemetery**

### 5 Jewish Cemetery
MAP H2 ■ Schönhauser Allee 23–25 ■ www.jg-berlin.org ■ 8am–4pm Mon–Thu, 7:30am–1pm Fri

The small Jewish cemetery is among the city's most beautiful. The tombstones stand amid dense scrub and high trees. The cemetery was set up in 1827, when the former Jewish cemetery in Große Hamburger Straße was closed. Two of the famous personalities who have found their final resting places here are the painter and printmaker Max Liebermann (1847–1935) and the composer Giacomo Meyerbeer (1791–1864).

### 6 Husemannstraße
MAP H1 ■ Between Wörther and Danziger Str.

The East German regime undertook a perfect restoration of this idyllic street for Berlin's 750th anniversary celebrations. A stroll through the leafy roads lined with houses from the Gründerzeit (the years after the founding of the German Empire in 1871) is one of the loveliest ways to experience Prenzlauer Berg. Ancient-looking street lamps and signs,

cobbled streets, antiquated shop signs and a few atmospheric pubs take the visitor back to the late 19th century.

### 7 Zionskirche
MAP G2 ■ Zionskirchplatz ■ (030) 449 21 91 ■ 8–10pm Mon, 1–7pm Tue–Sat, noon–5pm (tower: noon–5pm) Sun

Zionskirche, dating from 1866–73, and the square of the same name form a tranquil oasis in the middle of the lively district. The Protestant church has always been a political centre too. During the Third Reich, resistance groups against the Nazi regime congregated here and, during the East German period, the alternative "environment library" (an information and documentation centre) was established here. Church and other opposition groups who were active at Zionskirche played a decisive role in the political transformation of East Germany in 1989–90, which eventually led to the reunification of Germany.

### 8 Wasserturm
MAP H2 ■ Knaackstr.

The unofficial symbol of the district is this giant 30-m- (98-ft-) high water tower, built in 1877 as a water reservoir, but shut down in 1914. The engine house in the tower was used as an unofficial prison by the SA from 1933 to 1945, a period recalled by a memorial plaque. The water tower stands on Windmühlenberg (windmill hill), where some of the mills that had

**The Wasserturm**

made Prenzlauer Berg famous in the 19th century once stood. Today this round brick building has been converted into trendy apartments.

**Interior of Synagoge Rykestraße**

### ⑨ Synagoge Rykestraße
MAP H2 ■ Rykestr. 53 ■ (030) 88 02 83 16 ■ guided tours 2–6pm Thu ■ www.jg-berlin.org/en.html

Built in 1904, this synagogue is one of the few Jewish places of worship to have survived Kristallnacht on 9 November 1938, the violent attacks on Jewish property by the Nazis. The temple's historic interior was built from red bricks in the shape of a basilica. It is the largest synagogue in Berlin (see p59).

### ⑩ Gethsemanekirche
MAP H1 ■ Stargarder Str. 77 ■ (030) 445 77 45 ■ May–Oct: 5–7pm Wed–Thu (otherwise by prior arrangement)

Outside this red-brick church, dating back to 1891–3, East German secret police beat up peaceful protesters. It was the starting point for the collapse of the East German regime.

**Gethsemanekirche interior**

## A DAY IN PRENZLAUER BERG

### ▶ MORNING

Set off from the U-Bahn station in Senefelderplatz, one of the lively spots in Prenzlauer Berg. From here, explore the old tenement blocks and backyards. Now continue west along Fehrbelliner Straße to Zionskirchplatz with its eponymous church. There are numerous cafés on the square, such as **Kapelle**, where you could stop for a capuccino. Leave the square via Zionskirchstraße, then turn left into Kastanienallee. This is one of the most colourful streets in the quarter. At the end of the street you could pop into **Prater** (see p141). Then turn right into Oderberger Straße, one of the best preserved streets of the district. Continue east along Sredzkistraße until you reach **Husemannstraße**. Have a good look around the old Berlin streets, you may find something interesting to buy.

### AFTERNOON

You could have lunch at one of the numerous restaurants in **Kollwitzplatz** (see p136): Gugelhof (see p141) and **Zander** are both recommended, the former for German and French cuisine, the latter for imaginative fish specialities. After lunch, walk along Knaackstraße to the **Synagoge Rykestraße**. From here it is a few paces back to the **Wasserturm**. Give your feet a rest at the small green space around the tower before continuing along Belforter Straße and Kollwitzstraße to Schönhauser Allee. You will find perfect tranquility there in the **Jewish Cemetery**.

*See map on p137*

# The Best of the Rest

### ① Greifenhagener Straße
MAP H1

Not the most beautiful, but one of the best-preserved red-brick residential streets of old Berlin.

### ② Pfefferberg
MAP H2 ■ Schönhauser Allee 176 ■ (030) 44 38 30

This alternative cultural centre in a former brewery hosts concerts, performance art events and festivals.

### ③ Senefelderplatz
MAP H2

The wedge-shaped square is named after Alois Senefelder, a pioneer of modern printing techniques. At its centre is a "Café Achteck", housed in a historic octagonal public urinal.

### ④ Zeiss-Großplanetarium
Prenzlauer Allee 80 ■ (030) 421 84 50 ■ 9am–noon Tue–Thu, 6–9:30pm Fri, also pm Sat & Sun

Lose yourself amidst uncountable stars, planets and galaxies under the vast silvery dome of the planetarium.

### ⑤ Mauerpark
MAP G1 ■ Am Falkplatz

The vast park near the former border, comprising Max Schmeling Hall and Jahn Sports Park, was built for the Berlin Olympic bid in 2000. Today it hosts sports and music events, and a Sunday flea market.

**Buildings at Helmholtzplatz**

### ⑥ Helmholtzplatz
MAP H1

Apart from the trendy cafés and bars, time seems to have stopped here in 1925, with buildings reminiscent of a social housing programme.

### ⑦ Prenzlauer Berg Museum
MAP H2 ■ Prenzlauer Allee 227–228 ■ (030) 902 953 917 ■ 9am–7pm Mon–Fri, 10am–6pm Sat & Sun

This museum charts the history of the district and its poor working-class inhabitants in the 19th century.

### ⑧ Konnopke
MAP H1 ■ At the southern exit of U-Bahn Schönhauser Allee ■ (030) 442 77 65 ■ 10am–8pm Mon–Fri, noon–8pm Sat

This legendary *Currywurstimbiss* was opened in 1930 under the U-Bahn steel viaduct. The spicy sausages are among the best in the city.

### ⑨ Oderberger Straße
MAP G/H1

This leafy street is lined with cafés, boutiques and a few historic buildings. The old swimming baths of Prenzlauer Berg at No. 84 were renovated in 2015.

### ⑩ Thälmannpark
MAP H1 ■ Prenzlauer Allee

One of few parks in the northeast of the city, dominated by Socialist prefabricated buildings. It has a monument to Ernst Thälmann, a communist murdered by the Nazis.

**Toy stall, Mauerpark flea market**

# Restaurants

**1** **Oderquelle**
MAP G1 ▪ Oderberger Str. 27
▪ (030) 44 00 80 80 ▪ 6pm–1am daily
▪ €

Basic Berlin and German dishes are served up in an alternative, relaxed setting in this quaint little *Kiez* (neighbourhood) place.

**2** **Gugelhof**
MAP H2 ▪ Knaackstr. 37
▪ (030) 442 92 29 ▪ 4pm–1am Mon–Fri, 10am–1am Sat & Sun ▪ €€

Bill Clinton was once a guest at this restaurant, which attracts clients from all over Berlin. The menu features an original combination of German and French cuisine.

**Outdoor tables at Gugelhof**

**3** **Cotto e Crudo**
MAP G/H1 ▪ Eberswalder Str. 33 ▪ (030) 44 03 71 11 ▪ noon–midnight Tue–Sun ▪ €€

Homely little restaurant, Cotto e Crudo offers authentic Sicilian cuisine. It is located close to the southern end of Mauerpark.

**4** **Weinstein**
MAP H1 ▪ Lychener Str. 33
▪ (030) 441 18 42 ▪ 5pm–2am daily (from 6pm Sun) ▪ €€

A friendly, rustic wine bar with a great selection of Austrian and German wines and solid bistro fare.

**PRICE CATEGORIES**
For a three-course meal for one with half a bottle of wine (for equivalent meal), taxes and charges included.

€ under €30   €€ €30–60   €€€ over €60

**5** **Prater**
MAP H1 ▪ Kastanienallee 7–9
▪ (030) 448 56 88 ▪ 6pm–midnight Mon–Sat, noon–midnight Sun ▪ no credit cards ▪ €€

Surprises at the Prater include a beer garden (open noon Apr–Sep), a rustic restaurant in the courtyard and free live concerts.

**6** **Sasaya**
MAP H1 ▪ Lychener Str. 50 ▪ (030) 44 71 77 21 ▪ noon–3pm, 6–11:30pm Thu–Mon ▪ no credit cards ▪ €€

Head to Sasaya for some of Berlin's best sushi. Reservations needed.

**7** **Osmans Töchter**
MAP H1 ▪ Pappelallee 15
▪ (030) 32 66 33 88 ▪ 5:30pm–midnight daily ▪ €€€

This modern, family-run restaurant serves traditional Turkish cuisine.

**8** **Pasternak**
MAP H2 ▪ Knaackstr. 22 ▪ (030) 441 33 99 ▪ 9am–1am daily ▪ €€

Go Russian at this Moscow-style venue, with borscht, Russian music and vodka.

**9** **Café November**
MAP H1 ▪ Husemannstr. 15
▪ (030) 442 84 25 ▪ 10am–1am Mon–Fri, 9am–2am Sat & Sun ▪ €€

A Prenzlauer Berg institution with a small but tempting menu.

**10** **Mao Thai**
MAP H2 ▪ Wörther Straße 30
▪ (030) 441 92 61 ▪ noon–11:30pm daily ▪ €€

Berlin's first Siamese restaurant, this is one of the friendliest eateries in town, serving traditional and artistically presented food.

*See map on p137*

# TOP 10 Berlin's Southeast

Berlin's east and south are remarkably different in character. Friedrichshain, Lichtenberg and Hohenschönhausen in the east are densely built-up, with their old tenement blocks evoking stark memories of World War II and perhaps even more of life during the bleak days of the East German regime. Green Treptow and idyllic Köpenick in the far southeast, meanwhile, seem almost like independent villages and,

**Sculpture detail, Treptower Park**

together with Großer Müggelsee, are popular day trip destinations for visitors and Berliners alike.

## BERLIN'S SOUTHEAST

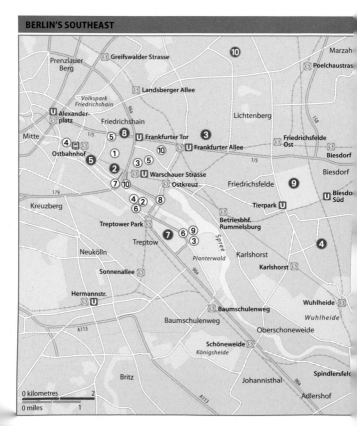

*revious pages* The Berliner Dom with the shimmering Sony Center in the background

**A view of the small town of Köpenick from the Spree River**

### 1 Köpenicker Altstadt and Köpenicker Schloss

Schloss: Schlossinsel ■ 11am–6pm Thu–Sun (to 5pm in winter) ■ Adm ■ www.smb.museum

The island community of Köpenick has a venerable history: as early as the 9th century, people had settled on Schlossinsel. The village stayed independent until 1920. Its coat of arms still features two fish, and the Altstadt (old town) on the Dahme River has 18th–19th-century fishermen's huts. On 16 October 1906, Wilhelm Voigt, dressed as a captain, led soldiers into the Rathaus (town hall) on Alt-Köpenick, arrested the mayor and "confiscated" the municipal coffers. The "Hauptmann von Köpenick" (Captain of Köpenick) is commemorated by a statue in front of the Rathaus. The 1904 structure is a good example of Gothic brick architecture from Brandenburg. The charming Baroque Köpenick palace, on Schlossinsel in the south of the district, was built in 1677–81 for the future King Frederick I by Dutch architect Rutger van Langervelt. It now houses collections from the Kunstgewerbemuseum (see p51).

### 2 Mercedes-Benz Arena

Mühlenstr. 12–30/O2-Platz 1 ■ Ticket hotline (030) 20 60 70 88 99 ■ www.mercedes-benz-berlin.de

The city's largest entertainment arena, seating 17,000 people, hosts pop concerts and shows of all kinds, as well as being home to the Alba Berlin basketball team and the Eisbären Berlin ice-hockey club.

Kaulsdorf

**S** Kaulsdorf

Mahlsdorf

1/5

1/5

Kaulsdorf Süd

Waldesruh

Mittelheide

**S** Köpenick

Friedrichshagen **S**

Köpenick
① ⑨
② ①
⑦

Friedrichs-hagen
Spree

⑧

⑥ Großer Müggelsee

Kämmereiheide

**The Mercede[s**

###  Stasi-Museum Berlin

Ruschestr. 103, Haus 1
■ 10am–6pm Mon–Fri,
noon–6pm Sat & Sun
■ Adm ■ www.
stasimuseum.de

**Button spy camera, Stasi-museum**

The former headquarters of the feared Stasi, East Germany's secret police, is now a memorial commemorating the victims of the East German regime and of Erich Mielke, the minister in charge of the secret police. Visitors can see his offices, the canteen and spying equipment used by the Socialist big-brother regime.

###  Deutsch-Russisches Museum

Zwieseler Str. 4 ■ 10am–6pm Tue–Sun ■ www.museum-karlshorst.de

World War II ended here on 8 May 1945, when Germany signed its unconditional surrender. Documents, uniforms and photographs, displayed in the former officers' casino, relate the story of the war.

### 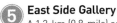 East Side Gallery

A 1.3-km (0.8-mile) section of the Berlin Wall was left standing next to the Spree River. In 1990, 118 artists from around the world painted colourful images onto the grey concrete, making it a unique work of art. Particularly famous is a mural by Russian Dmitri Vrubel showing Erich Honecker and Leonid Brezhnev kissing. Most murals were restored by the original artists in 2009 *(see p78)*.

###  Großer Müggelsee

Treptow-Köpenick district

Nicknamed Berlin's "Large Bathtub", the Großer Müggelsee is the city's biggest lake, covering 766 ha (1,892 acres). Müggelsee is not as popular as Großer Wannsee, mainly because it is so far from the centre of town. It is known for the beer gardens on its south side, which can be reached on foot or by boat from Friedrichshagen. You can swim in the lake, and around it are great walking and cycling paths.

### 7 Treptower Park

Alt-Treptow

Established in the 19th century for the city's working classes, Treptower Park is today best known for its Sowjetisches Ehrenmal (Soviet Memorial). In April 1945, 7,000 Red Army soldiers who died during the liberation of Berlin were buried here. Beyond the mass graves is a 12-m (39-ft) bronze statue of a Russian soldier holding a child and a sword with which he has destroyed the Nazi *hakenkreuz* symbol *(see p61)*.

### 8 Friedrichshain

MAP H2

This densely built-up area grew rapidly during the industrialization of the late 19th century. Its industries made it an Allied target during the war and it was one of Berlin's most damaged districts. After the fall of

...ty's East Side Gallery

the Wall, Friedrichshain attracted a vibrant young population, and it is now one of the city's most popular and bohemian areas, home to trendy design and media companies, bars, clubs, and cafés, mostly set around Boxhagener Platz and Simon-Dach-Straße. Its Volkspark is an oasis of tranquillity, with Ludwig Hoffman's charming Märchenbrunnen fountain, decorated with fairy-tale characters, and the wooded Großer and Kleiner Bunkerberg hillocks (see p61).

**Märchenbrunnen, Volkspark**

### ⑨ Tierpark Berlin
Am Tierpark 125 ■ (030) 51 53 10 ■ Opening times vary, check online ■ Adm ■ www.tierpark-berlin.de/tierpark

Located in the Friedrichsfelde Palace park, Europe's largest zoological garden hosts several rare species. The Siberian tigers in their rocky outdoor enclosures are worth a visit. The park is known for its successful elephant breeding programme. The 1695 palace sits in the middle of this 160-ha (400-acre) estate (see p61).

### ⑩ Gedenkstätte Hohenschönhausen
Genslerstr. 66 ■ English guided tours 11am & 2:30pm Apr–Oct, 2:30pm Nov–Mar ■ Adm ■ en.stiftung-hsh.de

This former secret police prison for political prisoners was in use until 1990. Before 1951, it served as a reception centre for the Red Army. You can visit the watchtowers and cells – particularly horrifying are the windowless "submarine cells" for solitary confinement and torture.

## A DAY IN BERLIN'S SOUTHEAST

### ▶ MORNING

Begin your tour of Berlin's Southeast at Alexanderplatz. Sights on this tour are not always near each other, so using public transport is recommended.

Take the U-Bahn line U5 to Magdalenenstraße station, from where it is a short walk to the **Stasi-Museum Berlin**. Return to the station and continue on U5 to **Tierpark Berlin**, where you can spend some time exploring both the zoological garden and the beautifully restored **Schloss Friedrichsfelde**, built in early Neo-Classical style. Then catch bus No. 296 from the Tierpark U-Bahn station to the **Deutsch-Russisches Museum**.

### AFTERNOON

From the museum, either walk (15 minutes) or take bus No. 296 southwest down Rheinsteinstraße to the S Karlshorst tram stop. No. 27 goes direct to **Rathaus Köpenick**. Stop for a typically German meal in the **Ratskeller** (see p149), the town hall's cellar restaurant. Afterwards explore **Köpenick Old Town** (see p145). The old fishing village is especially worth a visit. There are many cafés near **Köpenicker Schloss** (see p145) where you could stop for coffee and cake. Continue your journey by tram No. 60 to Friedrichshagen, the access po[int] for the **Großer Müggelsee**. Fr[om] here take one of the tourist b[oats] across the lake to **Müggelsee Terrassen**, where you ca[n round] off the day with an even[ing meal] at a choice of restaura[nts].

# Bars and Clubs

### 1 Berghain
Located in a former power station, this club has a strict door policy – be prepared to queue. A good sound system and cool crowds make the wait worthwhile *(see p75)*.

### 2 Arena
**Eichenstr. 4** ▪ **(030) 533 20 30** ▪ **Check opening days in advance**
This sprawling post-industrial riverside complex of concert halls, a club ship *(Hoppetosse)* and a moored swimming pool *(Badeschiff)* is unusual even by Berlin standards.

### 3 Cassiopeia
**Revaler Str. 99** ▪ **(030) 47 38 59 49** ▪ **From 7pm Wed–Sat**
Join hippies, punks and freestylers in this underground urban enclave for ungentrified clubbing and live gigs.

### 4 Holzmarkt
**Holzmarktstr. 25** ▪ **(030) 47 36 16 86**
A rejuvenated area by the Spree river that offers an eclectic mix of bars, clubs and cultural events.

### 5 CSA
**Karl-Marx-Allee 96** ▪ **(030) 29 04 47 41** ▪ **From 7pm daily** ▪ **No credit cards**
Named after the Czech Airlines office that was based here, CSA is a stylish cocktail bar serving perfect drinks to pleasant lounge music.

### 6 Festsaal Kreuzberg
**Am Flutgraben 2** ▪ **(030) 551 50 65 87** ▪ **From 4pm Mon–Sun**
One of Berlin's best live music halls, this all-in-one venue hosts rock, alternative and indie bands in the former White Trash and Food space. Has a lovely beer garden.

### 7 Monster Ronson's Ichiban Karaoke Bar
**Warschauer Str. 34** ▪ **(030) 89 75 13 27** ▪ **From 7pm daily**
At this lively bar, karaoke fans either practise their art in soundproof booths that can fit up to 16 people, or sing on a stage. Try the brunch on Sundays.

### 8 Salon zur Wilden Renate
**Alt Stralau 70** ▪ **(030) 25 04 14 26** ▪ **6pm–2am Wed–Thu, 6pm–8am Fri, 6pm–6am Sat & Sun** ▪ **No credit cards** ▪ **No disabled access**
Styled like a living room, this club is spread across several floors. It plays house and techno house music and often has a queue at the door.

### 9 Insel
**Alt-Treptow 6** ▪ **(030) 53 60 80 20** ▪ **Club 7pm–1am Wed, 8pm–late Fri & Sat**
This miniature castle on a Spree island houses a beer garden by day and a club by night. Live concerts in summer; poetry slams and ping pong in winter.

### 10 Matrix
**Warschauer Platz 18** ▪ **(030) 29 36 99 90** ▪ **10pm–7am daily**
Located in vaults under the Warschauer Straße train station, Matrix is one of the largest clubs in the city. Popular with a young crowd, it attracts Berlin's best DJs.

...r railway arches

# Restaurants

**PRICE CATEGORIES**
For a three-course meal for one with half a bottle of wine (or equivalent meal), taxes and charges included.

€ under €30   €€ €30–60   €€€ over €60

### ① freiheit fünfzehn
Freiheit 15 ▪ (030) 65 88 78 25 ▪ From 4pm Mon–Sat, 11am–midnight Sun ▪ €

German and French cuisine served aboard a schooner moored on the Müggelspree. If you prefer dry land, you can dine in the beer garden.

**Vast vaults of Ratskeller Köpenick**

### ② Ratskeller Köpenick
Alt-Köpenick 21 ▪ (030) 655 51 78 ▪ 11am–11pm daily ▪ €€

Traditional Berlin fare is served in the vaulted cellars where Wilhelm Voigt once famously conned gullible local civil servants *(see p145)*.

### ③ Klipper Schiffsrestaurant
Bulgarische Str. ▪ (030) 53 21 64 90 ▪ 10am–1am daily ▪ No credit cards ▪ €

This two-masted 1890 boat has been turned into a cosy restaurant; the menu features fish and game dishes.

### ④ Freischwimmer
Vor dem Schlesischen Tor 2 ▪ (030) 61 07 43 09 ▪ noon–midnight Mon–Fri, 10am–midnight Sat & Sun ▪ €€

This legendary restaurant and bar floats on a wooden terrace over the Flutgraben Canal. A great spot for weekend brunch.

### ⑤ Burgeramt
Krossener Str. 21–22 ▪ (030) 66 76 34 53 ▪ Noon–midnight daily ▪ €

A wide variety of burgers available for every palate, from beef patties cooked on a lava stone to several vegeterian options.

### ⑥ Restaurant Zenner
Alt-Treptow 14–17 ▪ (030) 533 73 70 ▪ 10am–10pm Mon–Thu & Sun, 10am–4am Fri & Sat ▪ No credit cards ▪ €

A classic day trip destination: once, families used to "bring and brew their own coffee". Today it is a popular outdoor café and beer garden.

### ⑦ Krokodil
Gartenstr. 46–48 ▪ (030) 65 88 00 94 ▪ 5pm–midnight Mon–Sat, 11am–11pm Sun (brunch 11am–3pm) ▪ €

Situated in Köpenick's Old Town, near the river baths in Gartenstraße, this is one of the nicest garden venues, especially in summer.

### ⑧ Bräustübl
Müggelseedamm 164 ▪ (030) 37 44 67 69 ▪ 11am–midnight daily ▪ €

This typical beer garden, belonging to the neighbouring Berliner Bürger-Brau brewery, serves game dishes.

### ⑨ Lehmofen
Freiheit 12 ▪ (030) 655 70 44 ▪ Noon–midnight daily (from 10am Sun) ▪ €

Meat and vegetarian dishes, freshly cooked in a clay oven, are the top attractions in this Anatolian restaurant with a summer terrace.

### ⑩ Leander
Jungstr. 29 ▪ (030) 29 00 48 03 ▪ Apr–Oct: from 10am daily; Nov–Mar: from 3pm Mon–Fri & from 10a Sat & Sun ▪ €

This romantic bistro with an old feel offers creative and cosmo food – and it is a bargain to b

*See map*

# TOP 10 Grunewald and Dahlem

Berlin's green southwest, which includes the districts of Grunewald and Dahlem, is dotted with lakes, rivers, residential villas, private estates and small castles. Grunewald and Dahlem have a charming suburban character that has always drawn affluent and famous Berliners. Visitors can enjoy extensive walks in the Grunewald forest, take a ferry ride across picturesque Wannsee to the romantic ruins at Pfaueninsel or relax at Europe's largest inland beach. Dahlem's Museum of Europäischer Kulturen has a terrific collection, while the Haus der Wannsee Konferenz and Alliiertenmuseum recall a more painful period in Berlin's history.

**Schloss Glienicke, detail**

## GRUNEWALD AND DAHLEM

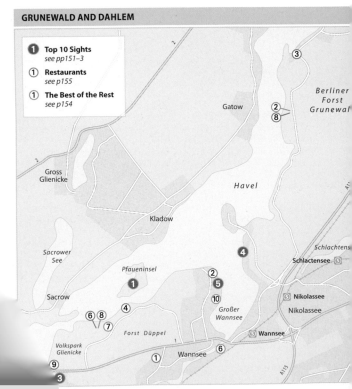

- ① Top 10 Sights
  see pp151–3
- ① Restaurants
  see p155
- ① The Best of the Rest
  see p154

**Friedrich Wilhelm II's charming ruined castle folly on Pfaueninsel**

### 1 Pfaueninsel
**Pfaueninselchaussee ▪ (030) 80 58 68 30 ▪ 10am–sunset daily ▪ Adm (castle) ▪ www.spsg.de**
Visitors to Pfaueninsel are immediately enchanted by the romantic palace ruins and the eponymous peacocks that run around here. The Wannsee island, which can only be reached by ferry, is one of the most charming spots for a walk in Berlin (see p60).

### 2 Museum Europäischer Kulturen
**Arnimallee 25 ▪ 10am–5pm Tue–Fri, 11am–6pm Sat & Sun ▪ Adm ▪ www.smb.museum**
Of three museums in Dahlem, only the Museum of European Cultures remains (the Museum of Asian Art and the Museum of Ethnology are moving to the Humboldt Forum, which is due to open in 2019, see p89). The museum's vast array of objects, including jewellery and graphic art, represent life in Germany and other European countries from the 18th century to the present day.

### 3 Schloss Glienicke
**Königstr. 36 ▪ (0331) 969 42 00 ▪ Apr–Oct: 10am–6pm Tue–Sun; Nov, Dec & Mar: 10am–5pm Sat & Sun ▪ Adm ▪ www.spsg.de**
One of Berlin's most beautiful Hohenzollern palaces, this romantic castle was built by Schinkel in 1824–60 as a summer residence for Prince Carl of Prussia. The landscaped garden, designed by Lenné, includes pavilions called "Große" and "Kleine Neugierde" (large and small curiosity), a teahouse and the Orangerie.

Halensee

Grunewald ⑤ ⑦

Grunewald

Schmargendorf

⑧

⑩ ⑨ ①
⑤ Ⓤ Dahlem Dorf
⑥ ⑦
Onkel Ⓤ Dahlem ②
Toms Hütte Ⓤ ④
③ Freie Universität

mme Ⓤ Lichterfelde West ⑤
anke

Zehlendorf

Mexikoplatz ⑤ Lichterfelde
Sundgauer Strasse
⑤
Zehlendorf

Schönow

0 kilometres 2
0 miles 1

**White-sand artificial beaches at the beautiful Wannsee lake**

### ④ Strandbad Wannsee
Wannseebadeweg 25
■ Call for opening times: (030)
803 54 50 ■ Adm

Europe's largest inland beach is
a picturesque spot on the edge of
the city, attracting up to 40,000 daily
visitors. The renovated swimming
baths were built in 1929–30 as a
recreation area for workers *(see p61)*.

### ⑤ Gedenkstätte Haus der Wannsee-Konferenz
Am Großen Wannsee 56–58
■ (030) 805 00 10 ■ 10am–6pm
daily ■ www.ghwk.de

It is hard to believe that something
as abhorrent as the Holocaust could
have been planned at this elegant
villa. Built by Paul Baumgarten in
1914–15 in Neo-Baroque style for
businessman Ernst Marlier, it hosted
the Nazi elite, among them the infamous Adolf Eichmann, on 20 January
1942. They met to discuss the details
of the mass extermination of Jews.
An exhibition documents the conference and its consequences,
as well as the history of the villa.

### ⑥ Alliiertenmuseum
Clayallee 135 ■ (030) 818 19 90
■ 10am–6pm Sun–Tue ■ www.
alliiertenmuseum.de/en

This museum recalls the 50 or so
years of partnership between West
Berliners and the Western Allies.
Based in a former US barracks, it uses
uniforms, documents, weapons and
military equipment to tell the story of
Berlin's post-war history, though not
only from the military point of view.

### ⑦ Grunewald Villas
Some of Berlin's most
attractive 19th-century villas are
found in the streets around the
Grunewald S-Bahn station. Especially
worth seeing are Nos. 15 and 11 in
Winklerstraße, the latter of which
was built by Hermann Muthesius
in the style of an English country
house. Villa Maren at No. 12 is a
beautiful example of the Neo-
Renaissance style. The villas on
Furtwänglerstraße and Toni-Lessler-
Straße are also worth a detour.

**PRUSSIA AND ANTIQUITY**

From 1821, Lenné and Schinkel tried to
turn the Potsdam countryside into an
"island paradise". Their idea was based
on Classical ideas of the
harmonious ensemble of
architecture and landscape,
in line with the idealized
views of antiquity
prevalent in the Neo-
Classical period. The
architectural style of
Prussian palaces such
as Sanssouci **(left)**
thus harks back to
Greek and Roman
models and the
Italian Renaissance.

### 8 Jagdschloss Grunewald

Hüttenweg 100, Grunewaldsee
■ (0331) 969 42 00 ■ Apr–Oct: 10am–
6pm Tue–Sun; Nov, Dec & Mar:
tours only, 10am–4pm Sat & Sun
■ Adm ■ www.spsg.de

This small white 1542 palace is the
oldest in the city area. It was once
a hunting lodge for the Electors.
Built in the Renaissance and
Baroque styles, it holds paintings by
Cranach the Elder and 16th–19th-
century portraits of Hohenzollern
rulers.

### 9 Museumsdorf Düppel

Clauertstr. 11 ■ (030) 802
66 71 ■ Apr–Oct: 10am–5pm
Sat & Sun ■ Adm ■ www.dueppel.de

This lively open-air museum is
a reminder that Berlin was once a
series of villages dating back to the
13th century. Costumed actors enact
the daily life of the Middle Ages, and
there are bread-baking, pottery
and basket-weaving demonstrations.
The gardens are fascinating.

**Villas of Mexikoplatz**

### 10 Mexikoplatz

Idyllic Mexikoplatz in the
southern district of Zehlendorf is
one of the most atmospheric and
architecturally fascinating squares
in Berlin. It is flanked by elegant
semicircular Jugendstil apartment
blocks, and in front of these stands
Berlin's last remaining Art-Deco-
style S-Bahn station. In summer,
the buildings' balconies are richly
decked with greenery and flowers.
Some of Berlin's most magnificent
mansion houses line Argentinische
and Lindenthaler Allee, the streets
leading into the magnificent square.

---

## A DAY IN THE SOUTHWEST

### ▶ MORNING

Start your morning walk through
Berlin's southwestern districts
by taking the S-Bahn (line S1)
to **Mexikoplatz**. Here you can
admire the beautiful villas and
the lovely green square before
dropping in at **Café Krone** (No.
2 Argentinische Allee) for a late
breakfast. Then take bus No.
118 southwards to the open-air
museum **Museumsdorf Düppel**.
From there, take bus No. 115
north to the **Alliiertenmuseum**.
Afterwards, a 20-minute walk
through the park opposite leads
right up to the beer garden **Luise**
(see p155) near the Free University,
where you may like to have lunch.

### AFTERNOON

Resume your explorations with a
stop at the **Museum Europäischer
Kulturen** (see p151), a 2-minute
walk south of the café, or discover
exotic flora in the giant greenhouses of the **Botanischer Garten**
(pp60–61), a 20-minute walk east.
The seasonal displays are spectacular at any time of year. Then
find your way to the Botanischer
Garten S-Bahn station to take the
train to the Wannsee station, gate-
way to the sights of southwestern
Berlin. When the weather is right,
head to the beaches of **Strandbad
Wannsee**. Alternatively, pay a visit
to the **Gedenkstätte Haus der
Wannsee-Konferenz** and then
admire the park and **Schloss
Glienicke** (see p151). After your
day out, allow yourself to be
tempted by coffee and cake or
supper at **Restaurant Remise im
Schloss Glienicke** (see p155). Your
best option for the return journey
is the S-Bahn from Wannsee.

See map on pp150

# The Best of the Rest

 **Open Air Museum Domäne Dahlem**

Königin-Luise-Str. 49 ▪ 10am–6pm Mon & Wed–Sun ▪ Adm ▪ www.domaene-dahlem.de

Learn about modern organic farming techniques at this historic working farm.

 **Grunewaldturm**

Havelchaussee

This Neo-Gothic brick tower was built in 1897 as a memorial to Kaiser Wilhelm I.

 **Onkel-Tom-Siedlung**

**Grunewaldturm**

Argentinische Allee

The "Uncle Tom's Hut" settlement, developed in 1926–32 according to designs by Bruno Taut and others, was intended to create a modern housing estate for workers, unlike the narrow and dark old tenement blocks they lived in.

**4 Free University**

Habelschwerdter Allee 45 ▪ Library: 9am–10pm Mon–Fri (to 5pm Sat & Sun)

The campus of Berlin's largest university, founded in 1948 as a rival to the East-Berlin Humboldt University, covers large parts of Dahlem. It is worth looking at the 1950s Henry-Ford-Bau and the Philological Library, designed by Lord Norman Foster.

**rman Foster's Philological Library**

 **Teufelsberg**

Both the hill and the dark green Teufelssee lake are popular destinations for flying kites and biking. Swimming and sunbathing at the lake is mainly nude.

**6 Heinrich von Kleist's Tomb**

Bismarckstr. 3, Am Kleinen Wannsee

German playwright Kleist and his companion Henriette Vogel committed suicide by shooting themselves in 1811; they are buried here together (near the S-Bahn overpass).

**7 St-Peter-und-Paul-Kirche**

Nikolskoer Weg 17 ▪ (030) 805 21 00 ▪ 11am–4pm daily

This charming stone church, built in 1834–7 by Stüler, resembles Russian-Orthodox churches and is used for marriage ceremonies.

**8 Blockhaus Nikolskoe**

Nikolskoer Weg 15 ▪ (030) 805 29 14 ▪ 10:30am–6pm daily (to 10pm summer)

This wooden, Russian-style *dacha*, built in 1819, was a gift from King Friedrich Wilhelm III to his daughter Charlotte and his son-in-law, the future Tsar Nicholas I. The house is now a restaurant.

**9 St-Annen-Kirche**

Königin-Luise-Str./Pacelliallee

This 14th-century Gothic church has attractive murals depicting scenes from the life of St Anna, as well as late Gothic figures of saints and a Baroque pulpit.

 **Liebermann-Villa**

Colomierstr. 3 ▪ Summer: 10am–6pm Wed–Mon; winter: 11am–5pm Wed–Mon

The home of Berlin painter Max Liebermann, on the Wannsee shore, is now a museum of his art.

# Restaurants

**PRICE CATEGORIES**
For a three-course meal for one with half
a bottle of wine (or equivalent meal),
taxes and charges included.

€ under €30   €€ €30–60   €€€ over €60

**The Blockhaus Nikolskoe restaurant**

### 1 Mutter Fourage
Chausseestrasse 15a ▪ (030)
805 23 11 ▪ Summer: 9am–7pm;
winter: 10am–6pm daily ▪ €

Hidden in the yard of a market
garden and an atelier, this charming
café has a delicious selection of
homemade cakes and snacks.

### 2 Haus Sanssouci
Am Großen Wannsee 60
▪ (030) 805 30 34 ▪ 11:30am–
11pm Tue–Sun ▪ €€

Offering great Wannsee views,
this idyllic cottage-style restaurant
offers up mostly German food,
but it has lobster nights and
other specials too.

### 3 Wirtshaus Schildhorn
Havelchaussee/Straße am
Schildhorn 4A ▪ (030) 30 88 35 00
▪ Summer: noon–midnight daily;
winter: noon–10pm Sat & Sun ▪ €€

In summer enjoy your *bratwurst*
outside, in this picturesque spot
on the Havel riverside.

### 4 Wirtshaus zur Pfaueninsel
Pfaueninselchaussee 100 ▪ (030)
805 22 25 ▪ Summer: 10am–8pm
daily; winter: 10am–6pm Wed–Mon
▪ €

A small venue serving rustic
German food in the open air. An
ideal place for a break before a
Pfaueninsel visit.

### 5 Alter Krug Dahlem
Königin-Luise-Str. 52 ▪ 10am–
midnight daily ▪ (030) 832 70 00
▪ no credit cards ▪ €

Relax in the porch swings of this
large beer garden. A barbecue
provides the food at mealtimes.

### 6 Blockhaus Nikolskoe
Nikolskoer Weg 15 ▪ (030)
805 29 14 ▪ from 10:30am daily
▪ no credit cards ▪ €€

Traditional German fare in a historic
log cabin, built as a Russian *dacha*.

### 7 Luise
Königin-Luise-Str. 40 ▪ (030)
84 18 88 0 ▪ 10am–1am daily ▪ €

One of Berlin's nicest beer gardens,
on the Free University campus,
Luise's is always crowded and
always has a good atmosphere. Try
the delicious salads and sandwiches.

### 8 Grunewaldturm-Restaurant
Havelchaussee 61 ▪ (030) 41 72
00 01 ▪ 10am–7pm daily ▪ €€

This restaurant is a great place to
relax after a long hike and enjoy
the views of Wannsee.

### 9 Restaurant Remise im Schloss Glienicke
Königstr. 36 ▪ (030) 805 40 00
▪ Mar–Jan: 11am–late daily ▪ €€

Sophisticated surroundings and
cuisine. Fish dishes and salads in
summer, game and roasts in winter.

### 10 Chalet Suisse
Clayallee 99 ▪ (030) 832 63 62
▪ noon–midnight daily ▪ €€

A cosy atmosphere and Swiss
hospitality are the order of the day.
Local and exquisite Swiss cooking
features strongly on the menu.

*See map on pp150–51*

# 🔟 Potsdam and Sanssouci

Potsdam is an important part of European cultural history – a splendid centre of the Enlightenment, which reached its climax in the 18th century in the architectural and artistic design of Frederick the Great's palace of Sanssouci. The palace complex, with its beautiful, extensive park, is both magnificent and playful. It has been designated a World Heritage Centre of Culture by UNESCO and enchants millions of visitors every year. The town of Potsdam, numbering more than 150,000 inhabitants, is the capital of the federal province of Brandenburg. This former garrison town has much to delight visitors, including small palaces and old churches, idyllic parks and historic immigrant settlements.

**Marmorpalais**

**POTSDAM AND SANSSOUCI**

- ① **Top 10 Sights** see pp157–9
- ① **Restaurants** see p161
- ① **The Best of the Rest** see p160

*Volkspark Potsdam*

*Paradies-Garten*

*Sizilianischer Garten*

*Park Sansoucci*

*Park Charlottenhof*

*Park Sanssouci*

*Charlottenhof*

0 metres    600
0 yards     600

4 km ⑦

*Havel*

### 1 Neues Palais

**Am Neuen Palais** ▪ (0331) 969
42 00 ▪ 10am–6pm Wed–Mon (Nov–
Mar: to 5pm) ▪ The visitor centre is at
the south gate; audio guide available
▪ Adm ▪ www.spsg.de

One of Germany's most beautiful
palaces, the Baroque Neues Palais
was built in 1763–9 for Frederick the
Great by Johann Gottfried Büring,
Jean Laurent Le Geay and Carl von
Gontard. The vast structure has 200
rooms, including the Marmorsaal
(marble hall), a lavishly furnished
ballroom, and the Schlosstheater,
where plays are once more performed today. Frederick's private
chambers are equally splendid,
especially his Rococo study, the
upper gallery with valuable parquet
flooring and the Oberes Vestibül,
a room clad entirely in marble.

**The beautiful Baroque Neues Palais**

### 2 Schloss Sanssouci

**Maulbeerallee** ▪ (0331) 969
42 00 ▪ Apr–Oct: 10am–6pm Tue–
Sun; Nov–Mar: 10am–5pm Tue–Sun;
guided tour obligatory ▪ Adm
▪ www.spsg.de

Frederick the Great wished to live
"sans souci" ("without worries") in
a palace outside the city. In 1745, he
commissioned his favourite architect
Georg Wenzeslaus von Knobelsdorff
to construct this magnificent Rococo
palace according to his own designs.
The structure rises proudly above the
former terraced vineyards, leading
up to the domed building and its
marble hall at the centre of the
complex. In both its design and
shape, the hall pays homage to
Rome's Pantheon. To its left and
right are attractive rooms designed
by von Knobelsdorff and Johann
August Nahl; these include the
famous concert room and the king's
library. In this wing, the monarch
liked to play the flute or to philoso-
phize with Voltaire. Works by the
king's favourite painter, Antoine
Watteau, adorn the palace walls.

### 3 Schloss Charlottenhof

**Geschwister-Scholl-Str. 34a**
▪ (0331) 969 42 28 ▪ May–Oct:
10am–6pm Tue–Sun ▪ www.spsg.de

A small Neo-Classical palace in Park
Sanssouci, built in 1829 by Schinkel
for the heir to the throne, Friedrich
Wilhelm IV. Particularly worth seeing
is the tent-like Humboldtsaal.

### ④ Schlosspark Sanssouci

**Chinesisches Haus: Am Grünen Gitter** ▪ (0331) 969 42 25 ▪ May–Oct: 10am–6pm Tue–Sun ▪ **Römische Bäder: Lennéstr.** ▪ (0331) 969 42 25 ▪ May–Oct: 10am–6pm Tue–Sun ▪ **Orangerie: An der Orangerie 3–5** ▪ (0331) 969 42 22 ▪ Apr: 10am–6pm Sat & Sun; May–Oct: 10am–6pm Tue–Sun ▪ www.spsg.de

It is easy to spend a day in the park, which covers 287 ha (709 acres). Among the many charming buildings hidden in the landscaped garden is the Rococo-style Chinesisches Haus, built in 1754–6 by Johann Gottfried Büring. It originally served as a teahouse and dining room, and now houses an exhibition of East Asian porcelain. The Römische Bäder (Roman Baths) are lakeside pavilions modelled on an Italian Renaissance villa. They were built as bath- and guesthouses between 1829 and 1840 by Schinkel. The Orangerie, built in 1851–60 by Stüler, was also originally intended for the king's guests. Today it houses a small gallery of paintings.

### ⑤ Schloss Cecilienhof

**Im Neuen Garten** ▪ (0331) 969 42 00 ▪ Apr–Oct: 10am–6pm Tue–Sun; Nov–Mar: 10am–5pm Tue–Sun ▪ www.spsg.de

The 1945 Potsdam Conference was held in this little palace, built in 1914–17 in the style of an English country house. It is a UNESCO World Heritage Site and is now used as a hotel. It also houses a small exhibition documenting the Conference and the palace's furnishings.

### ⑥ Marmorpalais

**Heiliger See (Neuer Garten)** ▪ (0331) 969 45 50 ▪ May–Oct: 10am–6pm Tue–Sun; Nov–Apr: 10am–4pm Sat & Sun ▪ www.spsg.de

This small, early Neo-Classical palace by the Heiliger See was built in 1791–7 by Carl Gotthard Langhans and others. It features an elegant concert hall as well as contemporary furniture and porcelain.

**House in the Holländisches Viertel**

### ⑦ Holländisches Viertel

**Friedrich-Ebert-, Kurfürsten-, Hebbel-, Gutenbergstr.**

A pleasant way to explore Potsdam is a walk through the historic Old Town. Built between 1733 and 1742, the area originally served as a settlement for Dutch workers after whom it is now named.

**THE POTSDAM CONFERENCE**

In July and August 1945, the heads of the governments of the United States (Harry Truman), the USSR (Joseph Stalin) and Great Britain (Winston Churchill) met in Schloss Cecilienhof in order to seal the future of Germany through a treaty. Vitally important points such as the level of reparations to be paid by Germany, the demilitarization of the country, its new borders, the punishment of war criminals, and the resettlement of Germans from Poland were decided here.

### ⑧ Marstall (Filmmuseum)
**Breite Str. 1a** ■ **(0331) 271 81 12** ■ **10am–6pm Tue–Sun** ■ **www. filmmuseum-potsdam.de**

This small museum in the Baroque former stable buildings of the king's town residence uses old cameras, props and projectors to document the history of German film.

### ⑨ Museum Barberini
**Alter Markt, Humboldtstr. 5-6** ■ **(0331) 23 60 14 499** ■ **11am–7pm Tue–Sun** ■ **www.museum-barberini.com**

The predecessor to this private art museum was Palace Barberini, built in 1771–72 by Frederick the Great. Destroyed at the end of World War II, it was reconstructed by Hasso Plattner, and opened to the public in 2017. The exhibition rooms showcase 250 exquisite paintings and sculptures from Mr. Plattner's collection and others on loan from international museums.

### ⑩ Nikolaikirche
**Am Alten Markt** ■ **(0331) 270 86 02** ■ **9am–6pm Mon–Sat, 11:30am–5pm Sun**

Potsdam's most attractive church was designed by Schinkel in 1830 in a Neo-Classical style. Its giant dome is particularly striking, and you can ascend it for a breathtaking view over the Stadtschloss that is now home to the parliament of Brandenburg.

**The Neo-Classical Nikolaikirche**

---

## A DAY IN POTSDAM

### ▶ MORNING

Begin your exploration in the Schlosspark Sanssouci as early as possible in order to get ahead of the daily influx of visitors. Start with **Schloss Sanssouci** *(see p157)* and **Neues Palais** *(see p157)* then visit the Chinesisches Haus, Römische Bäder and Orangerie. From the orangery's viewing terrace you will have magnificent views over the entire palace complex. If you are up for it, you could also climb up to **Schloss Belvedere** on top of the hill. From Schlosspark walk along Voltaireweg to Neuer Garten in the northeast of Potsdam, where you can recover over a tasty lunch at **Schloss Cecilienhof** *(see p161)*.

### AFTERNOON

Start the afternoon looking around **Schloss Cecilienhof** and stroll through Neuer Garten. Stop for a break at Heiliger See, then head to the centre of Potsdam, starting with the **Holländisches Viertel** (Dutch quarter) where you could pop into one of the numerous cafés. Stroll past the **St Peter-und-Paul Kirche** *(see p160)*, the **Französische Kirche** *(see p160)*, the **Nikolaikirche** and the **Altes Rathaus** *(see p160)* to the **Marstall** film museum and Museum Barberini. If you have the time, extend your tour by driving to nearby Babelsberg. You could either visit the **Filmpark**, admire **Schloss Babelsberg** *(see p160)* or walk up **Telegrafenberg** *(see p160)*. To round off your day, a delicious evening meal awaits you at **Pino** *(see p161)* in Potsdam.

*See map on pp156–7*

# The Best of the Rest

### ① Alexandrowka
**Russische Kolonie/Puschkinallee**

The Russian colony feels like a village in Tsarist Russia. Decorated log cabins with picturesque gardens were built here in 1826 for a Russian military choir. Don't miss the museum and the Alexander Newski church.

### ② Dampfmaschinen-haus Sanssouci
**Breite Str. 28** ■ **(0331) 969 42 25** ■ May–Oct: 10am–6pm Sat & Sun ■ www.spsg.de

This building, resembling a mosque with minarets, is the water pumping station for Sanssouci. The 1842 pump can be seen inside.

### ③ Telegrafenberg
**Albert-Einstein-Str.** ■ Einsteinturm tours Oct– Mar: (0331) 29 17 41 ■ Adm

The elegant Einstein tower on top of Telegraph Hill was designed by Erich Mendelssohn in 1920 to see the sun.

### ④ Schloss Babelsberg
**Park Babelsberg** ■ **Closed for renovation until 2018** ■ www.spsg.de

Built by Schinkel in 1833–5 as a summer residence for royalty, this Neo-Gothic palace sits in an idyllic park on the banks of the Havel River.

**Altes Rathaus**

### ⑤ Potsdamer Stadtschloss
**Neuer Markt**

The Hohenzollern palace that was once the residence of Frederick the Great was badly bombed in World War II and had to be demolished in 1960. It has since been rebuilt as a cultural centre and the seat of the Potsdam legislative assembly.

### ⑥ Altes Rathaus
**Am Alten Markt**

The old town hall, built in 1753, is decorated with sculptures and Potsdam's coat of arms – two gilded Atlas figures, each carrying a globe on its back. Today, it is home to the city's museum.

### ⑦ Filmpark Babelsberg
The Filmpark offers visitors a tour of the legendary UFA-Studios, which were among the world's most prestigious when they operated here in Babelsberg from 1917 to 1945. Exciting U-boat trips and thrilling stunt performances and special effects are shown *(see p65)*.

### ⑧ Französische Kirche
**Am Bassinplatz** ■ **(0331) 29 12 19** ■ late Mar–mid-Oct: 1:30–5pm Tue–Sun

In 1752, Johann Boumann built this elliptical Huguenot church with its columned portico; Schinkel designed the beautiful interior in the 1830s.

### ⑨ St-Peter-und-Paul-Kirche
**Am Bassinplatz** ■ **(0331) 230 79 90** ■ 10am–6pm daily (winter: to 5pm)

The Catholic church of saints Peter and Paul, modelled on Haghia Sophia in Istanbul, was built in 1867–70 by Stüler.

### ⑩ Brandenburger Tor
**Luisenplatz**

The most attractive of five former town gates was built by Gontard and Unger in 1770 to celebrate Prussian victory in the Seven Years' War.

**The Neo-Gothic Schloss Babelsberg**

# Restaurants

**PRICE CATEGORIES**

For a three-course meal for one with half
a bottle of wine (or equivalent meal),
taxes and charges included.

€ under €30   €€ €30–60   €€€ over €60

### 1 Speckers Landhaus
Jägerallee 13 ▪ (0331) 280 43 11
▪ noon–2pm, 6–11pm Tue–Sat ▪ €€

The combination of a Prussian
interior, friendly service and light
cuisine make Speckers Landhaus
one of Potsdam's best restaurants.

### 2 Schloss Cecilienhof
Neuer Garten ▪ (0331) 370
52 33 ▪ noon–11pm daily ▪ €€

The palace is now a luxury hotel. Its
restaurant serves solid German food.

### 3 Pino
Weinbergstr. 7 ▪ (0331) 270 30
30 ▪ 6pm–midnight Mon–Sat ▪ €€

Close to Park Sanssouci, Pino serves
a daily changing menu of exquisite
Sicilian fare. The wine list reads like
a Who's Who of Italian vintages.

### 4 Restaurant Juliette
Jägerstr. 39 ▪ (0331) 270 17
91 ▪ noon–3:30pm, 6pm–midnight
Wed–Mon ▪ Closed Jul ▪ €€

A former manor house is the setting
for this French restaurant, one of the
most charming in Potsdam. It serves
top-quality French classics.

### 5 Krongut Bornstedt
Ribbeckstr. 6–7 ▪ (0331) 550
65 48 ▪ 11am–10pm daily ▪ €€

This rustic restaurant, set in
the brewery of a historic country
manor, Krongut Bornstedt, serves
hearty meals with local fish, game,
sausages and home-brewed beers.

### 6 Maison Charlotte
Mittelstr. 20 ▪ (0331) 280 54
50 ▪ noon–11pm daily ▪ €€

An olde-worlde wine bar in a red-
brick Dutch house with outdoor
seating in a pleasant courtyard,
Maison Charlotte serves French
country fare and fine wines.

### 7 Friedrich Wilhelm
Im Wildpark 1 ▪ (0331) 550
50 ▪ 6–10pm Tue–Sat ▪ €€€

This Michelin-starred restaurant in
Hotel Bayrisches Haus (see p176)
is probably Potsdam's best. Light
German dishes are exquisitely prepared and presented by Alexander
Dressel. In summer, eat on a terrace
overlooking a wildflower meadow.

### 8 Waage
Am Neuen Markt 12 ▪ (0331)
817 06 74 ▪ noon–midnight Tue–Sun
▪ €€

Attractive historic restaurant in
central Potsdam. Regional meat
and fish dishes in unusual variations
are particularly worth trying.

**Café Heider's vintage car shuttle**

### 9 Café Heider
Friedrich-Ebert-Str. 29 ▪ (0331)
270 55 96 ▪ 8am–1am Mon–Fri,
9am–1am Sat, 10am–1am Sun ▪ €

This lovely café in the middle of
Potsdam's Old Town offers a
fantastic breakfast, which you
can enjoy outside on the terrace in
summer. A vintage Ford can be hired.

### 10 La Madeleine
Lindenstr. 9 ▪ (0331) 270 54 00
▪ noon–midnight daily ▪ No credit
cards ▪ €

A little bistro serving all sorts of
crêpes, such as sweet with jam or
savoury with ham – the ideal spot
for a quick snack.

*See map on pp156–7*

# Streetsmart

Interior of Berlin Hauptbahnhof

# Getting To and Around Berlin

### Arriving by Air

Berlin is served by two international airports, Tegel and Schönefeld. A new regional hub, Berlin-Brandenburg Airport (BER, or Willy-Brandt-Flughafen), is planned to open in late 2020 to replace them.

**Tegel Airport (TXL)**, located about 8 km (5 miles) northwest of the city centre, has excellent public transport links into town. Buses 109 and 128, and the express buses X9 and TXL (both of which stop right outside the terminal) connect to convenient S- and U-Bahn stops, and to the Berlin Hauptbahnhof (Berlin Central) and Zoologischer Garten stations, taking about 20 minutes.

**Schönefeld Airport (SXF)** is about 18 km (11 miles) southeast of the centre. The fastest way to get there and away is the S-Bahn commuter train or Deutsche Bahn's RB14 and RE7 Airport Express trains, which whisk you to Berlin Hauptbahnhof in around 30 minutes. City buses link the airport to the U-Bahn network.

### Arriving by Rail

The city's gleaming new main station, **Berlin Hauptbahnhof**, is centrally located and close to the government district. All long-distance trains arrive and depart from here. Other key stations include Gesundbrunnen on the northern side of town, Zoologischer Garten in the west, Ostbahnhof in the east and Südkreuz in the south. The stations connect seamlessly to the S- and U-Bahn and city bus networks.

The national railway, **Deutsche Bahn (DB)**, often gives steep online discounts on regular fares. Buy train tickets in advance, as onboard fares are more expensive. DB's high-speed ICE trains link Berlin to Hamburg (2.5 hrs), Munich (6.5 hrs) and Frankfurt (4.25 hrs). Private rail **Harz-Elbe Express (HEX)** has cheap fares for journeys to Magdeburg and Harz Mountains ski resorts.

### Arriving by Road

The central coach station, **Zentraler Omnibus-bahnhof (ZOB)**, is located near Charlottenburg's Funkturm (see p122) and offers good-value links from all major German and European cities. The ZOB website lists daily departures and arrivals as well as coach lines, which include **Eurolines**, **FlixBus** and **Berlinienbus**. Seats fill up fast during the summer and holiday seasons, so book early.

When driving to Berlin, you will arrive via the Berliner Stadtring, the orbital motorway around the city. From the south you come in on the A115 – the famous Avus Autobahn. From the north you arrive on the A111 via Stolpe in the direction of Autobahndreieck Funkturm. The speed limit on the Stadtring is generally 100 kmh (62.5 mph), and on urban motorways 80–100 kmh (50–62.5 mph). Drivers should be aware there are frequent radar checks.

### Travelling by Underground

The transport network is run by the **Berliner Verkehrsgesellschaft (BVG)** and Deutsche Bahn. BVG tickets are transferable between all modes of public transport in Berlin.

The Berlin U-Bahn, or underground railway, has one of Europe's largest networks and provides a fast, convenient means of getting around the city. There are 10 U-Bahn lines, each identifiable by number and colour. The U-Bahn runs from 5am to 1am; at weekends most lines run throughout the night. The station indicated on the platform is the train's final destination.

The Stadtbahn or S-Bahn (city commuter railway) has 15 lines connecting the centre with the suburbs. They run every 5 to 20 minutes. Many lines share tracks so you need to pay attention to indicator boards.

### By Bus and Tram

Buses and trams are also operated by BVG. Berlin has a dense bus network. All lines have three-digit numbers except for express services, which are preceded by "X". Buses and trams marked "M" go to areas that have no direct S- or U-Bahn links. Board via the front door (unless you have a buggy, in which case the back door will be opened) and present your ticket or fare money to the driver. Trams operate only in the eastern part of the city.

## Tickets

Berlin is divided into three fare zones: A, B and C. Most destinations are covered by an AB ticket, available from BVG ticket machines. For most visitors, the best value is an AB day ticket at €7, valid until 3am the following day. A single AB journey costs €2.80 and is valid for two hours in one direction. A *Kurzstrecke* (short distance ticket) is valid for up to three S- or U-Bahn stations or six bus stops, and costs €1.70. Children under 14 years pay a reduced rate; those under six travel free.

Tickets for buses and S- and U-Bahn trains are available at stations and from bus drivers. Trams and some buses have onboard ticket machines. At the station, you must validate your ticket in the red or yellow machine before boarding; on the bus, find the yellow validation machine after you board.

## By Taxi

There are taxi stands all over Berlin, and you can also hail a taxi in the street. Taxis from companies such as **Würfelfunk**, **City Funk**, **Taxi Berlin** and **Talixo** can also be booked on the phone or online. The starting price is €3.90, and a further €1.50–2 is charged per kilometre (0.6 mile). If you hail a taxi, you can travel up to 2 km (1 mile) for €5

but you must ask at the start for the *Kurzstrecke* (short distance tariff).

The **Velotaxi** (bicycle rickshaws) is an unusual way to explore the city. These can be found in the city centre at several popular visitor locations from April to October.

## By Car

All of Berlin inside the S-Bahn ring is a green zone, which means that only vehicles bearing a special environmental badge are allowed in. Order these in advance through **Green Zones**, which processes 24-hour rush orders for an extra fee. Drivers without this badge face a €40 fine.

To hire a car you'll need a valid full driving licence, passport and credit card; some agencies will only accept customers over 21 years. There are rental agencies at the airports and across central Berlin. Search websites such as **billiger-mietwagen.de** help find the best deals.

## By Bicycle

Berlin is bicycle-friendly, with an extensive network of cycle lanes, although most run directly along the street. The red-and-silver bikes of DB's **Call a Bike** scheme are found across the city. You have to pre-register and provide credit card details. The website is only in German, but the phone hotline usually has someone who can speak English. There are bike hire places all over town, and hotels and hostels often rent cycles to their guests for €5–10 per day.

# Practical Information

### Passports and Visas

Visitors from outside the European Economic Area (EEA), European Union (EU) and Switzerland need a valid passport to enter Germany. EEA, EU and Swiss nationals can use their national identity cards instead. Citizens of Canada, the US, Australia and New Zealand can visit Germany for up to 90 days without a visa as long as their passport is valid for 6 months beyond the date of entry. For longer stays, a visa is necessary and needs to be obtained in advance. Most other non-EU nationals need a visa, and should consult the German **Federal Foreign Office** website or their German embassy for details. Schengen visas are valid for Germany.

### Customs and Immigration

For EU citizens there are no limits on most goods, except weapons, some types of food, plants and endangered species, taken in or out of Germany as long as they are for personal use only. Non-EU citizens may import 200 cigarettes and a litre of spirits per adult, and can claim back VAT on EU purchases over €25 at the airport when leaving EU.

### Travel Safety Advice

Visitors can get up-to-date travel safety information from the **Foreign and Commonwealth Office** in the UK, the **State Department** in the US and the **Department of Foreign Affairs and Trade** in Australia.

### Travel Insurance

Travellers are advised to buy insurance against accidents, illness, theft and travel delays or cancellations. Germany has a reciprocal health agreement with other EU countries, and EU citizens receive emergency treatment under the public healthcare system if they have with them a valid European Health Insurance Card (EHIC). Prescriptions have to be paid for upfront. Non-EU visitors should check if their country has reciprocal arrangements with Germany.

### Emergency Services

There are hotlines for the police, fire brigade, emergency dentists, narcotics- and poison-related emergencies.

### Health

Berlin has one of the best health services in the world. Ambulances arrive swiftly when called. Those able to reach a hospital themselves should use the entrance marked *Notaufnahme* (Accident and Emergency). Less serious cases can be dealt with in one of the many private walk-in clinics. **Charité Krankenhaus**, Berlin's main central hospital, has a 24-hour emergency room. The US and UK Embassies can provide a list of English–speaking physicians.

No vaccinations are mandatory but basic flu jabs and routine vaccines should be kept up-to-date. *Apotheken* (chemists or pharmacies) are signalled by a red "A" sign. After 8pm, the address of the nearest all-night pharmacy is posted on the door of each outlet; alternatively, you can call the **Ärztlicher Bereitschaftsdienst der KV Berlin** to help locate the nearest doctors and open pharmacies. Those covered by private health insurance can also contact **Doctors on Call**.

Visitors who suspect they may have caught a sexually transmitted disease (STD) can have a "quick test" done at **Berliner AIDS-Hilfe**. Results are delivered in half an hour. Emergency contraception is available on prescription.

### Personal Security

As in most cities, use common sense when visiting Berlin. Beware of pickpockets and bag-snatchers in crowded trains, at stations and around tourist areas. At night, avoid: U-Bahn line U9 north of the Zoo; behind the Kaiser-Wilhelm-Gedächtnis-Kirche; and Görlitzer Park in Kreuzberg. The areas of Lichtenberg, Marzahn and Wedding are also best avoided after dark.

### Lost Property

The **Zentrales Fundbüro** (central lost property office) keeps anything that has been lost and found anywhere in Berlin. If you have left an item on public transport, enquire at the **Fundbüro der BVG**. Items lost on the S-Bahn or the national railways are sent to the **Fundbüro der Deutschen Bahn**.

## Women Travellers

Berlin is safe for women but avoid parks and dark streets at night. On trains or buses late at night, take a seat near the driver.

## Travellers with Specific Needs

Berlin is well-equipped for visitors with mobility issues. Nearly all streets and pavements are sloped at junctions for wheel-chair users. Most public buildings, malls and cinemas are fitted with lifts, ramps and extra-wide doors. The **German Red Cross** (DRK) rents out wheelchairs at a nominal daily cost.

S- and U-Bahn trains are wheelchair accessible, but not all stations are equipped with lifts. In the U-Bahn, wait at the head of the platform, and the driver will put up a ramp. In the S-Bahn, speak to the station manager to have a ramp set up. BVG network maps show all accessible stations.

Buses having a wheel-chair symbol are equipped for disabled access and have one door with a ramp that can be lowered down.

Over 160 of the silver *City Toiletten* public conveniences in central Berlin are fully accessible.

Those wishing to drive around Berlin and Brandenburg, or to share a ride with other visitors, can contact specialist travel agents **BBV Tours** or **Micky Tours**.

Berlin's charitable association for the blind and sight-impaired, the **Allgemeiner Blinden- und Sehbehindertenverein**, offers practical advice on suitable facilities.

## DIRECTORY

### PASSPORTS AND VISAS

**Federal Foreign Office**
w auswaertiges-amt.de/EN/

### EMBASSIES

**Australia**
MAP L6 ▪ Wallstraße 76–79
w germany.embassy.gov.au

**Canada**
MAP L3 ▪ Leipziger Platz 17
w germany.gc.ca

**UK**
MAP K3 ▪ Wilhelmstr. 70–71
w ukingermany.fco.gov.uk

**USA**
Clayallee 170
w berlin.usembassy.gov

### TRAVEL SAFETY ADVICE

**Australia**
Department of Foreign Affairs and Trade
w dfat.gov.au
w smartraveller.gov.au

**UK**
Foreign and Commonwealth Office
w gov.uk/foreign-travel-advice

**US**
US Department of State
w travel.state.gov

### EMERGENCY SERVICES

**Police**
( 110

**Fire Brigade**
( 112

**Emergency – Dentist**
( (030) 89 00 43 33

**Emergency – Narcotics**
( (030) 192 37

**Emergency – Poison**
( (030) 192 40

### HEALTH

**Ärztlicher Bereitschaftsdienst der KV Berlin**
( (030) 31 00 31

**Berliner AIDS-Hilfe**
MAP A5 ▪ Kurfürstenstr. 130
( (030) 885 64 00

**Charité Krankenhaus**
MAP J3 ▪ Charitéplatz 1
( (030) 450 50

**Doctors on Call**
( (030) 89 00 91 00

### LOST PROPERTY

**Fundbüro der BVG**
MAP E5 ▪ Potsdamer Str. 182, 9am–6pm Mon–Thu,

9am–2pm Fri
( (030) 194 49

**Fundbüro der Deutschen Bahn**
( (0900) 199 05 99

**Zentrales Fundbüro**
MAP F6 ▪ Platz der Luftbrücke 6, 9am–2pm Mon, Tue & Fri, 1–6pm Thu
( (030) 902 773 101

### TRAVELLERS WITH SPECIFIC NEEDS

**Allgemeiner Blinden- und Sehbehindertenverein**
Auerbacherstr. 7
( (030) 89 58 80
w absv.de

**BBV Tours**
Bizetstr. 51–55
( (030) 50 01 91 00
w bbv-tours.de

**German Red Cross**
Bundesallee 73
( (030) 60 03 00
w drk-berlin.de/reservierung.html

**Micky Tours**
Rhinstr. 7
( (030) 515 33 36
w mickytours.de

## Currency and Banking

Germany is one of the 19 European countries using the euro (€), which is divided into 100 cents. Paper notes are in denominations of €5, €10, €20, €50, €100, €200 and €500. Coins are €2, €1, 50c, 20c, 10c, 5c, 2c, 1c.

All large German banks have city centre branches. Cash machines or ATMs (*Geldautomaten*) are dotted throughout the city. A fee list should be posted next to the screen; if you withdraw cash from a bank not affiliated with your home institution, expect to pay a handling fee. Stiff fees are charged by "independent" ATMs for withdrawals. Inquire about credit card ATM cash withdrawal fees (which can be high) before departure. German banks charge up to 2% per credit card withdrawal.

**Mastercard** and **VISA** credit and debit cards are taken by many cafés, restaurants and shops but not all, so it is a wise to carry some cash. **Diners Club** and **American Express** are less common. Should your card be lost/stolen, it is essential you inform your bank immediately. Germany has a free 24-hour national **Lost Card Hotline** which will direct you to your bank.

Pre-paid currency cards (cash passports) are a more secure way of carrying money. They can be preloaded with euros, fixing exchange rates before you leave, and used like a debit card.

You'll be able to buy euros at *Wechselstuben* (banks and bureaux de change); many are based around train stations. Hotels will also change money but may charge higher fees.

Travellers' cheques can be exchanged at all larger banks or at branches of the issuers. Most banks charge a fee.

## Internet and Telephone

While connection speeds can lag behind those in some other European countries, Germans are more wired than ever. Berlin has over 400 wireless Internet hotspots – many free – in bars, cafés, department stores, hotels and public places such as the Sony Center. Deutsche Bahn gives you up to 30 minutes of free surf time per day at over 100 stations across the country. Kabel Deutschland, an internet services company, does the same thing at 75 outdoor Wi-Fi hotspots across town.

To use your mobile device in Germany, it will need to be equipped for GSM network frequencies 900 and 1800 MHz. It is advisable to sign up for an international usage plan to keep costs down. Europe-based companies such as Ortel also offer prepaid plans at competitive rates. Upon arrival consider buying a local SIM card or cheap mobile phone with a German number so you can take advantage of local rates. If needed, ask your home carrier for the unlock code to use a different SIM card/service.

There are public phones (both enclosed booths and open handsets) in the town centre, though they are slowly vanishing. Most are card-operated, but a few will take coins. Phone cards can be bought from post offices, department stores and kiosks.

## Postal Services

German mail is efficient, reliable and fast. Offices of Deutsche Post, the national mail service, usually open 8am–6pm (till noon on Saturday), with some variation for smaller outlets. Offices in train stations and airports open on Sunday as well. Buy stamps from the post office counter or vending machines (often outside the entrance). A standard letter weighing up to 20g or a postcard to anywhere outside Germany costs €0.75. For non-standard postcards and letters bigger than 235 x 125mm (9.25 x 4.9 in) the recipient incurs a charge.

Public postboxes in Berlin generally have two slots: *Postleitzahlen* (postal codes) 10000–169999 for addresses in Brandenburg and Berlin, and *Andere Postleitzahlen* (other postal codes) for destinations elsewhere in Germany and abroad.

## Television and Radio

Public television is built on two national networks, ARD and ZDF. Private channels such as RTL and SAT 1 have stolen a big chunk of their audience. The most authoritative news broadcasts are ARD's *Tagesschau* at 8pm and the 10:30pm ZDF evening news *Heute*. Thanks to satellite and cable you can tune into global English channels including CNN and BBC World. The most popular radio station is RBB's **Radio Eins** (livestream and 95.8 MHz), with pop, news, and chat shows.

## Newspapers and Magazines

Serious newspapers include the *Tagesspiegel*, *Berliner Morgenpost* and *Berliner Zeitung*, the only major East Berlin paper to survive reunification. The tabloid *BZ*, with the greatest circulation, is similar to the US *National Enquirer* or Britain's *Sun*. Another saucy broadsheet is the *Berliner Kurier*. The heavyweight nationals include the *Frankfurter Allgemeine Zeitung* and *Süddeutsche Zeitung*. The country's best-established weekly magazine is *Der Spiegel*, which has an English online edition.

Free event guides such as *030* are available in restaurants and cafés. For entertainment listings, try the twice-monthly magazines *Tip*, *Zitty* or *Prinz*; their online listings are updated more frequently. The *ExBerliner* magazine carries useful articles on Berlin life and culture, as does *The Local* online, both in English.

## Opening Hours

By law, Berlin retailers may conduct business 24 hours a day from Monday to Saturday. Few do so, however. On weekdays, small retailers generally open at 9am or 10am and shut by 7pm, while department stores close at 10pm. Large supermarkets open 8am–10pm. Most shutters go down at

4pm on Saturdays. Shops in large train stations and service stations and convenience stores (*Spätkauf*) stay open until at least midnight, and are also open on Sundays.

Banks in the city centre work 9am–4pm Monday–Wednesday, till 6pm on Thursday, and till 2pm on Friday. Small branches may take a hour's lunch break around 12:30pm. Larger post offices work 8am–6pm Monday–Friday, and till at least noon on Saturday. Pharmacies open 9am–7pm Monday–Friday, and until 4pm on Saturday. Public museums generally open 10am–6pm; many close on Monday, but stay open late on Thursday.

## Time Difference

Germany is on Central European Time (CET), an hour ahead of Greenwich Mean Time, 6 hours ahead of US Eastern Standard Time and 11 hours behind Australian Eastern Standard Time. The clock moves forward 1 hour during daylight saving time from the last Sunday in March until the last Sunday in October.

## Electrical Appliances

The electric current is 220 volts. Many electrical appliances such as hair dryers have 110/220V transformers built in, so converters may be less of a concern, especially if you're coming from North America. Bring an adaptor with two round pins. Some hotel bathrooms provide a lower current as a safety measure.

## Driving Licences

Germany recognizes UK, Australian, Canadian and US licences (see p165).

## Weather

The weather in Berlin is better than its reputation. The continental climate guarantees mild and dry weather from May to September. In spring and autumn it can be cold and wet, and from November to February it is often cloudy, with a biting cold, easterly wind whistling through the city.

(see p165)

### DIRECTORY

**CURRENCY AND BANKING**

**American Express**
📞 (069) 979 70

**Diners Club**
📞 (041) 587 508 008

**Lost Card Hotline**
📞 116 116

**Mastercard**
📞 (0800) 819 10 40

**VISA**
📞 (0800) 811 84 40

**TELEVISION AND RADIO**

**Radio Eins**
🅦 radioeins.de/livestream/

**NEWSPAPERS AND MAGAZINES**

**Der Spiegel**
🅦 spiegel.de/international/

**ExBerliner**
🅦 exberliner.com

**Prinz**
🅦 prinz.de

**Tip**
🅦 tip-berlin.de

**The Local**
🅦 thelocal.de

**Zitty**
🅦 zitty.de

## Visitor Information

The municipal **Berlin Tourist Info** service has seven offices in the city. Here you can book tickets for events and sightseeing tours, buy the Museum Pass and WelcomeCard (which gives unlimited access to the transport network and discounts on many attractions), and make reservations at hotels and hostels (for a €3 fee). The city-run websites **Berlin.de** and **VisitBerlin.de**, both available in English, provide useful information.

There is a wide variety of Berlin apps. Good ones in English include BVG Fahrinfo Plus (real-time public transport connections) and 360° Berlin (guided walks with panoramas), both on Android as well as iPhone, and WhatWasHere_Berlin (interactive historical city guide) for iPhone.

Some of the best English-language blogs exploring fashion, people, places, art and food are **Finding Berlin, I Heart Berlin** and **Stil in Berlin**.

## Excursions and City Tours

The watery landscape of the **Spreewald**, southeast of Berlin, is a unique, UNESCO-protected area of natural beauty. You can explore by traditional punt the old settlements of the Slavic Sorb peoples in the tree-lined waterways of Lübben and Lübbenau.

**Sachsenhausen**, the site of Germany's first Nazi concentration camp, where 100,000 people were murdered between 1936–45,

is a poignant experience. **Schloss Rheinsberg** in the Mecklenburg lakes district makes a splendid day trip. The summer residence of the young Frederick the Great can be visited by guided tour.

Near Potsdam lies the hamlet of Sacrow with its dreamy Saviour's Church, on the lake of the same name. Not far away, picturesque Caputh boasts the charming Baroque **Schloss Caputh** and Einstein's summer home, the **Einsteinhaus** (open only by guided tour at weekends in summer).

Hop-on-hop-off tours on double-decker buses, some of which are open-top in summer, are run by **City Circle, BEX, Berolina, Top Tour** and **Berlin City Tour**. The buses stop at all the main sights, and you can board at any one.

The cheapest, fastest way to see the city is to ride on buses No. 100 or 200. These double-deckers go from Bahnhof Zoo and Alexanderplatz right into Prenzlauer Berg, passing all the key sights for the price of a single fare.

**Berlin Walks** runs daily themed English-language walks, leaving from the taxi rank outside the zoo and Hackescher Markt. **Berliner Unterwelten** leads walks through the city's spooky underbelly into bunkers and tunnels. **Fat Tire Bike Tours** operates Segway and bike tours through Berlin.

Berlin's waterways – the Landwehrkanal, Havel and Spree Rivers, and the Wannsee and Müggelsee lakes – can all be toured by boat. **Reederei Riedel** and **Stern- und Kreis-Schifffahrt** take in historic

sights between the centre and Charlottenburg in the space of 2 to 3 hours.

## Shopping

Kurfürstendamm (see p30–31), Tauentzienstraße and Friedrichstraße are Berlin's main three shopping streets. Galeries Lafayette, Art and Fashion House Quartier 206 and Ku'damm are at the upper end of the scale, but you'll also find inexpensive shops around Tauentzienstraße and Alexanderplatz.

A good mix of shops can be found in the huge malls at Potsdamer Platz and Leipziger Platz, the Alexa shopping centre at Alexanderplatz, Schlossstraße in the south and the Gesundbrunnencenter in the north.

The best fashion and designer stores, selling coveted labels, are on Friedrichstraße and the west side of Ku'damm. Kaufhaus des Westens (KaDeWe) sells a grand range of fashions for men and women (see p76).

A great selection of CDs is at Kulturkaufhaus Dussmann (see p91). For gifts and souvenirs try KaDeWe and the souvenir shops on Unter den Linden near Pariser Platz, Potsdamer Platz and at Checkpoint Charlie.

Most antiques shops are clustered south of Nollendorfplatz (see p130) and in the smaller streets off Ku'damm. However, the antiques and flea market on the Straße des 17. Juni (see p76) and the antiques shops located in the S-Bahn arches between Friedrichstraße and the Museumsinsel offer better value.

## Dining

Berlin's culinary scene offers a huge range of well-priced restaurants and growing numbers of young, adventurous chefs. Old-style meaty, artery-clogging meals are giving way to inventive, lighter fare with global influences.

Vegetarians and people with specific dietary needs, such as gluten and lactose intolerances, will find suitable food in hip KreuzKölln. This trendy new area has seen a vegetarian foodie scene develop in recent years.

Other popular dining strips include Kurfürstendamm, Kastanienallee *(see p139)*; Oranienburger Straße in Mitte *(see p95)*; Wühlisch Straße in Friedrichshain; Oranienstraße *(see p130)* and Schlesische Strasse, both in Kreuzberg; and Akazientraße in Schöneberg. Berlin has more Michelin-starred restaurants than Munich or Hamburg, and this guide lists several two-star places: Fischers Fritz and Facil *(see p71)*, Lorenz Adlon Esszimmer *(see p117)*, Reinstoff *(see p70)* and Restaurant Tim Raue *(see p135)*.

## Where to Stay

Whatever your budget, finding a good, affordable place to stay generally isn't a problem, especially in eastern Berlin, where most of the main sights are located. There is a range of options from luxury and boutique hotels to B&Bs and quirky stays in camping trailers and former East German prison cells. Youth hostels are smartly equipped and attract guests of all ages. Kreuzberg has several *Pensionen* (guesthouses) and small hotels. Most business hotels are in west Berlin, particularly around the trade-fair grounds. Places outside the city centre can offer good value in green areas, and are often close to S- and U-Bahn lines. Sites such as **Berlin30.com, Airbnb, Trivago, HRS, TripAdvisor, lastminute. com, Expedia** and **Booking.com** are good places to look.

Rates are reasonable by European standards. Premium/middle/cheap double rooms in great locations are around €110 /75/50. The average hotel room price is around €90.

# Places to Stay

## PRICE CATEGORIES

For a standard double room per night (with breakfast if included), taxes and extra charges.

€ under €100    €€ €100–€200    €€€ over €200

## Luxury Hotels

### Hotel Intercontinental Berlin

MAP N6 ▪ Budapester Str. 2 ▪ (030) 260 20 ▪ www.berlin.intercontinental.com ▪ €€

A luxury hotel in the Tiergarten, nicely situated with great views over the central park, this establishment is popular with business travellers. The building itself is not particularly attractive, but the rooms are furnished in a timelessly elegant style. Its two restaurants offer first-class food – the elegant, fine-dining Hugos (see p70) has a Michelin star – and the Marlene Bar, the Cigar and Rum Lounge, and the pool and fitness area are also excellent.

### SAS Radisson Blu

MAP K5 ▪ Karl-Liebknecht-Str. 3 ▪ (030) 23 82 80 ▪ www.radissonblu.com/hotel-berlin ▪ €€

Conveniently located on the banks of the Spree between Alexanderplatz and the Museumsinsel, this modern hotel is ideal for exploring city sights. The centrepiece of the hotel is the AquaDom, the world's largest free-standing cylindrical aquarium (see p65). A ticket to the adjacent Sea Life Berlin lets guests take a lift ride through the centre of the AquaDom. The hotel's bright rooms offer views of either the aquarium or the Berliner Dom. Its chic restaurant HEat (see p109) is a bastion of Asian fusion cuisine. In the warmer months, you can enjoy alfresco dining on the elegant terrace, watching the boats go by.

### Sofitel Berlin Gendarmenmarkt

MAP L4 ▪ Charlottenstr. 50–52 ▪ (030) 20 37 50 ▪ www.sofitel.com ▪ €€

Relatively inexpensive and the smallest of the first-class hotels with just 70 rooms and 22 suites, the Sofitel is probably also one of the most attractive, with excellent views of the pretty Gendarmenmarkt. The classic Aigner (see p93) offers traditional Viennese cuisine.

### Grand Hotel Esplanade

MAP N6 ▪ Lützowufer 15 ▪ (030) 25 47 80 ▪ www.esplanade.de ▪ €€€

Glitzy and modern, with furnishings somewhere between Bauhaus style and functional sobriety. Service at this Sheraton group hotel is excellent and its first-class facilities include a state-of-the-art spa and fitness centre, with a pool, massage area, gym, solarium and three saunas. Harry's New York Bar, sister to the historic Harry's in Paris, is one of central Berlin's most popular venues, serving up cocktails with unexpected ingredients such as rosemary, pepper and paprika.

### Hotel Palace

MAP N5 ▪ Budapester Str. 45 ▪ (030) 250 20 ▪ www.palace.de ▪ €€€

This expensively restored hotel on the second floor of the Europa-Center is a real find – all the rooms are exquisitely designed and two suites – Panda and Zackenbarsch – were styled by the director himself. It boasts a spa and fitness centre, and a luxurious seventh floor Club Lounge serving snacks and sandwiches throughout the day and more substantial evening meals alongside spectacular views of Berlin's zoo. The hotel's House of Gin bar offers 150 varieties of gin. Staff are unobtrusive and very helpful.

### Hotel de Rome

MAP K4 ▪ Behrenstr. 37 ▪ (030) 460 60 90 ▪ www.roccofortehotels.com ▪ €€€

Located off Bebelplatz near the State Opera, just steps away from Unter den Linden, Hotel de Rome is sited within the historic 19th-century Dresdner Bank building. After World War II, the GDR State Bank used the structure. The interior is now a vision of postmodern ideas, while the Italian restaurant, the Opera Court café (see p93) and the spa area live up to the expectations of a hotel geared towards the international jet-set crowd.

## Kempinski Hotel Bristol Berlin

MAP P4 ▪ Kurfürsten-damm 27 ▪ (030) 88 43 40 ▪ www.kempinskiberlin. de ▪ €€€

One of Berlin's most famous hotels, the Bristol has it all – a magnificent, cosmopolitan blend of elegance and modern amenities. Among them is a luxury spa, a 2-hour health check at a private partner clinic, and the Kempinski for Kids pro-gramme, which arranges babysitting services and even child-sized robes and slippers. Its international reputation has attracted a host of famous guests, from Fidel Castro to Tina Turner.

## The Mandala Hotel Potsdamer Platz

MAP L2 ▪ Potsdamer Str. 3 ▪ (030) 590 050 000 ▪ www.themandala.com ▪ €€€

This apartment hotel, in a great spot at Potsdamer Platz, has suites of vary-ing sizes between 35–200 sq m (375–2,153 sq ft), each equipped with a kitchenette, fitness area, sauna, stereo, daily news-papers and anything else you could possibly wish for. The Michelin-starred, light-filled restaurant Facil (see p71) is a peace-ful haven from the hub-bub of Potsdamer Platz.

## Soho House

MAP H2 ▪ Torstr. 1 ▪ (030) 405 04 40 ▪ www.soho houseberlin.com ▪ €€€
This six-storey Bauhaus monument started life as a Jewish-owned depart-ment store before eventu-ally housing the archives of the East German Communist Party. The heated rooftop pool, fancy

art and a private cinema seem at home alongside exposed cement walls. An excellent spot for celebrity sightings.

## Westin Grand Hotel

MAP K4 ▪ Friedrichstr. 158–164 ▪ (030) 202 70 ▪ www.westin-berlin.com ▪ €€€
This Westin hotel offers luxury accommodation in a historic spot at the corner of Friedrichstraße and Unter den Linden, with large, elegant rooms and US-style service. The lobby and the grand stairs are breathtaking. There's also a café and a bar.

# Designer Hotels

## art'otel berlin-mitte

MAP L6 ▪ Wallstr. 70–73 ▪ (030) 24 06 20 ▪ www. artotels.com ▪ €€
This designer hotel emphasizes every detail and has styled everything, from the furniture to the soap in the bathroom. Blending architectural style with art-inspired interiors, each art'otel focuses on a contempo-rary artist. The historic building is decorated with paintings by the Neo-Expressionist postmodern artist Georg Baselitz. The hotel is centrally located, close to Nikolaiviertel.

## Casa Camper

MAP J5 ▪ Weinmeisterstr. 1 ▪ (030) 20 00 34 10 ▪ www.casacamper.com/ berlin ▪ €€
This modern hotel near Hackescher Markt in the hip part of Mitte is beauti-fully appointed. It offers excellent service and free Wi-Fi and iPod docking stations in every room. The small spa and snacks

and breakfast in the 24-7 rooftop bar are included in the price. Rooms on the upper floors have great views over the city.

## Dormero Hotel Berlin Ku'damm

MAP P4 ▪ Eislebener Str. 14 ▪ (030) 21 40 50 ▪ www.dormero.de ▪ €€
With a design that strikes a balance between clas-sical and modern, this boutique hotel mimics the city itself. Set in a historic building, the Dormero Hotel Berlin Ku'damm is located just a few steps from the shopping street Kurfürstendamm. Die Quadriga restaurant (see p127) serves up creative French cuisine.

## Hecker's Hotel

MAP B5 ▪ Grolmanstr. 35 ▪ (030) 889 00 ▪ www. heckers-hotel.com ▪ €€
The plain façade of this modern four-star busi-ness hotel, set in a side street just off Ku'damm, belies the much more sophisticated interior – you'll be greeted by mod-ern art, cool minimalism, clever lighting and first-class service.

## Ku'Damm 101

MAP G1 ▪ Kurfürsten-damm 101 ▪ (030) 520 05 50 ▪ www.kudamm101. com ▪ €€
This minimalist hotel, one of the few based on the Bauhaus design princi-ples of Le Corbusier, caters to an art-oriented, mostly European clientele, who appreciate the simple, comfortable rooms and large bathrooms, the stylish, modern interiors and the great views from the breakfast room. Prices are highly competitive.

### Maritim proArte Hotel Berlin
MAP K4 ■ Friedrichstr. 151 ■ (030) 203 35 ■ www.maritim.de ■ €€
Predominantly styled in tones of green and blue, this modern business hotel boasts almost 300 modern paintings decorating its rooms.

### nhow Hotel
Stralauer Allee 3 ■ (030) 290 29 90 ■ www.nhow-hotels.com/berlin ■ €€
A former warehouse on the Spree River is now a "music and lifestyle" hotel, complete with recording studio. Cutting-edge facilities in rooms include a flat-screen TV that doubles as a mirror.

### Park Plaza Wallstreet Berlin Mitte
MAP L6 ■ Wallstr. 23–24 ■ (030) 847 11 70 ■ www.parkplaza.com ■ €€
The New York Stock Exchange is the theme here, with dollar-bill carpets and murals of stockbrokers' and business maxims all around the building. A pleasant hotel in a central location.

### Q!
MAP P3 ■ Knesebeckstr. 67 ■ (030) 810 06 60 ■ www.hotel-q.com ■ €€
Stylish and discreet, this is a favourite among Hollywood stars. Its rooms are designed as "living landscapes" with furniture integrated into the walls.

### Lux Eleven
MAP J6 ■ Rosa-Luxemburg-Str. 9–13 ■ (030) 936 28 00 ■ www.lux-eleven.com ■ €€€
This stylish, modern apartment hotel is a designer's dream come true. Old townhouses have been converted into mostly white, sleek rooms with all the gadgets of a business hotel. The Prince restaurant and bar, with its understated elegance, adds to the upmarket flair of the hotel.

## Quirky Hotels and Guesthouses

### Eastern Comfort
Mühlenstr. 73–77 ■ (030) 66 76 38 06 ■ www.eastern-comfort.com ■ €
Moored on the Spree near the pretty Oberbaum bridge, this popular boat-hotel draws visitors aiming at the hard-partying districts of Kreuzberg and Friedrichshain. Some 24 snug berths are spread over two decks. White sandy beach and bits of old Berlin Wall nearby.

### Ostel
Wriezener Karree 5 ■ (030) 25 76 86 60 ■ www.ostel.eu ■ €
Located in Berlin's trendy Mitte district, Ostel is designed to look like a communist-era hotel. The choice of rooms includes doubles with shared or private bathrooms, rooms with double- or triple-decker bunk beds and apartments that can sleep up to six people. However, the hotel does not have an on-site restaurant.

### Scube Park Columbia Berlin
Columbiadamm 160 ■ (030) 69 80 78 41 ■ scubepark.berlin ■ €
These smartly-furnished wooden units in cool Scandinavian design have all the amenities including free Wi-Fi. Located on the grounds of a swimming pool near Tempelhofer Feld, each cabin can take up to four guests, year-round. An affordable hybrid of hotel and campsite.

### 25hours Hotel Bikini
MAP N5 ■ Budapester Str. 40 ■ (030) 26 36 95 94 ■ www.25hours-hotels.com ■ €€
Part of the new Bikini shopping mall, this smart 10-storey hotel offers guests the Monkey Bar, a rooftop restaurant with a 360º panorama and a ringside view of the primate enclosure and elephant house at the city's Zoologischer Garten (see pp42–3). The "jungle sauna" has windows overlooking the green expanse of the Tiergarten.

### Almodóvar Hotel
Boxhagener Str. 83 ■ (030) 692 097 080 ■ www.almodovarhotel.de ■ €€
Berlin's first biohotel flaunts its pedigree with flourish. The in-house Bardot bistro serves organic vegetarian dishes, as well as lactose- and gluten-free and vegan. Every room comes with its own yoga mat. Guests can also relax in the top-level spa and admire the Berlin panorama.

### Arte Luise Kunsthotel
MAP J3 ■ Luisenstr. 19 ■ (030) 28 44 80 ■ www.luise-berlin.com ■ €€
This charming hotel has 50 rooms all individually and imaginatively decorated by local artists, with themes that range from loud pop art to classic Modernism. Near Unter den Linden and the Hauptbahnhof.

### Hollywood Media Hotel
MAP P3 ■ Kurfürsten-damm 202 ■ (030) 88 91 00 ■ www.filmhotel.de ■ €€
Located right on glitzy Kurfürstendamm, this hotel has loads of cinematic knick-knacks including props, movie posters and photos of stars. Each of the 182 rooms is dedicated to a film legend. The owner is Artur Brauner, an esteemed Polish-born film producer.

### Michelberger Hotel
Warschauer Str. 39 ■ (030) 29 77 85 90 ■ www.michelberger-hotel.com ■ €€
Set right in the heart of the Friedrichshain entertainment district, the Michelberger Hotel offers guests quirky urban sophistication and a young, fun dynamic. Amenities include free Wi-Fi and a cool lounge area strewn with books and magazines.

### Propeller Island City Lodge
MAP B5 ■ Albrecht-Achilles Str. 58 ■ (030) 891 90 16 ■ www.propeller-island.de ■ No credit cards ■ €€
If you're staying at this unusual lodge, you will share it with the German audio-visual artist Lars Stroschen, who designed all the rooms himself, each in a unique style.

### Riverside City
MAP J4 ■ Friedrichstr. 106 ■ (030) 28 49 00 ■ www.riverside-mitte.de ■ €€
Housed in a former GDR car dealership, this small hotel combines Baroque features, a spa and an excellent location on the Spree. The interior decor and the excellent service make it a popular choice.

## Cosy Hotels

### Midi Inn City West Kurfürstendamm
MAP P2 ■ Wielandstr. 26 ■ (030) 881 64 85 ■ kudamm.midi-inn.de ■ €
This is Berlin's best small guesthouse close to Ku'damm – a handful of atmospheric rooms, retrofitted in a non-fussy, mock 1920s style. Free Wi-Fi and flatscreen TVs.

### Nürnberger Eck
MAP P5 ■ Nürnberger Str. 24A ■ (030) 235 17 80 ■ www.nuernberger-eck. de ■ €
A 5-minute stroll from Ku'damm, this handsome edifice has been a guest-house since the 1920s. The eight rooms are a time capsule of furnishings. A highlight is the early 20th-century bridal suite, with pink rose wall-paper, carved wooden bedstead and bird motifs.

### Pension Peters
MAP N3 ■ Kantstr. 146 ■ (030) 312 22 78 ■ www.pension-peters-berlin.de ■ €
Located just off café-filled Savignyplatz, this friendly little pension run by a German Swedish crew is thoughtfully furnished, with Belle Epoque details even in the marble fittings and frescoes. Rooms are large and bright – make sure you ask for one overlooking the peaceful rear courtyard.

### Derag Livinghotel Henriette
MAP L6 ■ Neue Roßstr. 13 ■ (030) 24 60 09 00 ■ www. deraghotels.de ■ €€
A stylish hotel with classic decoration – warm oak-panelled walls and thick carpets and curtains adorn the rooms, which are arranged around an inner courtyard. Few hotels in town are better than this, and the service is very friendly.

### Gorki Apartments
MAP G2 ■ Weinbergsweg 25 ■ (030) 48 49 64 80 ■ www.gorkiapartments. com ■ €€
Stylish, self-contained but serviced apartments in a renovated former East Berlin apartment complex. The house is located in the Mitte district so it can be a little noisy on the street-side of the apartments.

### Hotel Johann
MAP G5 ■ Johanniterstr. 8 ■ (030) 225 07 40 ■ www. hotel-johann-berlin.de ■ €€
This small hotel with friendly staff offers moderately priced comfort. It is located in a quiet street a 10-minute walk from the Jüdisches Museum, near an open-air swimming pool complex.

### Hotel-Pension Funk
MAP P4 ■ Fasanenstr. 69 ■ (030) 882 71 93 ■ www. hotel-pensionfunk.de ■ €€
Slightly antiquated guest-house close to Ku'damm, based in the apartment of the silent-film star Asta Nielsen. The rates are unbeatable, while furnishings and service are personal and friendly. There are only 15 rooms, so book in advance.

*For a key to hotel price categories see p172*

### Myer's Hotel
MAP H2 ▪ Metzer Str. 26
▪ (030) 44 01 40 ▪ www.
myershotel.de ▪ €€
A family-run hotel in
the centre of Prenzlauer
Berg ideal for families or
couples. Located in an
historic part of town, the
service is attentive and
the atmosphere relaxed.

### Sarotti Höfe
MAP F6 ▪ Mehringdamm
52–57 ▪ (030) 600 31
68 0 ▪ www.hotel-
sarottihoefe.de ▪ €€
Located in a converted
chocolate factory, this
unique hotel has rooms
with high ceilings and
vintage furniture. A series
of courtyards and stairs
lead to the rooms;
there are no lifts.

### Ackselhaus, Blue Home and Club del Mar
MAP H2 ▪ Belforter Str. 21
▪ (030) 44 33 76 33 ▪ www.
ackselhaus.de ▪ €€€
This small boutique with
a Mediterranean garden
has stylish themed rooms.
It is located near Kollwitzplatz, a popular area with
bustling bars and cafés.

## Hotels in Green Surroundings

### Das Andere Haus VIII
Erich Müller Str. 12
▪ (030) 55 44 03 31
▪ dasanderehaus8.de
▪ No credit cards ▪ €
After the fall of the Wall,
Communist leaders
were interned in this
comely 19th-century
ensemble. The five
guest rooms are, in fact,
converted prison cells
but surprisingly com-
fortable, with buffed
wood floors and sleek
modern bathrooms.

The Rummelsburger
Bucht, a bucolic arm
of the Spree, flows
past nearby.

### Hotel Bayrisches Haus
Im Wildpark/Elisenweg 2,
Potsdam ▪ (0331) 550 50
▪ www.bayrisches-haus.
de ▪ €€
Nestled in a former game
reserve outside Potsdam,
this deluxe take on
Bavarian country living
has marbled bathrooms,
gorgeous linens, the
Michelin-starred Friedrich
Wilhelm restaurant *(see
p161)* and an indoor pool.

### Hotel Müggelsee Berlin
Müggelheimer Damm 145
▪ (030) 65 88 20 ▪ www.
hotel-mueggelsee-berlin.
de ▪ €€
A comfortable hotel on
the Müggelsee, combin-
ing near-unspoilt nature
and closeness to the city.
There are tennis courts,
boat and bicycle hire and
plenty of leisure activities.

### Hotel Seehof am Lietzensee
MAP A4 ▪ Lietzenseeufer
11 ▪ (030) 32 00 20
▪ www.hotel-seehof-
berlin.de ▪ €€
Centrally located in
Charlottenburg, not far
from the Messegelände,
in a picturesque spot on
the Lietzensee. The well-
run hotel has a beautiful
indoor pool as well as a
delightful sun terrace.

### Landhaus Schlachtensee
Bogotastr. 9 ▪ (030) 809
94 70 ▪ www.hotel-
landhaus-schlachtensee.
de ▪ €€
A 20-minute walk from
the Schlachtensee *(see*

*p61)* and Krumme Lanke,
this villa oozes the charm
of old rural Berlin. The
furnishings in its rooms
are a little old-fashioned,
but the service is person-
able. The lovely beach at
Strandbad Wannsee is
just 4 km (2.5 miles away).

### Paulsborn am Grunewaldsee
Hüttenweg 90 ▪ (030) 818
19 10 ▪ www.paulsborn.
de ▪ €€
Sited in the southwestern
Grunewald forest, this hotel
is housed in an 1871
hunt-ing lodge used by
Kaiser Wilhelm II. There
is a restaurant and
lakeside terrace, as well
as riding stables nearby.

### Penta Hotel Berlin-Köpenick
Grünauer Str. 1 ▪ (030)
65 47 90 ▪ www.penta
hotels.com/en/berlin-
koepenick ▪ €€
The slightly sterile and
impersonal atmosphere
of this hotel is more
than made up for by its
location. It is right in the
centre of the southeast-
ern district of Köpenick,
on the banks of the
Dahme River, and
Müggelsee is not far
away. BER airport is
only a few minutes'
drive away by car or
S-Bahn. Free Wi-Fi.

### Spreeidyll-Hotel am Yachthafen
Müggelseedamm 70
▪ (030) 641 94 00 ▪ hotel-
spree-idyll.berlin ▪ €€
A small family-run house
on the Müggelspree, not
far from a bathing beach
and a boat-hire booth –
the ideal place to relax
and forget all about the
hustle and bustle of the
big city, which is, however,

only a short distance to the northwest. Come here to relax and take part in all kinds of watersports.

### Patrick Hellman Schlosshotel

MAP A6 ▪ Brahmsstr. 10 ▪ (030) 895 84 30 ▪ www. schlosshotelberlin.com ▪ €€€

This historic villa has been transformed into an exquisite boutique hotel with luxury furnishings, and a lovely garden, a pool and a sauna.

### Schlossparkhotel

MAP A/B3 ▪ Heubnerweg 2A ▪ (030) 326 90 30 ▪ www.schlossparkhotel. de ▪ €€€

The only hotel near Schloss Charlottenburg, next to the Schlosspark, this is just a few minutes from the west of the city centre. The facilities are good and service is impeccable.There are only 40 rooms.

### Medium-Priced Hotels

### Derag Livinghotel Großer Kurfürst

MAP L6 ▪ Neue Roßstr. 11–12 ▪ (030) 24 60 00 ▪ www.deraghotels.de ▪ €€

Close to the Spree south of the Museumsinsel, the hotel offers guests rooms as well as fully furnished apartments. It also has useful extras, such as a gym, sauna and bike hire.

### Henri Hotel Kurfürstendamm

MAP P4 ▪ Meinekestr. 9 ▪ (030) 88 44 30 ▪ www. hotel-residenz.com ▪ €€

Based in one of the most beautiful old Berlin townhouses near Ku'damm,

this hotel offers guests an intimate, characterful atmosphere. The late-19th-century rooms are tastefully furnished, and the restaurant has outdoor seating in summer.

### Honigmond Garden Hotel

MAP F2 ▪ Invalidenstr. 122 ▪ (030) 28 44 55 77 ▪ www.honigmond.de ▪ €€

Exuding nostalgia with a hint of luxury, this hotel is set within a listed 1845 building and has original antiques, stucco ceilings and a pretty courtyard with a Japanese fishpond.

### Hotel Amano

MAP G2 ▪ Auguststr. 43 ▪ (030) 809 41 50 ▪ www. amanogroup.com ▪ €€

In a narrow street lined with galleries, this chic hotel is an excellent base from which to explore the Hackescher Markt area, Scheunenviertel and the Museumsinsel. Rooms and fully serviced apartments are available. Open bathrooms make this a better choice for couples. The view from the roof terrace is spectacular, and extras such as bike hire, pedestrian navigation systems and iPod walking tours help guests make the most of their stay.

### Hotel Mani

MAP G2 ▪ Torstr. 136 ▪ (030) 53 02 80 80 ▪ www. amanogroup.de ▪ €€

A heartbeat from lively Rosenthaler Platz, this stylish hotel is a favourite with fashion models and weekend-breakers set to party. Its rooms are compact but beautifully appointed, with parquet

floors and ultramodern, open-plan bathrooms. Rent out bicycles from the reception and explore nearby modern art galleries, well-known landmarks and lovely cafés.

### Hotel-Pension Kastanienhof

MAP G2 ▪ Kastanienallee 65 ▪ (030) 44 30 50 ▪ www.kastanienhof.biz ▪ €€

A charming hotel set in a turn-of-the-20th-century building. The rooms are basic but well equipped. An ideal base for exploring Prenzlauer Berg.

### Riehmers Hofgarten

MAP F6 ▪ Yorckstr. 83 ▪ (030) 78 09 88 00 ▪ www.riehmershofgarten.de ▪ €€

Here you can live the life of a Prussian officer. This remarkable hotel is part of a large complex of 19th-century Neo-Gothic buildings – old Kreuzberg apartments, with sombre rooms and elegant bathrooms, are the perfect setting for trying out the 19th-century life-style. The hotel has free Wi-Fi and docking stations in every room. The restaurant has contemporary variations of traditional dishes.

### Bleibtreu-Hotel

MAP P3 ▪ Bleibtreustr. 31 ▪ (030) 88 47 40 ▪ www. bleibtreu.com ▪ €€€

The hotel's stylish inner courtyard – reminiscent of Tuscany and bright, tasteful rooms are an oasis of tranquillity. The international clientele is equally stylish. The hotel has its own restaurant, pool and sauna.

*For a key to hotel price categories see p172*

### Ellington Hotel Berlin

MAP P5 ▪ Nürnberger Str. 50–55 ▪ (030) 68 31 50 ▪ www.ellington-hotel.de ▪ €€€

This distinctive hotel is a beacon of modern design set within listed 1920s Bauhaus architecture. It is conveniently located close to the KaDeWe, Ku'damm and the zoo, offering a stylish alternative to a young, international clientele.

### Hackescher Markt

MAP J5 ▪ Große Präsidentenstr. 8 ▪ (030) 28 00 30 ▪ www.hotel-hackescher-markt.com ▪ €€€

A charming hotel in an unbeatable location right opposite Hackesche Höfe. Its large, bright, elegantly furnished rooms, friendly service, excellent restaurant and attractive patio guarantee a pleasant stay.

## Hotels for Business Travellers

### Leonardo Airport Hotel Berlin Brandenburg

Schwalbenweg 18 ▪ (030) 67 90 20 ▪ www.leonardo-hotels.com ▪ €

Conveniently situated near Berlin Brandenburg Airport in Schönefeld, this hotel is ideal for brief business trips or for budget visitors. Service is efficient and friendly.

### Arcotel John F

MAP K5 ▪ Werdescher Markt 11 ▪ (030) 405 04 60 ▪ www.arcotelhotels.com/JohnF ▪ €€

Very conveniently located within walking distance of Unter den Linden and the stores of Friedrichstraße, and midway between the

Museumsinsel and Gendarmenmarkt, this is a smart, modern hotel with a wealth of business and conference facilities. The breakfast includes their exclusive sparkling wine and vegan food options.

### Leonardo Hotel Berlin Mitte

MAP J4 • Bertolt-Brecht-Platz 4 • (030) 374 40 50 00 • www.leonardo-hotels.de • €€

This four-star hotel has modern, air-conditioned rooms, equipped with tea and coffee facilities. The hotel also offers 24-hour room service, a luxurious business lounge, a sauna and a fitness centre. It is located within walking distance of the Friedrichstrasse train station, the Reichstag building and many government institutions.

### The Mandala Suites

MAP L4 ▪ Friedrichstr. 185–190 ▪ (030) 20 29 20 ▪ www.themandalasuites.de ▪ €€

Sister establishment of the Mandala Hotel in Potsdamer Platz, this is also a central apartment hotel with suites elegantly equipped as offices and offering a secretarial service. A maid service is available and news-papers are delivered each morning.

### Wyndham Berlin Excelsior Hotel

MAP N4 ▪ Hardenbergstr. 14 ▪ (030) 315 50 ▪ www.hotel-excelsior.de ▪ €€

Located next to Amerika Haus, the hotel is decorated in a restrained style. Moderate prices, friendly staff, a gym and a brasserie make this a top choice.

### Estrel Residence Congress Hotel

Sonnenallee 225 ▪ (030) 683 12 25 22 ▪ www.estrel.com ▪ €€€

With more than 1,000 rooms, this hotel is one of Europe's largest, offering three- to four-star service. Its numerous conference rooms and latest technological equipment make it the perfect venue for international business meetings and the individual business traveller.

### Hilton Berlin

MAP L4 ▪ Mohrenstr. 30 ▪ (030) 20 23 00 ▪ www.hilton.de ▪ €€€

Executives favour this hotel because of its central location and the views across the Gendarmenmarkt and the Französischer and Berliner Doms, and specially designed executive rooms. There is a business centre, and a full secretarial service is included. The hotel also offers pet services, such as baskets and water and food bowls.

### NH Hotel Berlin-Kreuzberg

MAP H4 ▪ Heinrich-Heine-Platz 11 ▪ (030) 27 80 40 ▪ www.nh-hotels.com ▪ €€€

This hotel is the best choice if your business requires a longer stay in town. Not far from the Museumsinsel and Nikolaiviertel quarter, the apartments are equipped with desks and kitchens.

### Pullman Berlin Schweizerhof

MAP N5 ▪ Budapester Str. 25 ▪ (030) 269 60 ▪ www.pullmanhotels.com ▪ €€€

One of Berlin's top luxury hotels right in the centre of western Berlin, the

Schweizerhof features clean lines, elegant furnishings and a large, well-designed fitness area.

## Sofitel Berlin Kurfürstendamm

MAP P4 ■ Augsburger Str. 41 ■ (030) 800 99 90 ■ www.sofitel-berlin-kurfuerstendamm.com ■ €€€

Designed by star architect Jan Kleihues, this hotel boasts the largest rooms in Berlin and spectacular views over Ku'damm. Other perks include free Wi-Fi, efficient service and a helpful concierge desk.

## Budget Hotels and Hostels

### BaxPax Kreuzberg

MAP H5 ■ Schlesische Str. 18 ■ (030) 69 51 83 22 ■ www.baxpax.de ■ €

Much better than a youth hostel yet much cheaper than a guesthouse, this refurbished factory is an unusual place to stay – you may be sleeping in a decommissioned VW Beetle. Plus you'll meet friendly young people from around the world. BaxPax is in Kreuzberg, and less suitable for those over 30.

### BaxPax Mitte

MAP F2 ■ Chausseestr. 102 ■ (030) 28 39 09 65 ■ www.baxpax.de ■ €

Find 20 funky, themed rooms at this cool hostel close to Mitte's hotspots, complete with Internet café and laundry service but no breakfast.

### Bed and Breakfast Ring

www.bandb-ring.de ■ No credit cards ■ €

This hotel offers shared accommodation in private homes all over town. You'll normally have your own room with one or two beds or an apartment to yourself. The rooms are mostly priced moderately, from €25 per person.

### The Circus Hotel

MAP G2 ■ Weinbergsweg 1A ■ (030) 20 00 39 39 ■ www.circus-berlin.de ■ €

Near Alexanderplatz, this hostel offers great value accommodation close to many sights. Dorm beds and single, double and triple rooms are available as well as a rooftop apartment with good views. There is a restaurant, a garden courtyard, and bike and scooter rental.

### EastSeven Berlin Hostel

MAP H2 ■ Schwedter Str. 7 ■ (030) 93 62 22 40 ■ www.eastseven.de ■ €

In a lively Prenzlauer Berg neighbourhood brimming with bars and cafés, this friendly hostel is also just a 20-minute walk from Alexanderplatz and the Museumsinsel. There is a garden and free Wi-Fi.

### die fabrik

Schlesische Str. 18 ■ (030) 611 71 16 ■ www.diefabrik.com ■ No credit cards ■ €

This hotel, whose name means "the factory", is a guesthouse, youth hostel and an alternative youth and arts centre in deepest Kreuzberg. It attracts backpackers from around the world, hoping to meet locals and other travellers.

### Gay Hostel

MAP D5 ■ Motzstr. 28 ■ (030) 21 00 57 09 ■ www.gay-hostel.de ■ €

Located in the heart of Schöneberg's gay quarter, this clean, hospitable and well-equipped hostel plugs visitors into the local scene with a booklet of local discounts. There are shared and private rooms on offer, and all have lockers, flatscreen TVs, coffee and free Wi-Fi.

### Grand Hostel Berlin

MAP F5 ■ Tempelhofer Ufer 14 ■ (030) 20 09 54 50 ■ www.grandhostel-berlin.de ■ €

Housed in an 1874 building, this friendly hostel with helpful staff is in a central location in trendy Kreuzberg. It offers safe, clean, spacious dorms and private rooms, some with their own bathrooms. There is also a lounge with computers, free Wi-Fi, bike rental and a large buffet for breakfast.

### Hotel Transit

MAP F6 ■ Hagelberger Straße 53–4 ■ (030) 789 04 70 ■ www.hotel-transit.de ■ €

Housed on two floors of a former factory, this international youth hostel is located in a lively area close to the town centre. It has 50 large loft-style rooms, including singles, doubles and dorms.

### Hüttenpalast

MAP H6 ■ Hobrechtstr. 66 ■ (030) 37 30 58 06 ■ www.huettenpalast.de ■ €

Tucked away in an old Neukölln vacuum-cleaner factory, this unique boutique hotel lets you slumber in designer caravans and Alpine huts placed inside the factory. Relax in the peaceful green courtyard, or sample organic treats in the streetside café.

*For a key to hotel price categories see p172*

# General Index

# Acknowledgments

## Author
Historian Jürgen Scheunemann has published several documentary and photographic books on Berlin and other destinations. His award-winning articles are published in travel magazines and daily newspapers in Germany and the US, and have appeared in the Berlin daily *Tagesspiegel*, among others.

**Additional contributor**
Jeremy Gray

**Publishing Director** Georgina Dee

**Publisher** Vivien Antwi

**Design Director** Phil Ormerod

**Editorial** Ankita Awasthi-Tröger, Michelle Crane, Rachel Fox, Freddie Marriage, Fíodhna Ní Ghríofa, Scarlett O'Hara, Sally Schafer, Avijit Sengupta, Christine Stroyan

**Design** Richard Czapnik, Sunita Gahir

**Picture Research** Phoebe Lowndes, Susie Peachey, Ellen Root, Oran Tarjan

**Cartography** Dominic Beddow, Simonetta Giori, Mohammad Hassan, Suresh Kumar, Casper Morris

**DTP** Jason Little, George Nimmo, Azeem Siddiqui

**Production** Linda Dare

**Factchecker** Petra Falkenberg

**Proofreader** Anna Streiffert

**Indexer** Hilary Bird

**Illustrator** www.chrisorr.com
First edition created by DK Verlag, Munich

## Commissioned Photography
Dorota Jarymowicz and Mariusz Jarymowicz, Britta Jaschinski, Rough Guides/Tim Draper, Rough Guides/Diana Jarvis, Rough Guides/Roger d'Olivere Mapp, Rough Guides/Roger Norum

**Revisions** Hansa Babra, Subhadeep Biswas, Bharti Karakoti, Priyanka Kumar, Daniel Mosseri, Adrian Potts, Farah Sheikh, Anupama Shukla, Lucy Sienkowska, Aakanksha Singh, Rituraj Singh, Hollie Teague, Ajay Verma

## Picture Credits
The publisher would like to thank the following for their kind permission to reproduce their photographs:

(Key: a-above; b-below/bottom; c-centre; f-far; l-left; r-right; t-top)

**123RF.com:** Heike Jestram 150cla.

**4Corners:** SIME/Giovanni Simeone 2tr, 44-5.

**Alamy Images:** AA World Travel Library 13br; A. Astes 62bl; Agencja Fotograficzna Caro 30-31c; B.O'Kane 26tl; Pat Behnke 130cra; Bildagentur-online/Schickert 136tl, 139bl; Bildarchiv Monheim GmbH 89cla; Agencja Fotograficzna Caro 2tl, 8-9,
16cl, 20crb, 69cr, 125tl, 140tr; 153cl; David Davies 33cra; dpa picture alliance 88br, 115crb; dpics 11ca; epa european pressphoto agency b.v. 63bc; FineArt 40br; Hernis 57cr, 125br; 138tl; Peter Horree 32br, 59tl; image-BROKER 34bl, 36crb, 42cla, 47br, 89bc, 139tl; imageBROKER/Ingo Schulz 120t; INTERFOTO 37tl, 37b; Keystone Pictures USA 158bl; LOOK Die Bildagentur der Fotografen GmbH 14br; Lothar Steiner 155tr; MARKA 48; Barry Mason 100cla; Iain Masterton 25tr, 39tl, 146tc; Nature Picture Library 43cra; Novarc Images 137br; Stefano Paterna 42bl; Roussel Photography 121bl; Riccardo Sala 35crb; John Stark 99cla; travelstock44 107tl; Werner Otto 33cl; Westend61 GmbH 21bc; Julie G Woodhouse 23cl, 123clb; World History Archive 46br.

**Ankerklause:** olfgang Borrs 134tl.

**Becketts Kopf:** 72cr.

**Berlinale:** Andreas Teich 80tl.

**Berliner Kaffeerösterei:** 126cl.

**Borchardt:** 71cl.

**Bröhan-Museum:** 53b.

**Clärchens Ballhaus:** Bernd Schoenberger 75crb.

**Corbis:** Bettmann 47tl; Eye Ubiquitous/Stephen Rafferty 88tl; Hemis/Borgese Maurizio 116cra, / Ludovic Maisant © 2015 The Andy Warhol Foundation for the Visual Arts, Inc./Artists Rights Society (ARS), New York and DACS, London 2015 53tl; Hulton-Deutsch Collection 49tc; incamerastock /Iain Masterton 38-9; Ocean/John Harper 110-1; Reuters/Fabrizio Bensch 27tl; Reuters/Tobias Schwarz 152t; Schoening 16bl, 119tr; VCG Wilson 40cb, 52t.

**DDR Museum:** 90tl.

**Deutches Technikmuseum/ © SDTB:** C. Kirchner 64tl.

**Deutsche Kinemathek:** Hans Scherhaufer 22tl, Marian Stefanowski 20cb, 22crb.

**Deutsche Oper:** Marcus Lieberenz 66tr.

**Deutsches Historisches Museum, Berlin:** 18bl.

**Dreamstime.com:** Rostislav Ageev 11cr; Albo 27b; Andreykr 128tl; Atosan 15cr; David Beaulieu 1, 4cra; Michal Bednarek 86bl; Goran Bogicevic 21tl, 96tr; Gunold Brunbauer 107cb; Buschmen 33br, 118tl, 128cl; Carolannefreeling 15tl, 144tl; Ccat82 103t,113t; Claudiodivizia 7tl, 10bl; 11clb, 24br, 39bc, 41tl; Mikael Damkier 10clb; Digitalsignal 95tr; Matthew Dixon 10br, 32-3c; Dennis Dolkens 129cr; Christian Draghici 4crb, 46t, 55t, 79bl, 102tl, 151tl, 159bl; Elenaburn 86t, 104bl; Elxeneize 16-7c, 158cra; Alexandre Fagundes De Fagundes 16crb,17tl, 52crb; Joerg Franzen 55bc; Kevin George 61c, 84tl, 147cla; Simone Gobbo 11tl; Gudmund1 14cl; Jorg Hackemann 4clb; Hai Huy Ton That 133br; Hel080808 12bl, 87cl; Hugoht 146b; Juliane Jacobs 130bl; Dragan Jovanovic 13clb; Junede 122-3t; Tom K 58tl, 85tr; Katatonia82 98tl; Sergey Kelin 4b, 11crb, 17cb, 35c, 60bl; Jan Kranendonk 6cla; Axel Lauer 94tl; Miroslav Liska 34-5cla; Locha79 7cr; Markwaters 15bl, 56br, 114bl, 136cl; Mateuszolszowy 41b; Matteocozzi 114tr; Lucian Milasan 12cl; Mishkacz 96bl; Luciano Mortula 51tc, 129tr; 145t; Kalin Nedkov 3tr, 162-3; Noppasinw 56cl, 79tr; Olena Buyskykh 25clb; Andrey Omelyanchuk 61tr; Sean Pavone 24-5c, 157tr; Petarneychev 78tl; Andrey Popov 12-3c;

Peter Probst 60cr; Rhombur 81tr; Ricochet69 132cl; Romangorielov 10cra; Rudi1976 3tl,4t, 82-3; Mario Savoia 30cl; Spongecake 156tl; Petr Švec 124t; Svenverk 154bl; Totalpics 142-3; Anibal Trejo 59b, 98cb,112tl; Ference Ungor 138c; Mirko Vitali 80bc; Vojtech Vlk 145br; Vvoevale 7tr, 24cl, 26bc, 76tl; Jannis Werner 152br; Jeff Whyte 54cla; Anastasiia Ylitko 11br, 43tl; Alex Zarubin 116bc.

**Facil Restaurant:** Lukas Roth 71tr.

**©Filmpark Babelsberg:** 65bl.

**Restaurant Florian:** 127tr.

**Friedrichstadt-Palast:** Götz Schleser 67tr.

**Brauhaus Georgbrau:** 108bl.

**Getty Images:** 48cr b; DeAgostini 51bc; John Freeman 31cra; Sean Gallup 68clb; Heritage Images 19bc, /The Merchant Georg Gisze, 1532 by Hans Holbein, the Younger (1497-1543) collection of the Staatliche Museen, Berlin 40cla; Lonely Planet 36tl; Andreas Rentz 63ca; Travelstock44 - Juergen Held 20-1c; ullstein bild 132br.

**Gugelhof:** 141cl.

**Restaurant & Café Heider:** 161crb.

**Hotel Adlon Kempinski:** Restaurant Quarrè 117tr

**House of Weekend:** 74b.

**iStockphoto.com:** Robert Herhold 21bl.

**Klunkerkranich:** Julian Nelken 134br.

**Kulturforum Berlin:** © Philipp Eder 4cla, 38cl, 38crb, 38bl.

**Kunst-Werke:** 99br.

**Labyrinth Kindermuseum:** 64bl.

**La Lavanderia Vecchia:** 135tr.

**James MacDonald:** 73bl.

**Matrix:** 148bl.

**Museum für Naturkunde:** A. Dittmann 64cr.

**Nola's:** 101tr.

**Oxymoron:** 100br.

**Ratskeller Kopenick:** 149cl.

**Refugium:** 93tl.

**Reinstoff:** 70tl.

**Robert Harding Picture Library:** Hubertus Blume 31tl; Siegfried Grassegger 20bc; Karl Johaentges 42-3c; Thomas Robbin 13tl, 30clb; Ingo Schulz 28-9, 33tl; Urs Schweitzer 43br; Lothar Steiner 23b.

**Schwules Museum:** Tobias Wille 69b.

**Sra Bua Bar:** 92bl.

**SuperStock:** Javier Larrea / age fotostock 18ca.

**Victoria Bar:** 73t.

**Zillestube:** 109tr.

**Zoologischer Garten, Berlin:** 42crb.

**Zur Letzten Instanz:** 108tc.

### Cover
Front and spine – **iStockphoto.com** Deejpilot
Back – **Dreamstime.com:** minnystock.

### Pull out map cover
iStockphoto.com Deejpilot

All other images are: © Dorling Kindersley. For further information see www.dkimages.com.

*As a guide to abbreviations in visitor information blocks:* **Adm** = admission charge.

Penguin Random House

Printed and bound in China

First published in the UK in 2002 by Dorling Kindersley Limited 80 Strand, London WC2R 0RL

Copyright 2002, 2018 © Dorling Kindersley Limited

A Penguin Random House Company

18 19 20 21 10 9 8 7 6 5 4 3 2 1

**Reprinted with revisions 2004, 2006, 2007, 2008, 2009, 2010, 2011, 2012, 2013, 2014, 2016 (twice), 2017, 2018**

A CIP catalogue record is available from the British Library.

ISBN 978 0 2413 1158 5

MIX
Paper from responsible sources
FSC™ C018179

## SPECIAL EDITIONS OF DK TRAVEL GUIDES

DK Travel Guides can be purchased in bulk quantities at discounted prices for use in promotions or as premiums. We are also able to offer special editions and personalized jackets, corporate imprints, and excerpts from all of our books, tailored specifically to meet your own needs.

To find out more, please contact:

in the US
**specialsales@dk.com**

in the UK
**travelguides@uk.dk.com**

in Canada
**specialmarkets@dk.com**

in Australia
**penguincorporatesales@ penguinrandomhouse.com.au**

# Phrase Book

## In an Emergency

| | | |
|---|---|---|
| Where is the telephone? | Wo ist das Telefon? | voh ist duss tel-e-fone? |
| Help! | Hilfe! | hilf-uh |
| Please call a doctor | Bitte rufen Sie einen Arzt | bitt-uh roof'n zee ine-en artst |
| Please call the police | Bitte rufen Sie die Polizei | bitt-uh roof'n zee dee poli-tsy |
| Please call the fire brigade | Bitte rufen Sie die Feuerwehr | bitt-uh roof'n zee dee foyer-vayr |
| Stop! | Halt! | hult |

## Communication Essentials

| | | |
|---|---|---|
| Yes | Ja | yah |
| No | Nein | nine |
| Please | Bitte | bitt-uh |
| Thank you | Danke | dunk-uh |
| Excuse me | Verzeihung | fair-tsy-hoong |
| Hello | Guten Tag | goot-en tahk |
| Goodbye | Auf Wiedersehen | owf-veed-er-zay-ern |
| Good evening | Guten Abend | goot'n-ahb'nt |
| Good night | Gute Nacht | goot-uh nukht |
| Until tomorrow | Bis morgen | biss morg'n |
| See you | Tschüss | chooss |
| What is that? | Was ist das? | voss ist duss |
| Why? | Warum? | var-room |
| Where? | Wo? | voh |
| When? | Wann? | vunn |
| today | heute | hoyt-uh |
| tomorrow | morgen | morg'n |
| month | Monat | mohn-aht |
| night | Nacht | nukht |
| afternoon | Nachmittag | nahkh-mit-tahk |
| morning | Morgen | morg'n |
| year | Jahr | yar |
| there | dort | dort |
| here | hier | hear |
| week | Woche | vokh-uh |
| yesterday | gestern | gest'n |
| evening | Abend | ahb'nt |

## Useful Phrases

| | | |
|---|---|---|
| How are you? (informal) | Wie geht's? | vee gayts |
| Fine, thanks | Danke, es geht mir gut | dunk-uh, es gayt meer goot |
| Where is/are? | Wo ist/sind…? | voh ist/sind |
| How far is it to…? | Wie weit ist es…? | vee vite ist ess |
| Do you speak English? | Sprechen Sie Englisch? | shpresh'n zee eng-glish |
| I don't understand. | Ich verstehe nicht | ish fair-shtay-uh nisht |
| Could you speak more slowly? | Könnten Sie langsamer sprechen? | kurnt-en zee langsamer shpresh'n |

## Useful Words

| | | |
|---|---|---|
| large | gross | grohss |
| small | klein | kline |
| hot | heiss | hyce |
| cold | kalt | kult |
| good | gut | goot |
| bad | böse/schlech | burss-uh/shlesht |
| open | geöffnet | g'urff-nett |
| closed | geschlossen | g'shloss'n |
| left | links | links |
| right | rechts | reshts |
| straight ahead | geradeaus | g'rah-der-owss |

## Making a Telephone Call

| | | |
|---|---|---|
| I would like to make a phone call | Ich möchte telefonieren | ish mer-shtuh tel-e-fon-eer'n |
| I'll try again later | Ich versuche noch ein mal später | ish fair-zookh-uh nokh ine-mull shpay-ter |
| Can I leave a message? | Kann ich eine Nachricht hinterlassen? | kan ish ine-uh nakh-risht hint-er-lahss-en |
| answer phone | Anrufbeantworter | an-roof-be-ahnt-vort-er |
| telephone card | Telefonkarte | tel-e-fohn-kart-uh |
| receiver | Hörer | hur-er |
| mobile | Handy | han-dee |
| engaged (busy) | besetzt | b'zetst |
| wrong number | Falsche Verbindung | falsh-uh fair-bin-doong |

## Sightseeing

| | | |
|---|---|---|
| library | Bibliothek | bib-leo-tek |
| entrance ticket | Eintrittskarte | ine-tritz-kart-uh |
| cemetery | Friedhof | freed-hofe |
| train station | Bahnhof | barn-hofe |
| gallery | Galerie | gall-er-ree |
| information | Auskunft | owss-koonft |
| church | Kirche | keersh-uh |
| garden | Garten | gart'n |
| palace/castle | Palast/Schloss | pallast/shloss |
| place (square) | Platz | plats |
| bus stop | Haltestelle | hal-te-shtel-uh |
| national holiday | Nationalfeiertag | nats-yon-ahl-fire-tahk |
| theatre | Theater | tay-aht-er |
| free admission | Eintritt frei | ine-tritt fry |

## Shopping

| | | |
|---|---|---|
| Do you have/ Is there…? | Gibt es…? | geept ess |
| How much does it cost? | Was kostet das? | voss kost't duss? |
| When do you open/ close | Wann öffnen Sie? schliessen Sie? | vunn off'n zee shlees'n zee |
| this | das | duss |
| expensive | teuer | toy-er |
| cheap | preiswert | price-vurt |
| size | Grösse | gruhs-uh |
| number | Nummer | noom-er |
| colour | Farbe | farb-uh |
| brown | braun | brown |
| black | schwarz | shvarts |
| red | rot | roht |
| blue | blau | blau |
| green | grün | groon |
| yellow | gelb | gelp |

## Types of Shop

| | | |
|---|---|---|
| antique shop | Antiquariat | antik-var-yat |

| | | |
|---|---|---|
| chemist (pharmacy) | **Apotheke** | appo-**tay**-kuh |
| bank | **Bank** | bunk |
| market | **Markt** | markt |
| travel agency | **Reisebüro** | rye-zer-boo-roe |
| department store | **Warenhaus** | vahr'n-hows |
| chemist's drugstore | **Drogerie** | droog-er-ree |
| hairdresser | **Friseur** | freezz-er |
| newspaper kiosk | **Zeitungskiosk** | tsytoongs-kee-osk |
| bookshop | **Buchhandlung** | bookh-hant-loong |
| bakery | **Bäckerei** | beck-er-eye |
| post office | **Post** | posst |
| shop/store | **Geschäft/Laden** | gush-eft/lard'n |
| film processing shop | **Photogeschäft** | fo-to-gush-eft |
| self-service shop | **Selbstbedienungsladen** | selpst-bed-ee-nungs-lard'n |
| shoe shop | **Schuhladen** | shoo-lard'n |
| clothes shop store | **Kleiderladen Boutique** | klyder-lard'n boo-teek-uh |
| food shop | **Lebensmittelgeschäft** | lay-bens-mittel-gush-eft |
| glass, porcelain | **Glas, Porzellan** | glars, Port-sellahn |

## Staying in a Hotel

| | | |
|---|---|---|
| Do you have any vacancies? | **Haben Sie noch Zimmer frei?** | harb'n zee nokh tsimm-er-fry |
| with twin beds? | **mit zwei Betten?** | mitt tsvy bett'n |
| with a double bed? | **mit einem Doppelbett?** | mitt ine'm dopp'lbet |
| with a bath? | **mit Bad?** | mitt bart |
| with a shower? | **mit Dusche?** | mitt doosh-uh |
| I have a reservation | **Ich habe eine Reservierung** | ish harb-uh ine-uh rez-er-veer-oong |
| key | **Schlüssel** | shlooss'l |
| porter | **Pförtner** | pfert-ner |

## Eating Out

| | | |
|---|---|---|
| Do you have a table for . . .? | **Haben Sie einen Tisch für . . .?** | harb'n zee ine-uhn Tisch für . . .? |
| I would like to reserve a table | **Ich möchte eine Reservierung machen** | ish mer-shtuh ine-uh rezer-veer-oong makh'n |
| I'm a vegetarian | **Ich bin Vegetarier** | ish bin vegg-er-tah-ree-er |
| Waiter! | **Herr Ober!** | hair oh-bare! |
| The bill (check), please | **Die Rechnung, bitte** | dee resh-noong bitt-uh |
| breakfast | **Frühstück** | froo-shtook |
| lunch | **Mittagessen** | mit-targ-ess'n |
| dinner | **Abendessen** | arb'nt-ess'n |
| bottle | **Flasche** | flush-uh |
| dish of the day | **Tagesgericht** | tahg-es-gur-isht |
| main dish | **Hauptgericht** | howpt-gur-isht |
| dessert | **Nachtisch** | nakh-tish |
| cup | **Tasse** | tass-uh |
| wine list | **Weinkarte** | vine-kart-uh |
| tankard | **Krug** | khroog |
| glass | **Glas** | glars |
| spoon | **Löffel** | lerff'l |
| teaspoon | **Teelöffel** | tay-lerff'l |
| tip | **Trinkgeld** | trink-gelt |
| knife | **Messer** | mess-er |
| starter (appetizer) | **Vorspeise** | for-shpize-uh |
| the bill | **Rechnung** | resh-noong |
| plate | **Teller** | tell-er |
| fork | **Gabel** | gahb'l |

## Menu Decoder

| | | |
|---|---|---|
| **Aal** | arl | eel |
| **Apfel** | upf'l | apple |
| **Apfelschorle** | upf'l-shoorl-uh | apple juice with sparkling mineral water |
| **Apfelsine** | upf'l-seen-uh | orange |
| **Aprikose** | upri-kawz-uh | apricot |
| **Artischocke** | arti-shokh-uh | artichoke |
| **Aubergine** | or-ber-jeen-uh | aubergine (eggplant) |
| **Banane** | bar-narn-uh | banana |
| **Beefsteack** | beef-stayk | steak |
| **Bier** | beer | beer |
| **Bockwurst** | bokh-voorst | a type of sausage |
| **Bohnensuppe** | burn-en-zoop-uh | bean soup |
| **Branntwein** | brant-vine | spirits |
| **Bratkartoffeln** | brat-kar-toff'ln | fried potatoes |
| **Bratwurst** | brat-voorst | fried sausage |
| **Brötchen** | bret-tchen | bread roll |
| **Brot** | 'brot | bread |
| **Brühe** | bruh-uh | broth |
| **Butter** | boot-ter | butter |
| **Champignon** | shum-pin-yong | mushroom |
| **Currywurst** | kha-ree-voorst | sausage with curry sauce |
| **Dill** | dill | dill |
| **Ei** | eye | egg |
| **Eis** | ice | ice/ ice cream |
| **Ente** | ent-uh | duck |
| **Erdbeeren** | ayrt-beer'n | strawberries |
| **Fisch** | fish | fish |
| **Forelle** | for-ell-uh | trout |
| **Frikadelle** | Frika-dayl-uh | rissole/ hamburger |
| **Gans** | ganns | goose |
| **Garnele** | gar-nayl-uh | prawn/shrimp |
| **gebraten** | g'braat'n | fried |
| **gegrillt** | g'grilt | grilled |
| **gekocht** | g'kokht | boiled |
| **geräuchert** | g'rowk-ert | smoked |
| **Geflügel** | g'floog'l | poultry |
| **Gemüse** | g'mooz-uh | vegetables |
| **Grütze** | grurt-ser | groats, gruel |
| **Gulasch** | goo-lush | goulash |
| **Gurke** | goork-uh | gherkin |
| **Hammelbraten** | hamm'l-braat'n | roast mutton |
| **Hähnchen** | haynsh'n | chicken |
| **Hering** | hair-ing | herring |
| **Himbeeren** | him-beer'n | raspberries |
| **Honig** | hoe-nikh | honey |
| **Kaffee** | kaf-fay | coffee |
| **Kalbfleisch** | kalp-flysh | veal |
| **Kaninchen** | ka-neensh'n | rabbit |
| **Karpfen** | karpf'n | carp |
| **Kartoffelpüree** | kar-toff'l-poor-ay | mashed potatoes |

| German | Pronunciation | English |
|---|---|---|
| Käse | *kayz-uh* | cheese |
| Kaviar | *kar-vee-ar* | caviar |
| Knoblauch | *k'nob-lowkh* | garlic |
| Knödel | *k'nerd'l* | noodle |
| Kohl | *koal* | cabbage |
| Kopfsalat | *kopf-zal-aat* | lettuce |
| Krebs | *krayps* | crab |
| Kuchen | *kookh'n* | cake |
| Lachs | *lahkhs* | salmon |
| Leber | *lay-ber* | liver |
| mariniert | *mari-neert* | marinated |
| Marmelade | *marmer-lard-uh* | marmalade, jam |
| Meerrettich | *may-re-tish* | horseradish |
| Milch | *milsh* | milk |
| Mineral- wasser | *minn-er-arl- vuss-er* | mineral water |
| Möhre | *mer-uh* | carrot |
| Nuss | *nooss* | nut |
| Öl | *erl* | oil |
| Olive | *o-leev-uh* | olive |
| Petersilie | *payt-er-zee-li-uh* | parsley |
| Pfeffer | *pfeff-er* | pepper |
| Pfirsich | *pfir-zish* | peach |
| Pflaumen | *pflow-men* | plum |
| Pommes frites | *pomm-fritt* | chips/ French fries |
| Quark | *kvark* | soft cheese |
| Radieschen | *ra-deesh'n* | radish |
| Rinderbraten | *rind-er-brat'n* | joint of beef |
| Rinderroulade | *rind-er-roo- lard-uh* | beef olive |
| Rindfleisch | *rint-flysh* | beef |
| Rippchen | *rip-sh'n* | cured pork rib |
| Rotkohl | *roht-koal* | red cabbage |
| Rüben | *rhoob'n* | turnip |
| Rührei | *rhoo-er-eye* | scrambled eggs |
| Saft | *zuft* | juice |
| Salat | *zal-aat* | salad |
| Salz | *zults* | salt |
| Salzkartoffeln | *zults-kar-toff'l* | boiled potatoes |
| Sauerkirschen | *zow-er-keersh'n* | cherries |
| Sauerkraut | *zow-er-krowt* | sauerkraut |
| Sekt | *zekt* | sparkling wine |
| Senf | *zenf* | mustard |
| scharf | *sharf* | spicy |
| Schaschlik | *shash-lik* | kebab |
| Schlagsahne | *shlahgg-zarn-uh* | whipped cream |
| Schnittlauch | *shnit-lowkhk* | chives |
| Schnitzel | *shnitz'l* | veal or pork cutlet |
| Schweinefleisch | *shvine-flysh* | pork |
| Spargel | *shparg'l* | asparagus |
| Spiegelei | *shpeeg'l-eye* | fried egg |
| Spinat | *shpin-art* | spinach |
| Tee | *tay* | tea |
| Tomate | *tom-art-uh* | tomato |
| Wassermelone | *vuss-er- me-lohn-uh* | watermelon |
| Wein | *vine* | wine |
| Weintrauben | *vine-trowb'n* | grapes |
| Wiener Würstchen | *veen-er voorst-sh'n* | frankfurter |
| Zander | *tsan-der* | pike-perch |
| Zitrone | *tsi-trohn-uh* | lemon |
| Zucker | *tsook-er* | sugar |
| Zwieback | *tsvee-ba* | rusk |
| Zwiebel | *tsveeb'l* | onion |

# Numbers

| | German | Pronunciation |
|---|---|---|
| 0 | null | *nool* |
| 1 | eins | *eye'ns* |
| 2 | zwei | *tsvy* |
| 3 | drei | *dry* |
| 4 | vier | *feer* |
| 5 | fünf | *foonf* |
| 6 | sechs | *zex* |
| 7 | sieben | *zeeb'n* |
| 8 | acht | *uhkht* |
| 9 | neun | *noyn* |
| 10 | zehn | *tsayn* |
| 11 | elf | *elf* |
| 12 | zwölf | *tserlf* |
| 13 | dreizehn | *dry-tsayn* |
| 14 | vierzehn | *feer-tsayn* |
| 15 | fünfzehn | *foonf-tsayn* |
| 16 | sechzehn | *zex-tsayn* |
| 17 | siebzehn | *zeep-tsayn* |
| 18 | achtzehn | *uhkht-tsayn* |
| 19 | neunzehn | *noyn-tsayn* |
| 20 | zwanzig | *tsvunn-tsig* |
| 21 | einundzwanzig | *ine-oont- tsvunn-tsig* |
| 30 | dreissig | *dry-sig* |
| 40 | vierzig | *feer-sig* |
| 50 | fünfzig | *foonf-tsig* |
| 60 | sechzig | *zex-tsig* |
| 70 | siebzig | *zeep-tsig* |
| 80 | achtzig | *uhkht-tsig* |
| 90 | neunzig | *noyn-tsig* |
| 100 | hundert | *hoond't* |
| 1000 | tausend | *towz'nt* |
| 1,000,000 | eine Million | *ine-uh mill-yon* |

# Time

| | German | Pronunciation |
|---|---|---|
| one minute | eine Minute | *ine-uh min-oot-uh* |
| one hour | eine Stunde | *ine-uh shtoond-uh* |
| half an hour | eine halbe Stunde | *ine-uh hullb-uh shtoond-uh* |
| Monday | Montag | *mohn-targ* |
| Tuesday | Dienstag | *deens-targ* |
| Wednesday | Mittwoch | *mitt-vokh* |
| Thursday | Donnerstag | *donn-ers-targ* |
| Friday | Freitag | *fry-targ* |
| Saturday | Samstag/ Sonnabend | *zums-targ zonn-ah-bent* |
| Sunday | Sonntag | *zon-targ* |
| January | Januar | *yan-ooar* |
| February | Februar | *fay-brooar* |
| March | März | *mairts* |
| April | April | *april* |
| May | Mai | *my* |
| June | Juni | *yoo-ni* |
| July | Juli | *yoo-lee* |
| August | August | *ow-goost* |
| September | September | *zep-tem-ber* |
| October | Oktober | *ok-toh-ber* |
| November | November | *no-vem-ber* |
| December | Dezember | *day-tsem-ber* |
| spring | Frühling | *froo-ling* |
| summer | Sommer | *zomm-er* |
| autumn (fall) | Herbst | *hairpst* |
| winter | Winter | *vint-er* |